TOWARDS MYSTICAL UNION

JULIENNE McLEAN

Towards Mystical Union

A modern commentary on the
mystical text *The Interior Castle*
by St Teresa of Avila

ST PAULS

ACKNOWLEDGEMENTS

The Scripture quotations contained herein are from the New Revised Standard Version Bible, copyright © 1989, by the Division of Christian Education of the National Council of the Churches of Christ in the USA, and are used by permission. All rights reserved. Also RSV or KJV where indicated in the text.

All excerpts from *The Interior Castle* in **bold** type are from the Fount Paperbacks (HarperCollins) 1995 edition. Reprinted by permission of Zondervan, a division of HarperCollins Publishers.

Excerpts from St John of the Cross are from *The Collected Works of St John of the Cross*, translated by Kieran Kavanaugh and Otilio Rodriguez, copyright © 1964, 1979, 1991 by Washington province of Discalced Carmelites ICS Publications, 2131 Lincoln Road, N.E. Washington, DC 20002-1199 USA. www.icspublications.org Reprinted by permission.

Excerpts from the E. Allison Peers (trans), *The Complete Works of St Teresa of Avila*, vol 2, Sheed and Ward, 1946. Reprinted by permission from Rowman and Littlefield Publishers Inc.

Excerpts from *The Life of Saint Teresa of Avila by Herself*, translated by J.M. Cohen, Penguin Classics, 1957. Reprinted by permission.

Excerpts from Evelyn Underhill, *Mysticism*, Oneworld, 1993. Reprinted by permission.

Excerpts from Robin Amis, *A Different Christianity*, State University of NY Press, 1995. Reprinted by permission.

Cover Image: *The Apotheosis of St Teresa and St John*, D. Joseph Garzia, seventeenth century, Chapel of the Sepulchre of St John of the Cross, Dascalced Carmelite Friars, Segovia, Spain.

ST PAULS Publishing
187 Battersea Bridge Road, London SW11 3AS, UK
www.stpauls.ie

ISBN 085439 661 6

ST PAULS, Alba House
2187 Victory Boulevard, Staten Island, NY 10314, USA

ISBN 0-8189-0960-9

Set by Tukan DTP, Fareham, Hampshire, UK
Printed by Interprint Ltd, Marsa, Malta

ST PAULS is an activity of the priests and brothers
of the Society of St Paul who proclaim the Gospel
through the media of social communication

In the spiritual marriage with our Lord, the soul always remains in its centre with its God.

Union may be symbolised by two wax candles, the tips of which touch each other so closely that there is but one light; or again, the wick, the wax, and the light become one, but the one candle can again be separated from the other, and the two candles remain distinct; or the wick may be withdrawn from the wax.

Spiritual marriage is like rain falling from heaven into a river or stream, becoming one and the same liquid, so that the river and the rainwater cannot be divided; or it resembles a streamlet flowing into the ocean, which cannot afterwards be disunited from it.

This marriage may also be likened to a room into which a bright light enters through two windows – though divided when it enters, the light becomes one and the same.

The Seventh Mansion, *The Interior Castle*, St Teresa

In appreciation

Throughout the many years of prayer, reflection, preparation and writing, I would like to give special thanks to all those friends, companions, spiritual directors, colleagues and students who have given their encouragement, support and insights on the work, and have deeply enriched my ongoing spiritual pilgrimage. I am also particularly grateful for all the rich and diverse dialogue, sharing and mutual learning on the courses and retreats I have co-led with Peter Tyler at Sarum College, Salisbury and Spain.

I would like to especially thank Joyce Foxcroft for editing the manuscript, and Fr Andrew Pudussery at St Pauls for his kind and thoughtful assistance in preparing the book for publication. Finally, I want to express a depth of gratitude to three people in particular: Warren, Peter and especially David, for their companionship, wisdom and discernment over many years.

Contents

Introduction to the Christian Mystical Tradition   9

The Threefold Way   27
     Awakening   28
     Purification and Purgation   34
     Illumination   40
     Union   51

Who was St Teresa of Avila?   57
     Entering the Religious Life   60
     Reforming Carmel   64

Introducing the mystical text *The Interior Castle*   73
     The Seven Mansions   74
     St Teresa Today   85

THE FIRST MANSION
Toward Awakening to Love   87
     The Beauty and Dignity of the Soul   89
     Awakening to Life in the Spirit   94
     Metanoia   104
     Self-Knowledge   112
     Humility   123
     The Lizards and the Snakes   130

THE SECOND MANSION
Entering and Purifying   147
     Decision, Discipline, Effort   149
     The Call of Love   153
     Ascesis   155
     Patience and Perseverance   160
     Spiritual Companionship   165

THE THIRD MANSION

What must I do to Acquire Eternal Life?   173
   Surrendering to Love   175
   Dark Night of the Senses   182

THE FOURTH MANSION

Infused by Love   199
   Transition and Transformation   201
   The Two Fountains   212
   Threshold   220

THE FIFTH MANSION

Betrothed to Christ   227
   Fragments of Heaven   229
   The Silkworm and the Butterfly   238
   Love Uniting to Love   242

THE SIXTH MANSION

Becoming His Bride   249
   Tests and Trials   251
   Dark Night of the Spirit   256
   Locutions, Ecstasy and Rapture   261
   Visions of God   273
   The Wound of Love   282

THE SEVENTH MANSION

The Mystery of Union   289
   The Wedding   291
   Union   295
   Mystery of the Kiss   301

Resting in Eternity, Living in the World   307

Bibliography   317

Introduction to the Christian Mystical Tradition

How what is called union takes place and what it is, I cannot tell. It is explained in mystical theology, but I cannot use the proper terms; I cannot understand what mind is, or how it differs from soul or spirit. They all seem one to me, though the soul sometimes leaps out of itself like a burning fire that has become one whole flame and increases with great force. The flame leaps very high above the fire. Nevertheless, it is not a different thing, but the same flame which is in the fire. What I want to explain is the soul's feelings when it is in this divine union. It is plain enough what union is; in union two separate things become one.[1]

I used at times, as I have said, to experience the very fleeting beginnings of something which I am now going to describe. When I made that inward picture in which I threw myself at Christ's feet, and sometimes also when I was reading, there would come to me unexpectedly such a feeling of the presence of God as made it impossible for me to doubt that He was within me, or that I was totally engulfed in Him. This was in no type of vision; I believe it is called mystical theology.[2]

The Life of Saint Teresa of Avila

St Teresa, like other saints and masters of the Christian spiritual life, maintained that it is possible, in a real sense, for the human soul to attain union with God. She humbly claimed that she, like many others, had actually reached this state, and her teachings on these matters were an integral part of the tradition of Christian life and faith.

In her extraordinary autobiography, Teresa's pen flows spontaneously and creatively, expressing many of the most important experiences, meetings, situations, and spiritual transformations that God worked in her heart and soul in her journey towards divine union. Her detailed writings chronicle her long and blessed love affair with Jesus Christ, and the constant action of the Holy Spirit in her soul, that finally took her towards 'the highest state of intimacy with God possible on this earth – the spiritual marriage.'[3]

What does Teresa mean when she refers to mystical theology in her *Life*, and to the soul being in divine union in *The Interior Castle?* Why are these integral parts of the Christian tradition? Why is there now such a heightened interest in mysticism, particularly in Christian mysticism? Why is this subject of paramount interest, relevance and importance in present times? What does Teresa have to say to all those who are on the Christian contemplative path about the joy and perils of our journey towards divine union? What are the real difficulties and problems regarding mysticism and the contemplative life, and how can they be carefully discerned? How can we use the teaching and writings of our spiritual forebears to help us in our own spiritual journey today?

These and other related questions are the subject of the present book, which is primarily intended to be a modern commentary on one of the best-known texts of Christian mystical literature, St Teresa's *Interior Castle.* There are several related aims of the book, which include exploring the interface between modern depth psychology, spirituality and mystical tradition, as well as providing a manual for spiritual direction designed to reflect a similar intention, flavour and approach as that of Teresa's original text, penned more than 400 years ago.

This commentary aims to be somewhat different from other books on, or about Teresa, as it is not primarily an intellectual or scholarly pursuit. Essentially, it is an inspirational, instruction manual based on Teresa's original text, that will serve to encourage and assist pilgrims towards a more heart-centred, contemplative and intimate relationship with God, through the saint's own spiritual writings and guidance.

The book attempts to create a fusion, an 'experientially shared space', between our heart and the writings and wisdom of the original text of the saint; insofar as it is possible to communicate mystical self-consciousness, the text is trying to fuse feeling and knowing –*amore ipse intellectus est* (to love is, in itself, understanding), as a well-known expression of medieval Latin Christian mysticism puts it.[4]

Teresa of Avila was a truly remarkable woman. Born in the early sixteenth century into a noble Castilian family, with direct Jewish descent, she showed marked interest in spiritual matters as a child, and took up the religious vocation at the age of twenty-one. Teresa was popularly known during her lifetime as the 'Holy Mother' and was canonised as a saint forty years after her death.

Teresa was an acknowledged mystic in her own lifetime, and underwent a staggering range of supernatural experiences. Everything she wrote is based on her own direct experience of God, and her writings were essentially intended as spiritual direction manuals for her nuns, and have been used by many, many generations of spiritual pilgrims in their 'journey in Christ' ever since.

So direct and penetrating is her insight, knowledge and understanding, so unpretentious and straightforward is her language, that we cannot but see our own spiritual yearnings and longings, our own progress, and our own 'death and transfiguration' in the love of God mirrored in her writings. We can allow the life, writings and presence of the Holy Mother to assist our own soul towards divine union. Her writings reveal a powerful and penetrating honesty and intimacy, a complete integrity, an essential pragmatism and compassion, but above all, a deep humanity that have hardly been surpassed in the whole corpus of Christian mystical literature.

Teresa's life and her reform of the Carmelite tradition was a renewal of the fundamentals and essence of the ancient spiritual tradition of the Order of the Blessed Virgin Mary of Mount Carmel, and she has been regarded as one of the greatest contributors to the Christian mystical tradition.

Why this particular subject is so relevant and important is that a spiritual rebirth or awakening, strikingly similar to that in her lifetime, is underway in our own times.

Teresa's life spanned most of the sixteenth century, when the European Renaissance and the Reformation were beginning. It is fairly obvious to observe that similar cultural, political, economic, ethnic, religious and spiritual convulsions and transitions are happening in our own times, and they appear to be even more urgent and global than those of the sixteenth century. What is striking is that there are so many parallels and similarities between the events and movements of today and those of the time when Teresa lived and wrote her most important and influential mystical literature.

In these early days of the new millennium, it can seem that the very foundations of what it means to be a civilised human being, living in an ordered and purposive universe are being attacked, undermined and destroyed more systematically than ever before in so many areas of our global society. We are living in most interesting and tumultuous times – witness the well-documented worldwide ecological crisis and the constant threats and rumours of increasing terrorism similar to the September 11 bombing catastrophe.

Additionally, the rise and proliferation of fundamentalism, in all its forms, religious or otherwise, in ever extreme, concrete, and even violent ways, is a particularly worrying trend. Our times appear to be characterised by increasing polarisation and fragmentation within groups and institutions, within the very fabric of our society, and indeed, if we allow it, within our very own souls. There certainly does appear to be growing collective turmoil and chaos, no matter in which part of the world, or in what sphere of life you choose to look.

Historians have noted that there are certain periods which generally coincide with the beginning of the fall of cultures and civilisations, when part of the mass of humanity irretrievably lose their reason and begin to destroy what has been created by centuries of culture and civilisation. One wonders whether we are in such a time now, and whether we are witnessing the slow demise of certain religious structures and cosmologies that have been dominant in the collective over past millennia, in order to make way for something very new which is trying to emerge.

It is interesting to note that in the well known poem *The Second Coming,* by the Irish poet and writer at the turn of the last century, W.B. Yeats, appeared to refer prophetically to a time of impending collective turmoil and chaos, and the slow emergence of a new religious vision – 'And what rough beast, its hour come around at last, Slouches towards Bethlehem to be born?'[5] What could Yeats possibly be referring to, and what is slouching towards Bethlehem trying to be born in our own time?

Alongside the global chaos and turmoil, I believe that our times are also experiencing a wider evolutionary shift, a significant change in direction, a true *metanoia.* A vast proportion of humanity is hungry to explore, experience and taste for themselves, in a modern contemplative way, the spiritual, and mystical dimension of life. They are seeking, by diverse means, to incorporate and integrate the spiritual into every aspect of living and life.

Striking features of our time include this rekindling of a deepening interest in mysticism, and in the ways of experiencing more direct knowledge of spiritual realities, and also the related areas of depth psychology, in its myriad forms. More and more people are becoming spiritually aware and are awakening to self-consciousness, to the great potentials of interior development and spiritual transformation and to the pressing need for a deeper relationship of themselves to the whole of creation, to God, to the Holy Spirit, to their fellow man and the global community.

There also appears to be a much wider recognition of the need for training and guidance; learning from our ancient traditions and paths of spiritual knowledge,

understanding and love that facilitate and enable interior
growth, development and surrender towards, and in, God.
We are generally unable to achieve spiritual maturity, depth
and integration on our own. For many, their religious
experiences have awakened them to the mystical, contemplative core of their own religious tradition. Many people
who have gained new understanding of their nature from
using these methods are returning to Christian roots that
they now understand more deeply.

Very large numbers of people are involved in the spiritual
quest now, at the start of the new millennium, and life in
the West is beginning to take a new direction now that
such large numbers are rediscovering their essentially
spiritual nature. Even fifty years ago, talking about the
deeper spiritual realities so publicly was fairly taboo.

Already, virtually unnoticed, parts of our civilisation are
becoming very different, so that today we are able to speak
more openly of things that not so long ago had to be
spoken of in whispers, particularly regarding the contemplative life and the Christian mystical tradition. In a
civilisation that has for so long forgotten that we are essentially spiritual beings, there now appears to be an evolutionary change in direction, a true metanoia of humanity turning
towards the spiritual dimension of life.[6]

Some say that a new era of the Holy Spirit is rapidly
approaching. It appears that the unprecedented accessibility
of knowledge, from the secrets of science and space travel
to the opening up and commonplace availability of many
of the most important spiritual writings from every religious
tradition, is designed to 'feed' this tremendous spiritual
awakening and deepening which is occurring globally. This
encourages an increasing ability to perceive and sense and
act from a living faith, through knowledge of the fundamental reality of our profound interconnectedness, and the
interrelationship of all things within life and creation.

This new era is about the insistence of the reality of the
spiritual dimension in life. It is about allowing these dimen-

sions *to work continually within us* to enable ongoing spiritual and psychological transformation of our perception of ourselves, of others and of the wider world within a larger design, order and meaning in life. This entails being able to live in an awareness of the reality of the constant Presence of God in, and all around us.

It also involves continually being in, and living out of, a state of willingness, openness of heart and selfless service and charity in our lives springing from our dedication to the reality of our underlying unity, within which all of life is so delicately held and balanced. These changes are now occurring on a global scale, irrespective of dogma, denominational creed, nationality or religious affiliation. The possibility of a great transformation within the heart of each soul is underway. We are on the cusp of new times, when the Heavenly Waters of the Holy Spirit are being poured upon humanity.

There has been much comment concerning the difficulty of the mainline Christian institutions to be able to sufficiently respond to, and connect with, this profound spiritual awakening of our time. It is an accepted historical phenomenon now that the traditional institutional Church has been on the decline for some time. People in the west are far less 'outwardly' religious than previously; certainly if measured in terms of church attendance.

The number of people who regard themselves as Christians now seems to be a minority. Indeed, a recent article in a national newspaper reported the possibility of the Roman Catholic priesthood in Ireland 'facing the prospect of extinction after the country's oldest seminary shut its doors last week because of its failure to attract a single new recruit... Twenty-three years ago a third of Ireland's population welcomed Pope John Paul II and almost 90 percent attended Mass regularly. Attendance is now as low as five percent in some areas'.[7]

Has the institutional church had its day? Are we moving into a post-Christian civilisation? Are the wonderful

churches and cathedrals now simply becoming historical
monuments to a bygone phase in western Christendom?
As Lawrence Freeman, leader of the World Community
for Christian Meditation, recently noted:

> The malaise of institutional Christianity has not gone away.
> It is puzzling and frustrating to try to understand how the
> mainline churches, despite all their determination and
> resources, still seem unable to connect with the profound
> spiritual needs of our time. For so many of the young, ready
> for idealistic and sacrificial commitment, hungry for inspira-
> tion, the church could give the sense of belonging that they
> seek as citizens of the global village.
>
> But instead of finding an inclusive vision, a comprehensive
> philosophy of life, a spirituality, they dismiss what they find
> as narrowness of mind, intolerant dogmatism, internal feuding,
> interdenominational sectarianism, medieval sexism and so on.
> It seems disloyal to reiterate it all. Perhaps the best way of
> dealing with it is to ask why – the unkindest cut of all – the
> most damning criticism is that Christianity lacks spiritual
> depth. Indeed, for many, it seems to lack spirituality period.[8]

The unprecedented spiritual longing and emergency of our
own times is certainly fuelling an overwhelming need for
this depth dimension of the Christian tradition to become
much more widely known, understood and practised. The
writings of the great Christian mystics and saints, such as
St Teresa, have been ignored or concealed for so many
years, particularly within the Protestant tradition. In many
respects, the teachings of the mystics have been one of the
best-kept secrets of the contemplative and enclosed religious
orders of the Christian church over the centuries.

These orders, the Carmelites, Benedictines, Jesuits,
Franciscans, Dominicans, and the Visitandines, which were
founded in seventeenth-century France, have kept the flame
of their founders' inspiration very much alive, and have
lovingly preserved their teachings and spiritual direction over
many centuries. The mystical Christian tradition is certainly
alive and well in modern times, as Freeman describes:

I am fortunate to be in touch with another side of modern Christianity – the quiet but deepening and growing network of contemplative Christians, Christians with a practice of contemplative prayer. Their sincere, searching faith and the pressures of modern life have awakened in them a hunger for spiritual experience and for the depth dimension of their Christianity.

Many have found with delight and relief the Christian tradition of contemplative prayer after exploring the spirituality of the East. While conducting regular lives and generally looking quite normal they, like the catechumens and Christians of the primitive church, follow a seriously faithful and daily contemplative practice. This does not isolate them in any ivory tower of private spirituality. Overall, and over time, their spiritual life integrates this contemplative dimension with other forms of communal prayer and activity in a church and in ministry to others.[9]

This depth contemplative dimension of Christianity has always existed, and continues to exist, in every Christian order or organisation genuinely concerned with the conscious transformation and transfiguration of the soul towards union with God through prayer, contemplation and active service and charity towards others and the world. This mystical dimension is, of course, only one element of the Christian tradition, and is inseparable from the many other parts that constitute the fullness of the whole, such as worship, service, community and interfaith dialogue.

The contemplative Christian tradition has flowered in particular places, times and individuals over the past 2000 years. It flourished in the Celtic Church during the sixth to eighth centuries in Anglo-Saxon Britain, through some of its most famous saints – St Columba and St Aiden of Iona, and St Cuthbert of Lindisfarne. Its most obvious homes have been, and still are, in the ancient monasteries on Mount Athos, and throughout the Middle East.[10]

Some of the better-known bearers of the Christian mystical tradition in the West have been Pseudo Dionysius, (or Denys) the Areopagite, in the early sixth century; Bernard of Clairvaux in the eleventh century, one of the early spiritual fathers of the Cistercian order; Bonaventure; Meister Eckhart; Jan van Ruysbroec; Gregory Palamas in the thirteenth century; Catherine of Siena in the fourteenth century; the English anchoress, Julian of Norwich, author of *Revelations of Divine Love;* and the unknown author of the *Cloud of Unknowing.*

St Teresa and St John of the Cross continued the mystical tradition of Christianity in the sixteenth century as part of the major reform of the Carmelite Order. Marie of the Incarnation, Jeanne-Marie Guyon as well as Pierre Caussade, author of *Abandonment to Divine Providence*, carried the tradition in the seventeenth and eighteenth centuries. More recent well-known figures include Therese of Lisieux, Thomas Merton and Henri Le Saux. Probably the most famous collection of mystical writings is the *Philokalia*, containing texts on the ascetical life, prayer and the hesychast tradition, written by the ascetical Orthodox Christian fathers between the fourth and fifteenth centuries.

So, what is Christian mysticism, and what is mystical theology attempting to describe? Essentially, mysticism is describing the sort of knowledge of God that is obscure to the mind or the intellect. The meaning of 'mystical' lies in the Greek root '*mu-*', which has to do with hiddenness, that which is closed or concealed. Words such as *mystikon, mysterion, mystes* are derived from this root, and were originally used in connection with the Greek mystery religions.[11]

In his book *The Origins of the Christian Mystical Tradition*, Andrew Louth succinctly describes mysticism as

> characterised as a search for, and experience of, immediacy with God. The mystic is not content to know about God, he longs for union with God. 'Union with God' can mean different things, from literal identity, where the mystic loses all sense of himself and is absorbed into God, to the union that is experienced as the consummation of love, in which the lover and the beloved remain intensely aware both of themselves and of the other.

How the mystics interpret the way and the goal of their quest depends on what they think about God, and that itself is influenced by what they experience: it is a mistake to try to make out that all mysticism is the same. Yet the search for God, or the ultimate, for His own sake, and an unwillingness to be satisfied with anything less than Him; the search for immediacy with this object of the soul's longing; this would seem to be the heart of mysticism.[12]

To explore the Christian use of such terminology we need to look at the meaning of the word, *mysterion* – mystery, in Christian vocabulary – as this is what the Greek Patristic writers refer to when they use *mystikos*, or mystic. *Mysterion* means a secret, but in its use in the New Testament it very specifically refers to the mystery of God's love for us revealed in Christ. It is a secret, or a mystery, not because it is kept secret, but because it is the revelation of something that essentially remains hidden in its revealing, being inexhaustible and inaccessible in the very event of its being made known and accessible to us in the life, death and resurrection of Christ. Contrary to being kept secret, it is something to be proclaimed and made known, since it is the revealing of God's love for us.[13]

For the early Christian Fathers, understanding the scriptures was not a simply academic matter. It was something for which one prepared through constant prayer, purification, humility and love. Through attention to the scriptures, and by the power of the Holy Spirit, it was possible to enter into a transforming relationship with God by conforming to the image of God, the Son, enabling us to contemplate the Father.

In the doctrine of sanctifying grace Christian theologians have consistently referred to the uncreated presence of God in the soul. The Greek Fathers first conceived this presence as an *image* of God in the soul, as an active participation in the divine life. Spiritual life, then, consists in a never-ceasing process of assimilation to this divine presence in the soul, as a *growing toward the Image*.[14]

Thus, in Christian vocabulary *mystikos* refers to, and makes accessible to us, this mystery of God's love for us in Christ. It essentially has a three-fold meaning, referring to the 'mystic' meaning of scripture, to the 'mystic' significance of the Christian sacraments, or mysteries, and finally to 'mystical theology', which is knowing God as revealed in Christ, as belonging to the fellowship of 'the mystery' (Eph 3.9). This was summed up by the anonymous fifth-century writer, Denys the Areopagite, whose writings gathered up the patristic mystical heritage and vastly influenced posterity.[15]

Denys elucidated the three ranges of meaning of *mystikos,* referring to the deeper meaning of scripture in which God reveals the mystery of His love, looking at the significance of the sacraments through which we are able to participate in this mystery, and exploring 'mystical theology'. He said that mystical theology was not something different, but looks less to the means than to the end, where the soul surrenders to God and, passing into the meaning of the signs and concepts it uses to grasp the mystery of love, is itself grasped and transfigured into that love. Denys established the regular use of the three ways of purification, illumination and union in the Christian tradition.[16]

When Denys wrote his treatise on 'mystical theology', he was writing about the way in which Christian liturgy displays the 'mysteries' of God's action in relation to the created order – the mystery of God going out from the depths of the divine nature to create, and then to become incarnate in, our nature – God binding creation together in communion and drawing creation back to its divine source. To understand this divine movement is to receive it into ourselves in such a way that we are taken beyond all words and signs. This openness or passivity to God's movement, 'suffering divine things' is what 'mystical theology' means.[17]

More specifically, the mystical life begins, as Teresa writes in her autobiography, when our self is surrendered, at a radical level, to the action, activity and purposes of God, so that it can no longer be thought of as acting from a centre that is essentially separated from God. The mystical is the 'supernatural', as Teresa emphasises in the fourth mansion of *The Interior Castle*, meaning the state in which what we are doing coincides, more or less, with what God is doing, or, in theological terms, the mystical is the formation of our created selfhood in the likeness of Christ.[18]

Bernard McGinn succinctly presents many of the essential difficulties in defining mysticism in his three-volume collection of works, *The Foundations of Mysticism*. He concludes that it is much more useful to present different ways of understanding the term under three main headings – as a part of a religious tradition, as a process or way of life, and as an attempt to express a direct consciousness of the Presence of God.

He points out that, in his view, perhaps the greatest insight of von Hugel's book of the early twentieth century, *The Mystical Element of Religion*, is that mysticism is actually only one element in a tradition or in any particular religious personality. No mystics (at least before the twentieth century!) believed in or practised 'mysticism'. They believed in and practised Christianity (or Judaism, Islam, Hinduism or Buddhism) – that is, the mystical elements of religious traditions were always part of a much wider historical and spiritual whole.[19]

McGinn has come to find that the term 'presence' grasps the unifying note in the varieties of Christian mysticism most centrally. He summarises the mystical element in Christianity as those parts of the beliefs and practices that concern the preparation for, the consciousness of, and the reaction to, what can be described *as the immediate or direct presence of God*. However, the ways in which these special forms of encounter with God have been understood down the generations are multiple.[20]

One thing that all the Christian mystics have agreed on is that the experience in itself defies conceptualisation and verbalisation, in part or in whole, and can only be presented indirectly, partially by a series of verbal strategies. Language in this dimension can only be used transformationally, not so much to convey information or content but to assist the seeker to hope, yearn, and to know that it is possible to journey towards, and rest in, the same Unity of Being in Christ.[21]

From this perspective, there are a host of models, metaphors or symbols that mystics have employed in their accounts. Mystical union is one of the central ways of describing this mystical dimension, and of course, was primarily what St Teresa used. Among the other major mystical categories are those of contemplation and the vision of God, deification, the birth of the Word in the soul, ecstasy, or radical obedience to the present Divine Will.

So, one of the central claims of most mystical texts, and especially of *The Interior Castle,* is that it involves an immediate consciousness of the Presence of God. Teresa's writings are a powerful witness to the possibility of entering into a sense of divine presence within the context of the ordinary religious observances, and, of course, in our everyday ordinary life. What differentiates mystical texts, and this particular text, from other forms of religious writings is that the presentation is both subjectively and objectively more direct and more immediate. This is certainly part of the intention in presenting much of Teresa's original text in this book.

So, what is all this for? As Teresa, and all the Christian saints have testified to in their lives and writings, the aim of the Christian life is to restore to splendour the corrupted, darkened image of God within ourselves, through our devotion, love and, ultimately, union with Christ. As an unchanged, uncorrupted icon of God, Christ reworks the corrupted image to reveal the original beauty within us, continually teaching and guiding us towards our divine archetype. Transfigured, Christ restores the radiance of a creation made dark by the Fall, and in our continually becoming 'conformed to the image of Christ' we can slowly regain our divine inheritance and our own inmost spiritual nature.[22]

To recover the light of Christ within our soul is our task. It is because of this that the themes of incarnation, transfiguration and deification – or resurrection – are so crucial. The events in the life of Christ are not only, or even mainly, events that have happened once in the past. They are entirely and eternally present and are able to be experienced by everyone. Christ's life represents what we actually are and can become, as the incarnate symbol of each person's proper destiny in life.

Christ, or life, or light – the terms are interchangeable – was joined to the world, as St Simeon writes, 'as yeast, as a small offering in the dough of our nature, and He joined our nature with His own incomprehensible, unapproachable nature, and, to explain things better, He joined all the reality of His divinity substantially to our nature, and that human nature He mixed unmixably with His own substance, and He made it a holy temple to Himself.'[23]

Thus, the idea of transfiguration is central to the Christian understanding of our destiny, as well as to the destiny of the whole created world – the one intimately involves the other. We must understand that what is exemplified in the life of Christ, as recorded in the New Testament, provides the standard according to which each individual can assess the radical and transformative spiritual possibilities that are continually open to them. Transfiguration signifies the most intimate and exalted experience of which we are capable; our whole physical being can be so irradiated with divine light that it can shine like the sun.[24] This is the spiritual marriage Teresa is referring to in the centre of the castle.

It has to be said that modern studies of mysticism have tended to separate and differentiate between mysticism and mystical theology, moving the field more towards the study of the phenomenology of mystical states of mind and experience. The essential problem with these modern, often academic studies, is that this approach artificially splits the people and their writings off from the whole religious tradition of which they were an integral part, leaving the mystery of faith and other elements that constitute the full expression and living of the spiritual life quite separate. The theological framework of the 'mystics' is, I believe, absolutely critical to the study of their life and work.

How is it possible to ignore the whole context and milieu of their life, which is, of course, what nourished, fed, fuelled and gave expression to their particular unique spiritual flowering? It really is quite problematic to separate mysticism from mystical theology, particularly in the history and expression of the mystical life in the Christian tradition. The fact that the term mystical theology antedated the coining of the word mysticism by over a millennium points us in the right direction. We must appreciate the complex and unbreakable bonds between mysticism conceived of as a religious way of life and mystical theology.[25]

Teresa was an exemplar of the heart of the mystical life – the union of God in love – but it's probable that her analysing of states of prayer in accordance with their psychological characteristics has opened up an area of modern development that she would have hardly recognised, let alone approved of. Modern studies of mysticism have tended to define mystical experience, not in terms of the mystery of faith being worked out in the soul, but in terms of phenomenologically observed psychological states, leading to the possibility of cross cultural comparison between mystics of all faiths and none.[26]

This is precisely why, for the Church Fathers, and certainly in Teresa's own understanding, mysticism was never reduced

> to the level of a psychological experience, considered merely, or primarily, in its subjectivity.
>   It is always the experience of an invisible objective world: the world whose coming the Scriptures reveal to us in Jesus Christ, the world into which we enter, ontologically, through

the liturgy, through this same Jesus Christ ever present in the Church. For Denis, as for the Fathers who were contemporary with him, together with certain inseparable spiritual experiences, always represent the world to which they give access, this mystical world of which St John Chrysostom speaks, where all the angels sing to God a mystical melody.[27]

Of course, mysticism is certainly not a religious phenomenon peculiar to Christianity. Each religious tradition has its own mystical aspect and it is vitally important that the specific character of a particular mystical tradition be respected. As Rowan Williams has emphasised, the most useful generalisations about mysticism across different traditions concentrate on comparing the *function* of the lives of the mystics and the saints within their own tradition, rather than on the content of their mystical experience:

> These figures, [the mystics and saints in the Christian tradition] in written texts as well as the 'text' of their lives, serve as points of orientation, touchstones of integrity, for the language and hopes of other believers precisely because they witness to so broad and comprehensive an access to the 'sacred source' of Christian commitment, the action and passion of God in the whole event of Jesus Christ.[28]

NOTES

1. Teresa of Avila. *The Life of Saint Teresa of Avila by Herself*, trans J.M. Cohen, Penguin Classics, 1957, p.122
2. Ibid, p.71
3. Kavanaugh, K. and Rodriguez, O. (trans). *The Collected Works of St John of the Cross*, ICS Publications, Washington, DC, 1979, p.20
4. McGinn, B. *The Language of Inner Experience in Christian Mysticism*, Spiritis 1 (2001) pp.157-171
5. Yeats, W.B., *Collected Poems*, Picador, London. 1990, p.211.
6. Amis, R. *A Different Christianity*, State University New York Press, NY, 1995, p.62
7. *The Observer*, 2 September 2002
8. Lawrence Freeman, *The Grateful Church of the Future*, The Tablet, 21 January 2000
9. Ibid.

10. See Dalrymple, W. *From the Holy Mountain*, Henry Holt & Company, New York, 1997, and Hieromonk Alexander (trans). *The Living Witness of the Holy Mountain – Contemporary Voices from Mt Athos,* St Tikhon's Seminary Press, South Canaan, Pennsylvania, 1999

11. Wakefield, G (ed) *Dictionary of Christian Spirituality,* SCM, 1983, p.272

12. Louth, A. *The Origins of the Christian Mystical Tradition,* Clarendon Press, Oxford, 1981, p. xv

13. Wakefield, G. *op.cit.* pp.272-273

14. Dupre, L. *The Deeper Life – An Introduction to Christian Mysticism,* Crossroad, NY, 1981, p.87

15. Wakefield, G. *op.cit.* p.273

16. Ibid

17. Williams, R. *Teresa of Avila,* Geoffrey Chapman, London, 1991, p.143

18. Ibid, p.144

19. McGinn, B. *Foundations of Mysticism* Vol 1, SCM, London, 1990, p. xvi

20. Ibid, p. xvii

21. Ibid, p. xvii

22. Amis, R. *op.cit.* p.53

23. Sherrard, P. *The Sacred in Life and Art,* Golgonooza Press, Ipswich, UK, 1990, p.99

24. Ibid, p.86

25. McGinn, B. *op.cit.* xiv

26. Wakefield, G. *op.cit.* p.274

27 Bouyer, L. 'Mysticism. An essay on the history of the Word' in Woods, R. (ed). *Understanding Mysticism,* Athlone Press, London, 1981, p.52

28. Williams, R. *op.cit.* p.158.

The Threefold Way

The spiritual path – the journey towards, and in, God – is, and always has been, fraught with manifold difficulties, delusions, battles and shadows. Without an accurate road map of the spiritual terrain and wise spiritual direction, which the great Christian saints and mystics have provided, it is certainly a dangerous and perilous journey. The writings of these spiritual titans are indispensable in our post-modern, secular, individualistic age, so that as much knowledge and understanding of the Christian mystical tradition as possible is made available to as many pilgrims as possible.

It is for those seekers who have that insatiable longing, sincerity, passion, willingness and discipline to absorb and use the wisdom of our forebears in their journey towards, and in, God. This ancient classical map of the spiritual journey towards mystical union was slowly developed over years of inner experimentation by the early Christians and the Desert Fathers. It became crystallised through medieval mystics such as Hugh of St Victor, Blessed Jan van Ruysbroec and St Catherine of Siena, and reached a height of refinement with St Teresa and St John of the Cross. Variations and subdivisions multiplied, but the core of the doctrine remained the same.

One of the basic ideas in western mysticism is that spiritual life moves through stages in an ascending order. The classical division into purgative, illuminative and unitive stages was established in the early Christian centuries and has survived most of the transitional differences and school polemics in the following centuries. The first stage is known as the way of awakening, purgation and purification, *the via purgativa*, the second stage as illumination, *the via illuminativa*, and the third stage as mystical union, *the via unitiva*.

Each stage has clear characteristics and distinguishing signs, and each has an appropriate and different set of criteria for discernment. An experienced contemporary Jesuit spiritual director has written that

> Though based on the inherited tradition of the Christian community, these stages have indeed been confirmed by my own personal experience as a spiritual director. I have found this general classical pattern to be very much a part of the individuated experience of most of the people I have directed.[1]

AWAKENING

The beginning of the stage of spiritual awakening, *metanoia* or turning towards God, is usually an intense form of conversion. This is sometimes a gradual process, but more often than not it can be an abrupt awakening to the reality of the spiritual dimension of life, which usually, in the initial stages, is in greater or lesser conflict with our ordinary everyday perception, attitudes, lifestyle and way of living and being. In some cases, the process of conversion can be quite sudden, experienced as being clearly imposed from without, rather than being slowly developed from within through faith. It can even have a mystical or supernatural character. One of the most famous examples from Scripture is, of course, that of St Paul and his 'road to Damascus' conversion: the sudden light, the voice, the ecstasy, and the complete alteration of life.

The varied ways and means of conversion towards the spiritual life, whether sudden or gradual, are well-documented in the religious literature.[2] An experience of conversion can often develop as a result of a long period of restlessness, searching, uncertainty or trauma, or it can happen quite suddenly through a vivid, powerful or overwhelming experience of God's Love, Light or the Presence of Christ. The overall effect of any real conversion experience is that it breaks down, challenges and often completely overturns our habitual and normal conscious understanding and perception of ourselves, the world and our relationship to God.

These conversion experiences, or profound changes in the direction of our lives, normally begin to reveal the reality and existence of a very different spiritual dimension of life, and of ourselves, which had hitherto been hidden, unconscious, unknown and untouched. This is a familiar state for many young Christians at the beginning of their new relationship with God. Their initial prayer and worship are often enlivened by occasional moments, or tastes, of real and unmistakable awakening to the life changing touch, Presence and Love of God.

Indeed, Louis Dupre emphasises the necessity of true spiritual awakening to the love of God as one of the primary conditions of any significant progress in the process of purification and purgation, noting that:

> It is not sufficient for the novice to be full of spiritual desire. He or she must be 'awakened' to it in a manner over which he or she has no control. Many saints, as we know, have undergone rather abrupt conversions to spiritual life. It is generally assumed that mystics also experience a clear 'awakening' to a high state of spiritual awareness.
>
> Yet in the 'Psychology of the Mystics', the eminent philosopher Joseph Marechal claims that for most people that awakening occurs gradually in the course of ordinary prayer. It concludes a process that has started with meditation, has then moved into a more inward recollection which, in due time, has turned into a state of habitual dwelling in the presence of God... Love must come first, with the soul becoming more and more centred on God rather than on itself before any real purgation can begin.[3]

Fleeting spiritual illuminations are very common, especially in our own times. Many pilgrims have had wonderful 'opening' experiences to the Holy Spirit and the genuine taste of God's Presence and Love at some time in their prayer and spiritual journey. However, this early stage of awakening to the spiritual dimension is very much only the beginning. These moments, phases, or experiences of awakening to God belong to some of the most intimate and precious aspects of what it means to be human. They are the beginning of our long journey home to the heart of God.

What are the signs of our own awakening to the presence of the Holy Spirit, to the spiritual dimension of life? These include the sense of being absolutely alive, a tremendous vitality, a direct, immediate knowing, or understanding, of our religious creeds, a sense of great treasure, beauty and splendour. There can also be an overwhelming sense of dread, of tremendous fear and anxiety, of encountering the *mysterium tremendum* of God. There is a sense of breaking through to something quite Other. Something is shown to us that is very different, and it is not mediated by our usual ideas, thoughts, or cognitive structures.

Some of these early types of awakening experiences powerfully challenge, and exceed, all the usual ways that we apprehend ordinary reality. There are many descriptions from the saints, mystics or wise spiritual directors that comprise the more sudden conversion experiences. With a more intense presence of the Holy Spirit in our lives, we can experience a fire beginning to burn from within, an immense calm, a sense of eternal or limitless peace, of profound well-being and blessing, a sense of coming home or belonging, or waves of endless Love.

There can also be the sense of entering the nothingness from which all things come, of rhythmic surges of energy, or incredible, indescribable joy. We can have an experience of transcendent ecstasy, of water gushing as if 'my breath is the breath of God'. We might receive a touch or taste of absolute freedom and energy like electricity plugged into a Source of Life. There can be a markedly increased sense of the Presence of Christ, that life and existence seem to be in this very moment, now, alongside a real sense of the eternal. There can certainly be a change in our sense of time and space, and definitely a sense of the holy, or holiness.

In his famous text written nearly 100 years ago, *Varieties of Religious Experience,* William James explored some of the basic characteristics of encounters with the spiritual dimension.[4] Firstly, they have a quality of ineffability – they defy expression in logical rational terms, and are often only fully intelligible to those who have known some analogous experience.

Consider the smell of a rose, or the sensation of being in love, or the pleasure that comes while listening to a great symphony; none are amenable to adequate logical or intellectual description. Most utterances on such dimensions are really rather inadequate, except to those touched by a certainty of the reality of that dimension. The attempt to express the inexpressible is, of course, where psychology and theology go hand in hand.

Secondly, James pointed to the noetic quality of this dimension by defining these states as 'states of insight into depths of truth unplumbed by the discursive intellect, insights which carry with them a tremendous sense of authority'. We actually know something different in this dimension. It tends to break the subject/object dualism, and purely intellectual thinking, and introduces us into a transcendent reality.

Somehow, there can be a sense of insight, of knowing, touching, tasting, seeing the wholeness of things and life, of seeing and being within the profound interconnectedness of things which defies the mind, reason and the intellect alone. More importantly, our faculty for intuitively penetrating the veil of temporal reality seems to be activated by a source beyond ourselves. A consciousness can appear, a sense of unitive being, or non-duality. There can be a change in the sense of time and space, a sense of the eternal.

Thirdly, these states generally transcend our ordinary sense of ourselves, and can often be experienced as more real and awake than our ordinary waking consciousness. We feel much more alive. These experiences represent another level, or dimension, of reality that is deeper than the previous one. However, these transcendent states can seldom be sustained for long, and share the quality of transiency, requiring further inner work to make the state a lasting one. The following of a particular way of life can increase their frequency and make the states more permanent.

Fourthly, the sense of inner stillness, quietness, and surrender is vital. James called this passivity, which is a term that can be misunderstood. The implication of this characteristic is that ego-transcendent states almost always bring with them the feeling of something that is given. It is the preparation, the conscious surrender, in order to be receptive to the action of the Spirit – it is not possible to create or manipulate this state. There is a distinct quality of otherness.

The essential quality of stillness, of the body, mind, emotions, has the capacity to restore our ability to re-member, to recollect, to remain ourselves and not be distracted or identified with influences from the outside. That is why prayer, meditation and contemplation are the essential pathways to connecting to, and living within, this deeper dimension.

The touch of the mystical is often spoken of in terms of the five interior senses of the soul when she is becoming betrothed to Christ, through the Holy Spirit. Teresa speaks about the sweet smell or perfume of the Holy Spirit in the fifth mansion when the bride is becoming betrothed to the Bridegroom.

Other saints and mystics have spoken about the sense of the interior taste of the Holy Spirit, as if we have been invited as special guests to a heavenly banquet, where there are the particular flavours, sounds, scents, textures and colours of Paradise. It is like nothing that we have ever tasted before, and is impossible to truly convey or describe to those who have not been to such a banquet.

The main psychological and spiritual changes of attitude that need to occur during these initial stages are the increasing recognition of how ignorant we are, of how little we actually know, of how much psychological work needs to be done in order to progress and deepen our spiritual life, of how open and vulnerable we are to be to the pressures and influences of the outside world, and of how powerful and insistent our self-love and egotism is.

The best way of beginning to develop our sense of self, or soul, is by increasingly devoting ourselves to prayer, meditation, the study of Scripture and contemplative and mystical literature within a community, group or in solitude, as well as the cultivation of compassion, patience, humility and generosity in as many practical choices and opportunities in life as possible.

In his spiritual autobiography, *The Golden String*, the twentieth-century Catholic monk and mystic, Bede Griffiths described the nature of spiritual awakening:

> An experience of this kind (of spiritual awakening) is probably not at all uncommon, especially in early youth. Something breaks suddenly into our lives and upsets their normal pattern and we have to begin to adjust ourselves to a new kind of existence. This experience may come, as it came to me, through nature and poetry, or through art or music; or it may come through the adventure of flying or mountaineering, or of war; or it may come through simply falling in love, or through some apparent accident, an illness, the death of a friend, the sudden loss of fortune.
>
> Anything that breaks through the routine of daily life may be the bearer of this message to the soul. But, however it may be, it is as though a veil has been lifted and we see for the first time behind the façade, which the world has built around us.
>
> Suddenly we know we belong to another world, that there is another dimension of existence… We see our life for a moment in its true perspective in relation to eternity. We are freed from all the flux of time and see something of the eternal order that underlies it. We are no longer isolated individuals in conflict with our surroundings; we are parts of whole, elements in a universal harmony.[5]

The beginning of awakening to the spiritual dimension of life often has its roots in the earliest memories of childhood, where it is not uncommon to have spontaneous experiences, or moments, of a spiritual reality different to ordinary, everyday life, experiences pregnant with a depth of meaning, vitality, richness and significance far beyond the actual physical situation. Such moments of awakening are unforgettable and indescribable, as they are moments of recollection and remembrance of ourselves, and of our relationship to spiritual realities.

As a child, my own relationship to nature and the local community was central to my spiritual awakening. Much of my childhood and adolescence centred on my interest in religion and activities in the local Christian community. From a young age I always felt a particular connection and fascination with the religious life and spirituality. There were many moments as a child – either in church, on retreat, or in 'the bush' which I would now describe as religious or numinous experience, where a presence of something quite beyond me, which I recognised as a sense or touch of God, or something quite Other, had been unquestionably real and strong.

PURIFICATION AND PURGATION

> Purification is a perpetual process. That which mystical writers mean, however, when they speak of the way of purgation, is rather the slow and painful completion of conversion. It is the drastic turning of the self from the unreal to the real life: a setting of her house in order, an orientation of the mind to (spiritual) truth. Its business is the getting rid, first of self-love; and secondly of all those foolish interests in which the surface consciousness is steeped. The essence of purgation, says Richard of St Victor, 'is self simplification'.[6]

This stage has to do with what is traditionally called ascesis, the ongoing work on, and purification of, oneself in order to overcome the effects of the past, and to heal our psyche and soul. In all religious traditions, ascetical practices have been deemed to be necessary in order to purify ourselves, so as to enter and taste the delights of the garden of Paradise.

There are different kinds of ascesis – physical ascetical practices, such as particular prayer postures, and psychological and spiritual ascetical practices, of which prayer, meditation and contemplation usually form the core. Psychotherapy, psychoanalysis and the many therapeutic endeavours that are now available are also potent tools to help individuals successfully work through childhood trauma, and all kinds of psychological and emotional difficulties and obstacles.

This stage usually becomes more serious and necessary when the initial awakening phase has slowed down, or stopped happening. For many people, the beginning of purification stage can bring on growing disappointment and disillusionment. It is only if the pilgrim seriously engages in, and commits themselves to undergoing the real difficulties and rigours of their internal purification process that such 'spiritual' disappointment can be overcome by a change of heart. This intense emotional purification of the heart can then lead on to the deeper phase of illumination.

This ongoing and ever-present process of self-purification entails a tremendous inner analysis; a continual commitment to uncover and take full responsibility for our unconscious patterns and games; a constant facing of our past wounds and traumas and their continuing effects on us and an ongoing confrontation with all the forms of subtle betrayal and sabotage of self and others. Only through a developed and stable practice and rhythm of prayer, meditation and service, and only if we have truly aroused devotion in our heart towards God, is it possible to endure and travel through the tremendous rigours and difficulties of this period.

The primary aim of the purification stage is the production of real repentance, of a deepening *metanoia,* the essential 'change of mind' away from ourselves and towards God; to become evermore deeply engaged in that fundamental transformation of our heart and outlook towards new, spiritual ways of looking at ourselves, at others and at God.

For some, the deeper conversion towards the reality of the spiritual life will be from the motivation of the fear and wrath of God. However, fear, an anxious and negative state, can, given generosity and openness towards it, give way before long to the deepening realisation of the love of God, and the turning away from a selfish, ego-centred life and attitudes. This change comes not from fear of punishment, but through recognising the rebellion against His Love that the old life essentially is – a state that we long to change and have transformed within our heart.[7]

Of course, at this stage, deeper engagement in self-knowledge and rigorous self-examination is indispensable, as Teresa emphasises in the first mansion. The purpose is not to undermine or to destructively criticise oneself, but to enter the process of self-enquiry, of ruthless openness, self-honesty and personal integrity so as to arrive at a real knowledge of oneself in the sight of God, becoming naked, open, receptive, surrendered, ready in His sight.

There is no substitute for the patient, slow psychological and psychotherapeutic work of exploring, understanding and learning to accept ourselves the way we are. In this regard, knowledge of God presupposes, and is intimately connected to, knowledge of self.

The depth and progress of our spiritual life does not necessarily depend on our mental health or capacities. However, a deepening union with God is generally accompanied by an increasingly more integrated personality and a greater focus of energy in the service of God.

The yearning and desire to move towards deepening states of contemplative prayer and meditation must be complemented and augmented by the ongoing struggle to develop an in-depth understanding of ourselves, and by an increasing ability to reflect on, sense, articulate and adequately respond to what is going on within our psyche, both from the conscious and the unconscious levels.

Spiritual transformation today is not only a matter of moving towards the innermost dwelling places, but also of ever more precise and technical self-knowledge, which begins at the earliest stages on the path and continues at all times, at all points and at all stages toward the mystery of union, as Teresa so clearly states.

There is a constant re-evaluation of our life, where the attachments, identifications and projections onto exterior life are waning, as we are slowly entering the 'life of our soul towards union with God, in Christ'.

As the pilgrim's senses, passions and spiritual perception are steadily able to become more emptied of an emphasis on our own personal gratifications, and able to become more refined, purified and objective through the action of the Holy Spirit in our heart, what were previously visionary 'glimpses' can become a more permanent recognition of, and being in, the Presence, mystery and mercy of God.

Slowly, as we are able to more fully face what is untransformed, addicted and still desperate inside, and are able more and more to expose ourselves to God's beauty and mercy, then His Presence and Love is able to infuse or install itself in increasingly steady ways in our heart and lives.

Essentially, in this purification stage, we are continually being placed, face to face, with our life, both conscious and unconscious, with all our soluble and insoluble problems, and one of the major tests of spiritual discrimination and discernment is the objective distinguishing between the permanent, eternal influences, and the personal, temporary influences.

As soon as we turn towards the interior world in prayer and reflection, we usually encounter whole dimensions of ourselves that have previously been unconscious, hidden and unknown. In modern psychological parlance, these refer to the shadow parts of the psyche, which describe all the psychic contents that have been driven back into the unconscious, including all the neglected, undeveloped, unacknowledged parts of ourselves.

At these early stages, rigorous self-knowledge and humility need to be growing. Humility is one of the most powerful forces of spiritual growth and development. No effort, and no teaching, is true and transformative if it does not lead to increasing humility, if it does not turn us around and, closing us off from the pressures of the world, begin to open us to the constant pressure of the Love of God.

We cannot hope to achieve right and true relationship with others, the world or with God unless we have such a sense of that reality, which alone enables us to see and understand ourselves and our real condition in these outer edges of the castle in their true spiritual perspective, which can only grow in the soil of deepening humility.

The purgative way is fraught with difficulties, blocks, distractions and obstacles, often seemingly overwhelming, that constantly pull us away from God. In the active purgative stage, our efforts need to be marshalled to overcome the major obstacles that obstruct our spiritual progress.

In her classic book, *Mysticism,* Evelyn Underhill describes the two main forms of active purgation: the slow process of detachment, which is intended to sever the existing ties of desire, and mortification, the deliberate choice of what is disagreeable, painful or humiliating which is intended to reverse habitual patterns of affection and behaviour.[8] The Christian monastic tradition has institutionalised the active pursuit of spiritual detachment through the vows of poverty, chastity and obedience that every nun and monk has to take on fully entering the religious life.

John of the Cross describes the purgative process in terms of the active and passive night of the senses in his writings entitled the *Ascent of Mount Carmel* and the *Dark Night of the Soul,* which are discussed in more detail in the third mansion. In this stage, John focuses on the importance of detachment from our desires and passions, which enables us to enter more deeply into the relationship with God through stillness and silence.

John insists that it is the inner detachment that matters, not the physical privation:

> John explicitly warns against excessive mortification, which focuses undue attention on bodily desires. Not the pleasure, but the desire of pleasure, its self-contracting aspect by which I turn back into myself, must be renounced. Pleasure is a necessary component of physical life. For one who is hungry, not to enjoy eating is neither natural nor desirable. But to eat merely for the sake of pleasure deflects the soul from its upward moment.
>
> Significantly John posits the love of Christ, not the pursuit of personal perfection as the main motive of all mortification... The renunciation of desire must, from the beginning, be motivated by what lies beyond man, rather than by an egocentric concern with moral progress. An ascetic pursuit of virtue for its own sake has no part in Christian mysticism. Even the desire of spiritual perfection must be God centred from the start.[9]

So, we can have all the best of intentions at this stage, but we are not yet stabilised in virtue, and the attraction of the world, the flesh and the devil is commonly very strong – our love for God is weak and fitful, alternating with periods of weariness and tepidity, and from time to time we are often severely tempted to give up the hardness of this increasingly narrow way:

> The Slough of Despond, the Hill of Difficulty, the Valley of Humiliation, and Vanity Fair are all met in this way, and the soul needs much encouragement if it is to persevere valiantly. A large part of ministry and spiritual direction with the cure of souls is spent sitting on a stone near the top of the Hill of Difficulty encouraging pilgrims.
>
> For the Hill of Difficulty is the grind of the whole thing which none of us can escape, the grind of resisting sin, of turning a deaf ear to temptation, of sticking to the necessary rules, the grind of the early morning alarum, of monotonous days, the grind of helping people about their weaknesses, of seeing their suffering, a grind disfigured by the failure of

losing one's passport through sins of infirmity and sins of surprise, and of having to climb down to find it in penitence and to climb back again forgiven once more.[10]

If our ascetical efforts are intense enough, the process of purification of the heart can lead to a reawakening of the presence of the Holy Spirit at a deeper level in our being. The essential attitudes at this stage, of patience and perseverance and being grounded in self-knowledge, enable us to hold on, in deepening faith, through the very difficult and often harrowing chasm of the dark night of the senses in order to make more and more purgative efforts, so that the rare and fleeting awakening spiritual experiences will eventually begin to *catch fire in the heart* and turn into illumination.

The stage of purgation, or purification relates to the second and third mansions of Teresa's *Interior Castle*. Her emphasis on the prayer of recollection, or active remembrance, at this stage relates to all forms of contemplative prayer that involve some active technique, such as specifically focusing on a holy image, or sacred literature, or focusing on recollection with imagination on Scripture, such as Ignatius' Spiritual Exercises.

ILLUMINATION

Though He has frequently entered into my soul, I have never at any time been sensible of the precise moment of His coming. I have felt that He was present, I remember that He has been with me; I have sometimes been able even to have a presentiment that He would come: but never to feel His coming nor His departure... It is not by the eyes that He enters, for He is without form or colour that they can discern; nor by the ears, for His coming is without sound; nor by the nostrils, for it is not with the air but with the mind that He is blended...

By what avenue then has He entered? Or perhaps that fact may be that He has not entered at all, nor indeed come at all from outside: for not one of these things belongs to outside. Yet it has not come from within me, for it is good, and I know that in me dwelleth no good thing. I have ascended higher than myself, and lo! I have found the Word above me still. My curiosity has led me to descend below myself also, and yet I have found Him still at a lower depth. If I have looked without myself, I have found that He is beyond that which is outside of me; and if within, He was at an inner depth still.

St Bernard of Clairvaux[11]

This is the way for those who have made some progress in the spiritual life, where faith, loyalty and longing for God is deepening into love, where we are spiritually moving towards becoming His friend, towards a deeper, more intimate friendship with Jesus. This is now the beginning of the truly interior life where we are assured of His friendship – 'I do not call you servants any longer, because the servant does not know what the master is doing; but I have called you friends, because I have made known to you everything that I have heard from my Father' (Jn 15:15).

We have been preparing for this by becoming so stripped away, naked, vulnerable and open, becoming small, humble and transparent enough, waiting in expectation, quietly, passively, being as receptive as possible to the movement of the Holy Spirit so that when He begins to touch, to enter into and ultimately transform our soul, we are able to respond to His call, His touch, His hand of friendship, in order to be able to be created afresh in His ineffable peace and silence.

Now, in this cyclical rhythm of the spiritual journey, the purgative phase is giving way, at different times with different intensities, to the perception of a new spiritual, transcendent reality, a new expanded consciousness of the reality, and love, of God, alongside a definite sense of His Presence in our soul. The increasing awareness of divine Presence at this stage is now becoming impressed and infused on the soul so directly, so firmly, and so clearly that there is no mistaking that something quite new is beginning to enter and transform our heart, mind and perception. Spiritual guidance and discernment are becoming even more important at this stage in order to understand and accept these new and wonderful graces that God is beginning to bestow.

The intensive experience of divine Presence is considered the most characteristic mystical phenomenon of this part of the way. This can have a distinctive, almost physical quality. The term 'physical' may be misleading, since the highest, exclusively mystical visions are not physical at all. However, it conveys an even more intense feeling of Presence. The ordinary feeling of God's Presence occurs at a lower degree of intensity than the awareness of a physical presence, while the mystical occurs at the same or at a higher degree (indeed it frequently has all the characteristics of an awareness of physical presence).[12]

Closely connected with the sense of the Presence of God is the definite sense of moving into a different dimension of life, of time, of perception, of knowing, of understanding. It is as if we begin to move into eternal time, where we are intimately touched by, and begin to truly know, with different interior senses, with the centre of our heart and soul, so to speak, the reality of the unity of God and His creation. We begin to live within, breathe, exist, see and understand the paradox of how all of life and creation is simultaneously in constant dynamic movement, and absolutely still, silent, at peace, stationary, all at the same time.

This sense of eternity, of His time, is quite real and tangible, and we realise that this dimension of eternity, God's time, has always been, is, and will always be intersecting our own human ordinary time. Yet, up until this stage, we have been asleep to its living existence. We have not as yet been able to fully live, breathe, and participate in both, simultaneously, until we have been graced to receive the touch, the illumination of the Holy Spirit in this stage of the path.

George Fox describes this beautifully:

> Now, I was come up in spirit through the flaming sword into the Paradise of God. All things were new; and all the creation gave another smell unto me than before, beyond what words can utter… The creation was opened to me; and it was showed me how all things had their names given them, according to their nature and virtue. And I was at a stand in my mind whether I should practise physic for the good of mankind, seeing the nature and virtue of the creatures were so opened to me by the Lord… Great things did the Lord lead me unto, and wonderful depths were opened unto me beyond what can by words be declared; but as people come into subjection to the Spirit of God, and grow up in the image and power of the Almighty, they may receive the word of wisdom that opens all things, and come to know the hidden unity in the Eternal being.[13]

It is important to note that illuminative experiences can occur in many different ways in many different circumstances. Such a revealing of divine Presence and the eternal life may go side by side with daily life and normal mental activities, without any ecstatic or visionary expressions. It does not usually occur in a sudden flash. However, one of the defining characteristics of this way is that a deeper love of, and need for, prayer and silence is developing. As we are becoming more wholehearted in our desire for, and our need to be with, Him, we now strive after more time and space in prayer, solitude and peace in order to enter the intimate chambers of the heart with Him.

Through time, discourse in prayer will become less necessary and finally impossible, and we will pass to affective prayer, pure and simple, which is the normal prayer of souls in this way. This should be a natural spiritual interior development, and this deepening movement of prayer should not be pressed for before we are truly ready for it. It is possible, though uncommon, for a soul to reach contemplation by discursive meditation or vocal prayer alone, and these ways must not be regarded as too elementary for this stage. [14]

With the deepening practice of prayer goes increased love of it. A deeper desire for silence and solitude slowly develops. Thus, in the illuminative way, we begin to love being with Him more than anything else, and consequently want to be alone with Him all the time. This interior aloneness with Christ is becoming a primary necessity of life.

Our aim is not, of course, to become anti-worldly, reclusive, or to retire into seclusion away from life or society. Quite the reverse – the challenge is to become contemplatives in the world, truly in the world but 'not of it' in our heart and soul, as non-attached and non-identified as is psychologically and spiritually possible.

Our usual preoccupations, perceptions, thoughts, ideas, affects and anxieties about the world in this stage are profoundly changing, as our sense and perception of life and of ourselves begin to open up to a strange new fullness of the spiritual life, in this dimension of His Presence and His Eternal Time.

This stage is often characterised by an increased intensity of infused contemplation. A sense of the passive prayer of recollection is deepening towards what Teresa describes in the fourth and fifth mansions as the prayer of quiet – a greater sense of interior stillness and silence. As prayer and contemplation deepen and the gradual process of interiorisation stabilises, a more or less permanent state of interior quiet is beginning to develop slowly.

We are entering into an increasingly more passive state of consciousness, a 'self forgetting attentiveness, a profound concentration, a self merging, which operates a real communion between the seer and the seen'.[15] We begin to love recollection and interior silence and we will want to be with Christ not only in prayer, but also in every part of our life.

Thus, at this stage of illumination, intense love for God is slowly becoming a wholehearted commitment of the whole of our being in an increasingly deepening transformation in God. Our ordinary rhythm of life and our personality, of course, remain, but are slowly becoming subordinate to the sense of increasing openness to Love and Presence and to the expression of His Love in all aspects of our life and living, in body, mind and soul.

So, in the illuminative way, there is a deeper sacrifice of our personal self, wishes and desires. The way of love is essentially the way of sacrifice and surrender, as the interior purification process is constantly uncovering the subtly hidden places of selfishness and egotism. In the earlier stages, our wilfulness and selfish desires have been fought directly, but here they are put in their proper place by the deliberate exercise of humility. Now that God is becoming the centre of our being, our soul is being quietly changed, transformed and transfigured.[16]

In the eastern Orthodox tradition, this stage is known as magnetisation, or gravitation, to God. St Theophan, a well-known Russian ascetic, described this as the beginning of an inner realignment that changes the strength and quality of everything that comes from our being. Our life's centre of gravity begins to change and revolve around God much more wholeheartedly.

We are able to do this through the formation of what is called a magnetic centre. The reality of the spiritual impulse within us is now becoming much more formed. We are able to dwell more deeply within our interior castle, this ark that separates us from the influence and distractions of the world, and leads to the flowering of a life of spontaneous prayer of the heart.[17]

St Theophan describes this spiritual progress from one stage to the next:

> When iron clings to a magnet it is because the power of the magnet draws it. In spiritual matters the same thing is true; it is only clear that God is touching us when we experience this living aspiration; when our spirit turns its back on everything else and is fixed on Him and carried away.
> At first this will not happen; the zealous person is still

turned wholly on himself. Even though he has 'decided' for God this is only in his mind. The Lord does not yet let Himself be tasted, nor is the man yet capable of it, being impure. All he can do is to serve God without tasting Him, so to speak.

Then as his heart begins to be purified and set right, he begins to feel the sweetness of a life pleasing to God; so that he begins to walk in His ways gladly and with love. It becomes his natural element, in which he delights. Then the soul starts to withdraw from everything else as from the cold, and to gravitate towards God, Who warms it. This principle of gravitation is implanted in the fervent soul by divine Grace.[18]

In *The Interior Castle*, Teresa describes the fourth mansion as this critical transition between the stages of purification and illumination. Here, as she describes so eloquently and passionately, mystical experiences often increase instead of dwindling, and their meaning starts to become clearer. The many small illuminations begin to take 'fire in the heart', and can lead, in time, to a permanent union with Christ, our Beloved, in the innermost mansion.

With the illuminative phase, there is also a growing sense of being increasingly more transparent. We are able to become more immediately open, honest and direct as we have less that is unconscious, hidden from view and based on our own personal agenda. Basically, we are surrendering in order to become more God-centred and less 'I'-centred. This is the fulfilment of John's words:

> He who has the bride is the bridegroom. The friend of the bridegroom, who stands and hears him, rejoices greatly at the bridegroom's voice. For this reason my joy has been fulfilled. He must increase, but I must decrease. (John 3:29-30)

What is the nature of this mysterious illumination? Apart from the certitude it imparts, what form does it usually assume in the consciousness of the self? The saints and mystics assure us that its apparently symbolic name is really descriptive; that they do experience a kind of radiance, a flooding of the personality with new light. A new sun rises above the horizon and transfigures their twilit world. Over and over again they return to light imagery in this connection.

Frequently, as in their first conversion, they report an actual and overpowering consciousness of radiant light, ineffable in its splendour, accompanying their inward adjustment. Underhill summarises different descriptions of illumination:

> 'Light rare, untellable!' said Whitman. 'The flowing light of the Godhead,' said Mechthild of Magdeburg, trying to describe what it was that made the difference between her universe and that of normal men. 'Lux vivens dicit' said St Hildegarde in her revelations, which she described as appearing in a special light, more brilliant than the brightness around the sun. It is an 'infused brightness', said Teresa 'a light which knows no night; but rather, as it is always light, nothing ever disturbs it.'[19]

In this quite mysterious divine embrace of the soul by His Presence and Light, the enjoyment of God is beginning to fill the spirit, as well as the body. It is penetrating and awakening the depths of our habitually unconscious existence. Between sleep and wakefulness, when the frontier that separates the conscious from the unconscious can be crossed, and when the body within the body is exposed, ecstasy and joy, which can be humanly overwhelming and unbearable, begin to seize hold of the whole personality.[20]

John Cassian explains:

> It is not easy to know how and in what respects spiritual tenderness overwhelms the soul. Often it is by an ineffable joy and by vehement aspirations that its presence is revealed. So much so that the joy is rendered unbearable by its very intensity, and breaks out into cries that carry tidings of your inebriation as far as a neighbouring cell.
>
> Sometimes on the contrary the whole soul descends and lies hidden in abysses of silence. The suddenness of the light stupefies it and robs it of speech. All its senses remain withdrawn in its inmost depths or completely suspended.

> And it is by inarticulate groans that it tells God of its desire.
> Sometimes, finally, it is so swollen with a sorrowful tenderness
> that only tears can give it consolations.[21]

The main characteristics of the illuminative way are the
deepening of the infused virtues of faith, hope and charity.
The power of spiritual insight into the workings of the
Holy Spirit and a real knowledge of the things of God are
developing in the soul through the graces our Lord is
beginning to bestow. This infused virtue of faith in God
enables us to experience the very real sense of God, by
means of which He begins to enlighten and guide us in His
ways. Our life begins to be more and more genuinely
irradiated by faith and joy. The spiritual insight that comes
by love is not a substitute for intellectual effort to those
who are intellectual, but it is its guide and completion; for
them the two works must go on simultaneously and
harmoniously.[22]

In the purgative way, hope is usually not very strong.
There will be many times when the interior work against
our resistance and negativity is very difficult, when the
odds seem overwhelmingly against the soul and we come
perilously near to despair. Now, in the illuminative way,
hope begins to become a reality to the soul. Love and
knowledge of God are beginning to issue in that certain
trust in Him which is hope. Our life is becoming centred
on Christ. We have an increasing desire to become like
Him.[23]

Mystic illumination takes place on several levels. It may
be a perception, a vision of the senses, a physical awareness
that is not provoked by an ordinary sense stimulus. The
saints and the mystics actually 'see' with their interior eyes
what other people cannot 'see'.[24] The illumination stage
can also be characterised by an often bewildering series of
visions, ecstasies and illuminations that can tremendously
expand the pilgrim's self-knowledge, through the action of
the Holy Spirit.

Teresa's name and reputation are associated with the

more extreme and unusual mystical experiences that she had herself. She writes about these in the latter sections of *The Interior Castle*, particularly in the sixth mansion, detailing the means that God uses to waken the soul – through different sorts of visions, locutions, wordless prayer, 'flight of the spirit' and even levitations. It is obviously difficult for those with no experience of such mystical states to make sense of these, but her text is essentially a spiritual discernment manual with specific guidance on how to understand, interpret and integrate such phenomena.

It is important to note that sensory illumination need not necessarily be mystical in the strictest sense. In the exercises called 'application of the senses', Ignatius Loyola invites the spiritual pilgrim to see with his eyes what is happening in the stable at Bethlehem, to hear the words that are spoken, to smell and taste the sweetness of God, to kiss the holy places where God is present. Yet, these exercises are not intended for mystics only and continue a long, mainly Franciscan, tradition. Here the mystic builds firmly on the foundation of ordinary Christian piety.[25]

At the level of the imagination, other forms of illumination take place. St John refers to infused, passive states that affect the imagination as visions, revelations, voices and spiritual feelings. In these clearly mystical states, the person sees visions or hears words while remaining fully conscious of their 'imaginary', that is, their non-sensuous character. Teresa clearly distinguishes between sensory visions and those visions that she 'sees' without eyes. In general though, mystics do not rank visions, imaginary or sensory, among the higher forms of divine illumination.

Long before our present knowledge of the unconscious, these more dramatic phenomena of altered consciousness were easily suspected as allusions to the devil and were hence confronted with a critical mind. Only their practical effects would reveal whether they came from God or not. Our more advanced knowledge of the unconscious has rendered us even more hesitant to accept visions and voices as direct expressions of God. Not surprisingly, when the soul is shaken to its depths by mystical alteration, certain archaic forms and types, barely veiled in the accepted symbols of the mystic's faith, can often rise to the surface.[26]

There are good reasons to distrust any religious visions – hallucinatory or imaginary – that are not solidly anchored in an overall religious context. Even to visions that illuminate, rather than deceive, John of the Cross advises that we should not attach any importance. In all circumstances it remains difficult to distinguish the epiphenomena of an unconscious transformation from an authentic divine illumination. At best, sensory and imaginary visions or voices play a supporting role in the mystical development. They may strengthen or concretise a mystical insight.[27]

However, with these expansions and enhancements come a new set of difficulties and temptations, which need careful and wise discernment. One of the greatest dangers to the seeker is the tendency to inflation and grandiosity. Unless there is ever more humility, surrender, letting go, detachment and disidentification from the spiritual experiences and ecstasies, this stage can be very destructive.

It is important that our intentions and motivations for the journey towards God have been thoroughly tested for their sincerity, through constant purification, so that essentially we do not want anything for ourselves. Our desire is for God alone, above and beyond anything He can give us or do for us.

The deeper we go on the spiritual path, the more subtle, invisible and powerful the tests and temptations can become. Our safety lies in remaining self-aware, humble, awe-struck before the indescribable and boundless glory of God, and as detached and unidentified as possible by all the new insights and revelations that are being given by Him.

The highest form of mystical illumination is that dark contemplation which, often in an instant, transforms the soul and fills it with lasting insight. Here we are confronted with the kind of intellectual vision where even the cautious

John of the Cross says no illusions can deceive the visionary. We are in the realm of what John calls 'dark contemplation', dark because no distinct vision occurs.

There is nothing to be seen, smelled or heard. Purely, senseless, imaginationless illuminations of this nature have been called 'intellectual' visions, yet they are neither visions nor 'intellectual'. Here the term stands for the purely mental, as opposed to the sensory or imaginary. It implies no kind of discursive understanding.

This transition to a more unitive state of consciousness, towards mystical union or the sacred marriage, involves nothing less than what the Christian mystics described as the 'dark night of the spirit', or, in more modern language, dismemberment of the created self. This annihilation is at once the greatest grace and the most protracted agony on our spiritual journey.

John of the Cross is the great expert on this stage. He speaks of the active and passive night of the spirit in the second book of the *Dark Night of the Soul*. Teresa focuses on this stage of illumination in the fifth and sixth mansions of *The Interior Castle*.

He analyses these deeper states of infused contemplation and refers to them as an inflowing of God into the soul. At this height of awareness, the mind's normal powers of cognition no longer function. In the *night* of the active powers of the mind, illumination means utter darkness. Teresa refers to the 'ligature of the faculties' while God makes His Presence felt 'in the most secret region of the soul, which has but a slight knowledge of it'.[28]

UNION

Teresa described mystical union in the innermost mansion or chamber:

In the spiritual marriage with our Lord, the soul always remains in its centre with its God. Union may be symbolised

by two wax candles, the tips of which touch each other so closely that there is but one light; or again, the wick, the wax, and the light become one, but the one candle can again be separated from the other, and the two candles remain distinct; or the wick may be withdrawn from the wax.

Spiritual marriage is like rain falling from heaven into a river or stream, becoming one and the same liquid, so that the river and the rainwater cannot be divided; or it resembles a streamlet flowing into the ocean, which cannot afterwards be disunited from it.

This marriage may also be likened to a room into which a bright light enters through two windows – though divided when it enters, the light becomes one and the same. (Seventh Mansion, Chapter 4, 2)

This is the way of Christ's lovers, and represents, in its highest manifestations, the climax of Christian perfection and wholeness. It is seen in its fullness in the selfless charity and complete union of the saints. However, there is considerable variation between souls in this way, and even the saints, like the stars, differ from one another in glory.[29]

In the illuminative way, the soul has learned to walk with Christ as friend, and in process of time this has become more and more interior, until we are in continual communion with Christ within the depths of our heart and soul. This mysterious knowledge of 'union with God' in the deepest part of the soul is now being made clearer and clearer, and an ever-steadier understanding of it is progressively deepening.

This knowledge, understanding and unitive state is nothing less that a new birth, or the second birth. It is the place where the Betrothed, or Brides of Christ, are ready to meet their Heavenly Bridegroom, where the soul is beginning to be transfigured in God's Light and Love. The old man/woman has truly died, for the new man/woman to be raised up by the grace of God.

The pilgrim now knows and realises that the lover, the soul, and Christ, the Beloved and His Love, which is all-encompassing, are 'not two', are not separate any longer, but are now conjoined, 'two becoming one', united in marriage, are now of one being and essence, and nothing can ever separate them again.

The external, transcendent Christ is not lost, but as we now dwell in continual interiorisation, Christ is known and worshipped as immanent within the soul itself, who is 'clothed in the wedding garment of Light', where 'the wick, the wax and the light become one' in the seventh dwelling place of our interior castle. There is habitual interior union with Him, and with the Holy Trinity through Him.

This knowing, experience and understanding is lived and breathed in every conceivable way and from every conceivable angle. There is the definite sense of a unity of being, which is like nothing that has gone before, as if all the small parts of life and creation have somehow been profoundly restored and reconnected into one whole, through a power of Love which is, at the same time, utterly transcendent and immanent.

In the illuminative way, the soul has become more recollected and has deliberately striven to become so. Now we are conscious of a fundamental habitual recollection, which, though not always conscious, is yet always there. We desire to possess God always, and never to depart from His Presence; there are no parts of life that we want to keep for ourselves, for we live our whole life in God's sight.[30]

The defining characteristic of sacred marriage is not raptures, visions, or any supernatural phenomena, but a steady possession of awareness of God's Love and His Light which is beginning to radiate from, and transfigure, the centre of our being. Wherever 'I' am and in whatever 'I' may be doing, there is a stable indwelling of the Presence of God.

Once this highest mystical awareness has been reached, the distinction between ordinary states of consciousness and transitory, mystical states, so clear in the earlier dwelling places, recedes without vanishing completely. There can still occur flashes of special illumination, but the general condition has become 'illuminated'.[31] Even while occupying ourselves with all the demands and expectations that the world makes on us, we retain the persistent awareness of God's Presence.

Our consciousness has become transformed and transfigured so as to dwell in the constant awareness of His Presence in the midst of ordinary life, work and service, neither distracting from the other. Both John and Teresa lived their later years in this state of union and became more and more efficient as their work became infused with a mystical inspiration. Because of the permanent character of the highest state of contemplation, Teresa and other saints and mystics refer to it as a 'marriage', that is, a state of being, rather than a singular experience.[32]

In the eleventh century, one of the most famous mystical theologians of the Orthodox tradition, St Simeon the New Theologian, wrote about mystical union as being clothed in the wedding garment of the Light of Christ:

Blessed are those who are clothed in light,
For they are wearing the wedding garment,
Their hands and feet shall not be bound,
Nor shall they be thrown into everlasting fire.
Blessed are those who have kindled the light
In their hearts, who keep it unquenched,
For as they joyfully depart from this life,
They will meet the bridegroom, torch in hand,
As he leads them into the bridal chamber.
Blessed are those who have approached the divine light,
Who have entered it and been absorbed by it,
Mingled in its brightness, sin has no more power,
They will weep bitter tears no more.
Blessed is the monk, offering his prayers to God,
Who sees Him, and is seen near to Him,
Who feels himself out of time and space,
For he is in God alone, knowing not
If he is in or out of the body;
He hears ineffable words, not to be spoken;
He sees what no eye has seen or ear heard,
Nor has it entered the heart of man.

> Blessed is he who has seen the Light of the world
> Formed in himself, for he has conceived Christ
> Within himself; he will be counted as his mother,
> As Christ, in Whom there is no lie, has said.[33]

The purpose of the contemplative journey, and the blessings of His wedding gifts in the bridal chamber, is certainly not for our own personal use. Very much on the contrary, the water is for the flowers, and the whole purpose of our contemplative journey is to return to the world around us, able to engage in the struggle of God's creation, confident that in our innermost selves we are united with Christ, our Lord, in His bridal chamber.[34]

There is the abandonment of our will to the will of God, the purified yearning that the will of God be done in all things, as Teresa emphasises so strongly in the latter mansions. There is a fundamental simplification in life and prayer; the soul becomes unable to practise any virtue separately, for that virtue is simply a manifestation of charity, while in prayer we are not really capable of making forced acts of the virtues because they all become acts of love.

We are able to express the constant deepening of our love and charity to others and the world. The virtues are now no longer actively sought and practised; we have entered upon the intuitive possession of the gifts of the Spirit, and willing to love God in all things, the gifts find expression in action, and everything is seen and done in God.

So, in these final stages of the contemplative journey, we are able to rest in the Presence of God and simultaneously be engaged in the activities and works of loving action, charity and service to our neighbour and the world. Even more wonderfully, we are able to deepen our activities in new ways now that our heart and mind are completely centred in God. The constant blessings of resting and being in divine union overflows and penetrates others' lives, through the union of our being and action.

NOTES

1. Houdek, F. *Guided by the Spirit – a Jesuit Perspective on Spiritual Direction*, Loyola Press, Chicago, 1996, p.37
2. Ibid, pp.78-88
3. Dupre, L. *op.cit.* p.69
4. James, W. *Varieties of Religious Experience,* Penguin, NY, 1985
5. Griffiths, B. *The Golden String,* Templegate, Illinois, 1954, p.11
6. Underhill, E. *Mysticism – the Nature and Development of Spiritual Consciousness,* Oneworld, Oxford, 1996, p.202
7. Harton, F.P. *The Elements of the Spiritual Life – A Study in Ascetical Theology,* SPCK, London, 1957, p.307
8. Underhill, E. *op.cit.* p.220
9. Dupre, L. *op.cit.* p.71
10. Harton, F. *op.cit.* p.309
11. Underhill, E. *op.cit.* p.244
12. Dupre, L. *op.cit.* p.77
13. Underhill, E. *op. cit.* p.258
14 Harton, F. *op.cit.* p.318
15. Dupre, L. *op.cit.* p.76
16. Harton, F. *op.cit.* p.321
17. Amis, R. *op.cit.* pp.285-294
18. Ibid, p.293
19. Underhill, E. *op.cit.* p.249
20. Clement, O. *The Roots of the Christian Mysticism,* New City, London, 1993, p.235
21. Ibid, p. 255
22. Harton, F. *op.cit.* p.315
23. Ibid, p.316
24. Dupre, L. *op.cit.* p.77
25. Ibid, p.78
26. Ibid
27. Ibid, p.79
28. Ibid, p.82
29. Harton, F. *op.cit.* p.323
30. Ibid, p.327
    See also Waaijman, K. *The Mystical Space of Carmel – A Commentary on the Carmelite Rule,* Peeters, Louvain, 1999
31. Dupre, L. *op.cit.* p.84
32. Ibid.
33. Bishop of Nafpaktos Hierotheos, *A Night in the Desert of the Holy Mountain,* Birth of the Theotokos Monastery, Greece, 1995, p.137
34. Tyler, P. *The Way of Ecstasy,* Canterbury Press, Norwich, 1997, p.123

Who was St Teresa of Avila?

Teresa de Cepeda y Ahumada was born on the 28 March 1515 into a noble Castilian family. Spain, at the beginning of the sixteenth century, was newly triumphant. The country had been recently united under the reign of Ferdinand and Isabella, the new Catholic Monarchs, who sent into exile large sections of the Spanish population, predominantly the Jews and the Moors, under their policy of ruthless ethnic cleansing. Across the Atlantic, the wars and triumphs of the conquistadors in the New World were beginning to amass untold wealth for Spain. Within this new political and economic stability in Spain was also a growing movement towards cultural and spiritual instability. This was not confined to Spain, of course, as the Reformation in Northern Europe was at this time in its infancy.

The Spanish religious authorities were becoming increasingly concerned about the activities of recent Jewish and Muslim converts to Christianity, who were derogatorily named *conversos* or *marranos* (meaning pigs). The authorities attempted to strictly enforce the new policy for maintaining religious and ethnic purity. To check that the converted Jews and Moors were not lapsing into old habits, the Spanish Inquisition was given wide-ranging powers to investigate, torture and try those found backsliding.

In 1948, the Jewish ancestry of Teresa was discovered when documents came to light in Valladolid concerning her grandfather, Juan Sanchez. He had been a *judeoconverso*, a Spanish Jew forced by the Inquisition to convert to Christianity on pain of death or expulsion. In 1485 the Inquisition in Toledo had suspected Teresa's grandfather of having 'lapsed into the secret practice of Judaism'. He was subsequently 'reconciled' to the Church.

Sixteenth-century Spain's statutes of 'Purity of Blood' –

limpieza de sangre – created a vulnerable climate for these new Christians, excluding them from many levels of society in education, the military and in the political arena. A veritable litany of camouflages now became necessary for the new Christian converts. Aristocracy of a sort could be bought at great cost, and Teresa's grandfather purchased his certificate of *hidalguia*, a quasi-knighthood, sometime around 1500.[1] He then moved his family from Toledo to prosperous Avila on the Castilian plain to begin a new life where his humiliating Jewish past would not be known. There he could be assimilated into society and resume his merchant profession.

He was successful in creating a new life and image for himself and inventing a fictional lineage. His sons married well into established old Catholic families. Teresa's father, Alonso Sanchez de Cepeda married first Catalina del Peso y Henao, and, after her death, the fourteen-year-old Beatriz de Ahumada, Teresa's mother. In 1528 Beatriz died, exhausted, having borne Alonso nine children. Thus, Teresa was brought up in a climate that was deeply conscious of its Christian heritage, whilst being slightly uneasy and apologetic about its more ambiguous roots. Her family was certainly a microcosm of Spanish society and ethnic racial mix, which was common at this time.

Teresa was by nature passionate and, from all accounts, a rather attractive and charming young lady. She suffered a devastating blow when her mother died at the young age of thirty-three, worn out by childbearing. Teresa was only thirteen at the time, and she sought consolation by appealing to the motherhood of Our Lady. In her autobiography, the *Life of Saint Teresa of Avila by Herself,* she confesses to certain youthful indiscretions of the flesh, which seem quite unexceptional to us today, but were cause for scandal in the closeted Spain of her time.

After her mother died, and her only elder sister – a half-sister, Dona Maria – married, her father grew concerned about her. He sent her as a boarder, at the age of 16, to a local finishing school, St Mary of Grace, which was attached to the Augustinian convent at Avila. During the eighteen months that she spent at the school, her strong antipathy to the religious life at this age had weakened to a vague distaste.[2]

Teresa entered the Carmelite Convent of the Incarnation at Avila in November 1536 at the age of twenty-one. Although the latter stages of the five-year conflict with herself, from the age of sixteen to entering the Incarnation, had been excessively painful, her entry into the religious life heralded an almost miraculous change in her state:

> When I left my father's house I felt such a dreadful distress that the pain of death itself cannot be worse. Every bone in my body seemed to be wrenched asunder. For, as I had no love for God to subdue my love for my father and relatives, the whole action did me such violence that, if the Lord had not helped me, my resolution would not have been enough to push me forward.
>
> At the moment of my entrance into this new state I felt a joy so great that it has never failed me even to this day: and God converted the dryness of my soul into a very great tenderness. All the details of the religious life delighted me. In fact, sometimes when I used to sweep the house at hours that I had once spent on my indulgence and adornment, the memory that I was now free from these things gave me a fresh joy, which surprised me, for I could not understand where it came from.[3]

The Spanish Carmelite order of the sixteenth century was the offspring of a regularisation of the order that had occurred in Palestine at the beginning of the thirteenth century. Toward the end of the twelfth century, a number of crusaders, pilgrims and holy people settled on the western slopes of Mount Carmel, near modern-day Haifa, desirous of imitating Elijah the Prophet by living a hermit-like life in the grottoes of the mountain.

Sometime between 1206 and 1214, their Prior, St Brocard, solicited a written rule of life from the then Patriarch of Jerusalem, St Albert. The result was the drafting of the Primitive Rule of the Order of the Blessed Virgin

Mary of Mount Carmel, which incorporated them into the diocese of Jerusalem and initiated the history of what was to become the Carmelite Order.[4] It is ironic that legend has placed the origins of the Carmel hermits with devotion to the prophet Elijah, and that Teresa inadvertently reclaimed part of her Jewish heritage through entering the Carmel in Avila.

ENTERING THE RELIGIOUS LIFE

Her twenty or so years at the Convent of the Incarnation were filled with incident. She writes in her *Life* that she was only half converted: 'But You, my Lord, were prepared for me to misuse Your grace for almost twenty years, and to accept the injury so that I might become better.'[5] Not until she was about forty-two years of age did the beginnings of sanctity appear in her. To use a favourite image of her own, she was a plant of slow growth, and needed a great deal of watering.[6] It is perhaps difficult to conceive of the life of the nuns in Spanish convents such as the Incarnation at this time. The nuns had a great deal of freedom; they could go out of the convent, could receive visitors and accept presents.

There was also a great disparity in wealth and living conditions of the women entering the religious life. The daughters of the wealthy families of Avila would live in a series of spacious apartments, whereas their less well-off sisters would be expected to be little more than skivvies to them. The local townsfolk would frequently come to the convent and the general chatter, gossip and flirting contributed to the overall 'salon' atmosphere.

Needless to say, Teresa revelled in it all and proved immensely popular and sociable, but admits in her autobiography that she was not able to progress any further in the contemplative life, and that she was 'ashamed to return to God and to approach Him in such intimate friendship as that of prayer.'[7]

Below the surface ran a darker strain. Just after her profession of vows in 1538, Teresa's health totally collapsed. Even before entering the Incarnation, she had suffered from serious fainting fits and various fevers. Her entry into the religious life increased their frequency. She developed heart trouble and other ailments. In August 1539 she fell into a serious decline after a series of well-meant but mis-guided attempts to cure her and experienced a prolonged cataleptic fit.

The young nun was pronounced dead. Her requiem mass was celebrated in one convent of the order, and a grave was dug for her in the convent grounds! Thankfully, she escaped being buried alive, and at the end of four days came to herself, remaining in a greatly debilitated state for nearly eight months. For almost three years more her paralysis, though gradually improving, crippled her and when she began to crawl on her hands and knees, she praised God. Not until her fortieth year did the effects of it entirely leave her.

During this time she began to turn back to her life of prayer and forsake some of the diversions she had previously indulged in with such gusto. To counterbalance her debili-tating health, Teresa began to enjoy spiritual experiences. She was greatly influenced by a popular devotional book of the time called the *Third Spiritual Alphabet* by the Franciscan, Osuna.

Previously, the contemplative life had been a sealed book to her. Following Osuna's leading, she passed through the stage of meditation and in time was raised to the prayer of quiet, and 'occasionally even to union'. During the whole of these twenty years, she confined her spiritual exercises to meditation, and except after communion, she writes that she 'never dared begin to pray without a book'[8], finding that whenever she discarded the book she experienced distractions and aridity. More importantly, for those twenty years, she did not find even one spiritual director who understood her.

From the late 1550s accounts of 'Teresa the Mystic' and her locutions, visions, levitations and ecstasies begin. The quickening of Teresa's spiritual life is often described as her 'second conversion', beginning about 1555[9]. She describes the return of a sense of God's Presence more vivid than anything she had known before:

> There would come to me unexpectedly such a feeling of the presence of God as it made it impossible for me to doubt that He was within me, or that I was totally engulfed in Him. This was no kind of vision; I believe it is called mystical theology. The soul is then so suspended that it seems entirely outside itself. The will loves; the memory is, I think, almost lost, and the mind, I believe, though it is not lost, does not reason – I mean that it does not work, but stands as if amazed at the many things it understands.[10]

She had passed from the prayer of quiet to the threshold of the state she later describes as the fifth mansion – the spiritual betrothal or the prayer of union.

As early as 1539, Teresa also began to experience a series of visions and voices, which were to become a normal part of her life. She writes how, when she was unsure about a new friendship that was developing:

> Christ appeared before me, looking more severe, and giving me to understand that there was something about this (friendship) that displeased Him. I saw Him with the eyes of my soul more clearly than I could ever have seen Him with the eyes of the body, and the vision made such an impression on me that, although it was more than twenty six years ago, I seem to see His presence even now.[11]

At this time she was particularly influenced by studying St Augustine's *Confessions*, and St Ignatius' *Spiritual Exercises*. She also consulted the Jesuit fathers, who had recently founded a house in Avila. One of these priests, Fr Juan de Pradanos, greatly encouraged her. Teresa writes that

> He said that my experiences were quite patently the work of the spirit of God, and that what I needed was to start praying

again, because I had not laid a good foundation, nor had I yet begun to understand the nature of mortification... He said that I must never on any account abandon prayer, on the contrary I must work hard at it, since God was granting me such special favours. How did I know, he asked me, that the Lord did not wish to benefit many people and to do much else through me?[12]

Teresa began to have her first experiences of rapture. After her confessor had been moved from Avila, she took a matter of some concern to his successor. Following the spiritual advice he gave to her to 'put the matter before God for some days and to recite the hymn *Veni Creator*, that God might show me the better course', she 'spent the greater part of one day in prayer, beseeching the Lord to help me content Him in every way.'

She goes on to write what then happened:

> I began the hymn; and as I was reciting it a rapture came on me so suddenly that it almost carried me away; it was so plain that I could make no mistake about it. This was the first time that the Lord had granted me this grace of ecstasy, and I heard these words: 'I want you to converse now not with men but with angels.' This absolutely amazed me, for my soul was greatly moved and these words were spoken to me in the depths of the spirit.[13]

From that time on, Teresa was only able to make firm friends with those who, like herself, loved God passionately and were trying to serve Him: 'These words have been fulfilled. For I have never since been able to form a firm friendship, or to take comfort in, or feel particular love for, any people except those whom I believe to love God and be trying to serve Him. This has been something beyond my control; and has made no difference if the people have been relatives or friends.'[14]

Teresa, herself, became matter of fact about the visions, ecstasies and unusual experiences which God was giving her, and saw these 'incidentals' as only having meaning and value within the context of a simple life of prayer and good works.

REFORMING CARMEL

Teresa was about to embark on an extraordinary phase in her life, taking on the reform of the religious life of Spain. This would finally force her to withdraw from the Incarnation with its somewhat gossipy atmosphere to eventually form a new community, much simpler and smaller, and based around the austerity of the original Rule of St Albert.

After her initial visions, ecstasies and the previous encouraging spiritual direction, she now suffered from inept and critical spiritual directors. She felt more alone than ever in discerning the will of God for her life and spiritual path, and for her religious community

However, her difficulties and ordeals developed in her a force of tough determination, a decisive aptitude and a depth of spiritual courage which were destined to set her apart from her contemporaries and which served her well in the difficult times to come.

She writes movingly of this time in her life:

> It happened at times that I was greatly tried and maligned about a certain matter by almost everyone in the town where I live and by my Order. I was greatly distressed by many things, which arose to disturb me. But the Lord said to me then: 'what are you afraid of? Do you not know that I am all-powerful? I will fulfil my promises to you'. And they were fulfilled shortly afterwards. Then I began to have such strength that I believe I could have undertaken new enterprises in his Service, even if they had cost me more trials and caused me to suffer afresh. This has happened to me so many times that I cannot count them.[15]

Her visions continued and Teresa set down her under-standing as it grew, listing three kinds of spiritual visions in ascending order of perfection. The first is the corporeal vision, which is manifested to the bodily eye. The second is the imaginary vision, which is a representation by the action of the imagination alone, without the intervention of the eye. Thirdly, the intellectual vision is spiritual perception by the understanding alone, without the production of any sensible image.[16]

Teresa never had a corporeal vision, but writes of her first intellectual vision, which happened in 1558:

> At the end of two years, during the whole of which both other people and myself had prayed continually that the Lord might either lead me by another path or reveal the truth – and all the time the locutions which, as I have said, the Lord was giving me were very frequent – I had the following experience.
>
> One day when I was at prayer, I saw Christ at my side – or, to put it better, I was conscious of Him, for I saw nothing with the eyes of the body or the eyes of the soul. He seemed quite close to me, and I saw that it was He. As I thought, He was speaking to me. Being completely ignorant that such visions were possible, I was very much afraid at first, and could do nothing but weep, though as soon as He spoke His first word of assurance to me, I regained my usual calm, and became cheerful and free from fear.
>
> All the time Jesus Christ seemed to be at my side, but as this was not an imaginary vision I could not see in what form. But I most clearly felt that He was all the time on my right, and was a witness of everything that I was doing.'[17]

An imaginary vision of Christ in His Resurrection Body is another of her well-known visions:

> Once when I was at Mass on St Paul's Day, there stood before me the most sacred Humanity, in all the beauty and majesty of His Resurrection body, as it appears in paintings...
> I will only remark that if there were nothing in Heaven to delight the eye but the great beauty of glorified bodies, that alone would be a very great bliss, particularly if it were the Humanity of our Lord Jesus Christ... For in its whiteness and radiance alone it exceeds anything that we can imagine.

She gives an extraordinary description of the nature of the divine light of God, which she was graced to perceive, although she says that the writing of it was greatly distressing to her because of the 'great violence to oneself':

> It is not a dazzling radiance but a soft whiteness and infused radiance, which causes the eyes great delight and never tires

of them; nor are they tired by the brilliance which confronts them as they look on this Divine beauty. The brightness and light that appear before the gaze are so different from those of earth that the sun's rays seem quite dim by comparison, and afterwards we never feel like opening our eyes again.

It is as if we were to look at a very clear stream running over a crystal bed, in which the sun was reflected and then to turn to a very muddy brook, with an earthy bottom, running beneath a clouded sky.

Not that the sun or anything like sunlight enters into the vision; on the contrary, its light seems the natural light, and the light of this world appears artificial. It is a light that never yields to darkness and, being always light, can never be clouded. It is of such a kind, indeed, that no one, however great his intellect, could imagine its nature in the whole course of his life.[18]

One of her most famous mystical experiences is the vision called the transverberation of her heart, which happened in 1559. This has been immortalised in the famous Bernini sculpture, found in St Paul's Cathedral in the Vatican. Here she describes what happened to her:

Our Lord was pleased that I should sometimes see a vision of this kind. Beside me, on the left hand, appeared an angel in bodily form; such as I am not in the habit of seeing except very rarely. Though I often have visions of angels, I do not see them. They come to me only after the manner of the first type of vision that I described.

But it was our Lord's will that I should see this angel in the following way. He was not tall but short, and very beautiful; and his face was so aflame that he appeared to be one of the highest ranks of angels, who seem to be all on fire. They must be of the kind called cherubim, but they do not tell me their names.

I know very well that there is a great difference between some angels and others, and between these and others still, but I could not possibly explain it. In his hands, I saw a great golden spear, and at the iron tip there appeared to be a point of fire. This he plunged into my heart several times so that it penetrated to my entrails.

When he pulled it out, I felt that he took them with it, and left me utterly consumed by the great love of God...

> The sweetness caused by this intense pain is so extreme that
> one cannot possibly wish it to cease, nor is one's soul then
> content with anything but God. This is not a physical, but a
> spiritual pain, though the body has some share in it – even a
> considerable share.[19]

At the time of the transverberation of her heart, Teresa was
nearing the end of more than twenty years as an obscure
nun. She stood at the threshold of her spiritual destiny to
reform the Carmelite monastic order. She befriended an
elderly friar, St Peter of Alcantara, who had been a part of
the discalced reform movement among the Franciscans. It
seems that he was one of the first to whom she turned to
discuss the possibility of reforming her own order. Teresa
records other early conversations she had about reform.

But it was the experience of a direct command from
God which set things in motion and clearly showed that
reform was the will of God. This is how she describes what
happened:

> One day, after Communion, the Lord earnestly commanded
> me to pursue this aim with all my strength. He made me
> great promises; that the house would not fail to be established,
> that great service would be done Him there, that its name
> should be St Joseph's; that he would watch over us at one of
> its doors and Our Lady at the other; that Christ would be
> with us; that the convent would be a star, and that it would
> shed the most brilliant light.
>
> This vision had a very great effect on me. For these
> words spoken to me by the Lord were of such a kind as to
> leave me in no doubt that they were from him. They
> distressed me very deeply, because they gave me a partial
> glimpse of the great anxieties and labours that the task entailed
> for me.[20]

Needless to say, as soon as the proposal became generally
known, it met with the most severe opposition and
persecution, the strongest resistance coming from her own
nuns at the Incarnation! There were even threats that she
might be denounced to the Inquisition! It was an extremely
difficult time for Teresa, and she decided to wait for several

months, during which all those in spiritual authority rejected the project and forbade her to set up a new convent.

Only one of her advisors supported her – Peter of Alcantara. His experience with the Discalced Franciscans made him probably the only spiritual guide and friend who had intimate understanding and knowledge of what God was commanding her to do. Finally, after deciding to go ahead and make the new foundation, she began to experience renewed visions:

> One day, when I was earnestly commending my project to God, the Lord told me to let nothing dissuade me from my purpose of founding the convent in poverty, for that was His Father's will and His own, and He would help me. I was in a profound state of rapture at the time, the effects of which were so great that I could not doubt its divine origin.[21]

Amidst the greatest secrecy, Teresa's first foundation was made on St Bartholomew's Day, 24 August 1562. Her convent of St Joseph's opened with four new nuns of the Discalced (literally shoeless) reform. Her triumph was short-lived, however. Two days later, a meeting of the city council at which representatives of all the town's Religious Orders were present, decided that the convent must be shut down. After an unsuccessful attempt at a forced eviction that afternoon, the council took to the law courts.

Almost immediately following the foundation, Teresa was plunged into a long interior conflict within her soul which lasted until she made a vow to do everything in her power to obtain the necessary permission to enter the new convent and undertake a vow of enclosure: 'The moment I had made this vow, the devil fled, leaving me quiet and happy, and so I remained, as I have done ever since... Indeed I am so very happy that I sometimes wonder whether I could possibly have chosen any place on earth more delightful.'[22] Although her own interior conflict subsided, the exterior conflict raged about her, and for several years she had to fight against legal proceedings which had been instituted against her.

She was greatly encouraged in her determination not to yield to the lawsuit by a vision of St Peter of Alcantara, who had recently died. Concerning her vision, she writes:

> On the same night [of the day that the discussion of the terms had begun] the blessed friar Peter of Alcantara, who was dead, appeared to me. Knowing what great resistance and persecution we were encountering, he had written to me before his death to say how pleased he was that the foundation was being heavily opposed, since all these efforts that the devil was making to prevent the foundation were a sign that great service would be rendered to the Lord in the new convent.
>
> I had seen him twice already since his death in a state of great glory, and so I was not afraid. Indeed, his appearance made me very happy, for he always came in his glorified body, full of great bliss, and it made me most blissful to see him.[23]

Two years later, in 1563, Teresa finally won and settled into her new home. The reform of the Carmelites had begun. She called the next four and a half years, from 1563 to 1567, 'the most restful years of my life', and indeed they were. She devoted herself with all her motherly skills to the establishment of her new little convent. She also began her writing career in earnest and completed her first two works – *The Life* and the *Way of Perfection,* both now spiritual classics.

From then until the end of her life, she was concerned with the establishment and spread of the reform that she had begun. Thus, in 1567, a new house was founded at Medina del Campo. In the next few years foundations at Valladolid, Malagon, Toledo, Salamanca, Segovia and elsewhere followed. The remarkable stories of all these foundations are contained in her *Book of Foundations.*

1567 was also significant as the year of Teresa's first encounter with one of the most influential people in her life, the mystic and saint, John of the Cross. Although he was only twenty-five when they met in Medina, Teresa, at fifty-two, immediately recognised his great spiritual gifts and proposed that he help her in establishing a male branch of her reform – which he duly did. The two of them got on famously, yet sadly their correspondence has not been preserved, so we can only guess at the insights these two spiritual giants shared.

July 1571 saw Teresa elected as Prioress of her old *alma mater* at the Convent of the Incarnation. The convent was exactly divided as to those who supported her and those who opposed her – when she arrived on 10 July to take up her position there were riots both inside and outside the convent!

Being no stranger to such situations, she simply began the lengthy and not unsuccessful process of reconciliation. She even sought an audience with Phillip, the King of Spain, who had become favourably disposed towards her situation. He took an active interest, and became involved in establishing the Reform.[24]

Further troubles were ahead though – moves were afoot to have the Reform suppressed. In April 1575, a General Chapter of the Carmelites was held in Spain and it was decided to suppress her twelve convents and prohibit her from founding new ones. It was recommended that she herself should 'retire' indefinitely to a convent of her choice in Castile – effectively becoming a prisoner.

Remarkably, she obeyed her superiors but continued to battle from behind the walls of the Toledo convent. John of the Cross was spared even that luxury. He was kidnapped by fellow monks on 3 December 1577, and held prisoner in a cell at the Discalced monastery in Toledo for nine months. His cell was 10ft by 6ft, and had once been used as a latrine. He was publicly beaten each day and given little to eat or drink.

Yet as this reign of terror and persecution towards her Reform was at its height, these two mystics, separately and intensely, turned within themselves to their spiritual resources and produced two of the greatest works of all Christian spiritual literature. John's poems would later form the basis of the *Dark Night of the Soul* and the *Ascent of Mount Carmel*, and Teresa wrote her own mystical masterpiece *The Interior Castle* in Toledo.

She was reluctant to write it, because she didn't want to be exposed to the increased attacks and persecution that would inevitably follow, but she was ordered to do so by her confessors. It was originally only intended for the nuns of the Reform. The writing took three months, and the companions who were looking after her at the time said that she wrote it as if in an intoxicated state, in a kind of ecstasy.

By 1580, peace had been declared and Teresa, sixty-five by now and calling herself 'an old crone', set off on the road to continue founding convents. John, having escaped, began to write and preach in earnest (however, the toll had been taken on his health and he died at the age of 49 in 1591). Teresa struggled on, and by Spring 1580 she had made the thirteenth of her foundations in Villanueva de la Lara, near La Mancha. In 1581 she heard that the conflict within the Carmelite Order had ended in partition.

By mid 1582, however, it was clear that she was coming to the end of the road, and in the autumn of that year she was asked by the Duchess of Alba to attend the labour of her daughter-in-law so that the delivery would be blessed by the presence of the saint. After a very difficult journey she arrived at the Duchess's castle, only to be told that the child had already been born and she would no longer be required. Exhausted and totally worn out, she retired to her convent at Alba de Tormes and there sank quickly.

Her nuns came around her bedside and begged her for some words that would be of help to them in the years to come. But, practical to the last, she only charged them always to keep strictly to their Rule and Constitutions. After that she said little more, except for repeating again and again a verse from Psalm 51: 'A sacrifice to God is an afflicted spirit; a contrite and humbled heart, O God, Thou wilt not despise.'[25]

She died at nine o'clock on 4 October 1582, having

exclaimed, as she received the Blessed Sacrament the evening before:

> Oh my Lord and my Spouse! This is the longed-for hour, it is time now that we should see each other again, my Beloved and my Lord, it is time now that I should go to Thee; let us go in peace and may Thy holy will be done. Now the hour has come for me to leave this exile, and to enjoy thee whom I have so much desired.[26]

The hidden one was about to reveal Himself.

NOTES

1. Orell, L.H. *Teresa's Jewish Mysticism*, in Spiritual Life – A Quarterly of Contemporary Spirituality, Vol 36, No. 2, Summer 1990
2. Allison Peers, E. *Mother of Carmel – A Portrait of St Teresa of Jesus*, SCM, London, 1948, p.13
3. Teresa of Avila, *The Life of Teresa of Avila by herself*, op.cit. p.33
4. Welch, J. *The Carmelite Way*, Gracewing, UK, 1996, p.9
5. Teresa of Avila, *The Life of Teresa of Avila by herself*, op. cit. p.34
6. Allison Peers, *op. cit.* p.14
7. Teresa of Avila, *The Life of Teresa of Avila by herself*, op.cit. p.50
8. Ibid, Chapter 4
9. Allison Peers, *op.cit.* p.19
10. Teresa of Avila, *The Life of Teresa of Avila by herself*, op.cit. p.71
11. Ibid. p.53
12. Ibid. p.168
13. Ibid, p.172
14. Ibid, p.172
15. Ibid, p.184
16. Allison Peers, *op.cit.* p.26
17. Teresa of Avila, *The Life of Teresa of Avila by herself*, op.cit. p.198
18. Ibid, p.198
19. Ibid, p.210
20. Ibid, p.237
21. Ibid, p.260
22. Ibid, p.269
23. Ibid, p.273
24. Allison Peers, *op. cit.* p.124
25. Ibid, p.139
26. Obbard, E.R. *La Madre, The Life and Spirituality of Teresa of Avila*, St Pauls Publishing, 1994, p.149.

Introducing the mystical text
The Interior Castle

Teresa wrote *The Interior Castle* in 1577, five years before she died. It was to become one of the best-known treatises of Christian contemplative literature and is the product of mature reflection on her journey towards, and in, God, and of a lifetime of observing and directing her spiritual daughters – the nuns of Carmel. In this work, she speaks with a degree of assurance and maturity not found in her other writings. After the Inquisition had seized her autobiography, her confessor suggested that she 'write a fresh book, and expound the teaching in a general way, without saying to whom the things that you describe have happened'.

Teresa describes a vision in which she saw the soul as:

> **resembling a castle, formed of a single diamond or very transparent crystal, and containing many rooms, just as in heaven there are many mansions.** (I, Chapter 1, 2)

The text is essentially a description of and guide to, spiritual change, progress, surrender and transformation throughout seven mansions, which represent three main stages in the life of interiorisation and prayer.

In the first three mansions, she tells of what the soul can do to move towards the inner mansions where God dwells. The fourth mansion is the transitional stage where the soul begins to undergo interior transformation, and God begins to take over. The most interior mansions are where Teresa describes God as increasingly purifying the soul towards His Likeness, leading to a state of spiritual marriage in the seventh, and innermost, mansion.

Teresa's experience and expression of spirituality, her description of the stages of the spiritual life and, indeed, many of her contemplative writings are suffused with the language of symbols and imagery. In the text, she says that certain experiences and descriptions of the important stages in the spiritual life could only be expressed in image, metaphor or allegory.

Her symbolism is a living, dynamic mix of a variety of images that arose within her in response to her own direct spiritual progress and surrender to God. For her, the soul was, at different times, a garden, a tree, a castle, a butterfly, in addition to a whole range of other imagery throughout the text e.g. water, fountains.

THE SEVEN MANSIONS

In *The Interior Castle* Teresa maps out the contemplative path towards union with God. Much preliminary preparation must occur before the pilgrim is ready to fully surrender to the Love and the will of God in their life.

In the initial stages, the journey entails the growth and nurturing of a sense of soul, or self in the modern Jungian sense. This sense of individuation is called the 'journey towards God'. Often tremendous pain and suffering over a long period of time accompany the disintegration of false, outmoded patterns and conditioning as we move towards the innermost dwelling places and our surrender to the Love and Light of God.

The purpose of the psychological journey is to bring us to a place of relative balance in ordinary life. This place lies at the outskirts of an unknown interior castle inside which another journey can begin. Mystical tradition speaks about that 'other journey', the 'journey in God' that begins at the place of the soul.

The interior castle symbolises our soul. Teresa gives an account of the mystical journey of the soul through each of the mansions until the centremost mansion is surrendered to, where, she tells us, 'the most secret things pass between

God and the soul. In the seventh and innermost mansion is the King of Glory in the greatest splendour, illumining and beautifying all the mansions.'

In the first mansion, she describes the castle as containing:

> **many rooms, some are above, some below, others at the side; in the centre, in the very midst of them all, is the principal chamber in which God and the soul hold their most secret intercourse.** (I, Chapter 1, 4)

She says that each mansion is inside the other:

> **Consider how a palmito tree [which is indigenous to that area of Spain] has many layers of bark, which surround the savoury pith, and must be removed before it can be eaten.** (I, Chapter 2, 8)

It is important to emphasise that Teresa is not advocating a strictly hierarchical model of different stages of the spiritual life. The scheme of the three ways, or stages, of progress in the spiritual life – purification, illumination and union - dates back to the influential writings of the fifth-century monk Pseudo Dionysius, author of *Divine Names, Mystical Theology* and *Celestial Hierarchy.*

Two medieval theologians, St Bonaventure and Hugh of Balma, took up the Dionysian triad and wrote famous mystical treatises on the interior life. Each took opposing views as to whether the stages are primarily hierarchical or are mainly different ways to access God.[1]

Bonaventure wrote the mystical treatise *On the Three Ways* in the thirteenth century. He saw the three stages as different types of contemplative exercises to be put into practice as ways of access to the experience of God:

> There are three forms of exercise in these three ways: meditation (with reading), prayer and contemplation. In each one of these three forms of prayer, the soul is purified, illumined and perfected.[2]

However, Hugh of Balma, writing in *Theologia Mystica* in the second half of the thirteenth century, conceived of the three ways as successive stages of the spiritual life, where each stage is consolidated before moving on to the next:

> Three ways must be followed if a person is to possess this excellent wisdom; the first cleanses the heart, the second enlightens it, and the third unites it with God.[3]

Teresa's perspective was certainly a blend of these views of the mystical life, and she guided her 'daughters of Carmel' with particular discernment, according to the different dispositions and needs of the individuals in her spiritual care. Doubtless she would have been fully conversant with differing perspectives, having had John of the Cross and Peter of Alcantara to guide her, two of the greatest mystical saints and ascetics of the era.

For Teresa, God is the Beloved – the Spouse within the innermost chamber of the heart. The contemplative journey inward is the journey to a place where God's Love fuses, melts, and dissolves into the life of the soul. She is also very careful to describe this castle as having an abundance of rooms. She does not want us to be deceived and think that we have encountered the Love and Presence of God when we have not.

Outside the castle are those who feel no attraction to God or the spiritual life, who are entirely caught up in the life of physical ambition, pursuit and gratification. She says that the first dwelling place represents the awakening of our spiritual life through devotion and the longing for God, and that prayer, meditation and reflection are the gateways into this castle.

In these early stages of the spiritual life, Teresa counsels perseverance, humility and self-knowledge in equal measure, the spiritual task here being how to learn to enter ourselves. Knowing ourselves, in this context, is about being increasingly familiar with, and accepting of, our own fallibility, our needs, vulnerabilities, our blocks, pain, limitations, and ultimately our complete dependence on God.

She discusses the difficulties in turning away from

worldly appearances and outward life towards the spiritual life and a relationship to God. This also begins with the loosening of thousands of our attachments and identifications – of who we think we are; our image of ourselves; our perceived status; our need to achieve and be seen in a particular way, in whatever form that may take.

In order to penetrate more deeply into our interior castle, she advises us to:

> **withdraw from all unnecessary cares and business, as far as is compatible with the duties of one's state of life.** (I Chapter 2, 16)

She advises that it is essential to keep close to spiritual directors and mentors in the outer mansions. The soul is not strong enough to defend herself alone where she needs protection, guidance, and the nurturing of hope and faith in God. Teresa constantly emphasises the importance of humility, which, of course, is the antidote to self-importance, grandiosity, pride, arrogance and egotism.

In the second dwelling place, Teresa concentrates on the role of prayer as the doorway into our interior castle, and on the importance of perseverance. She says that God reaches us here mainly through objective means, such as literature, sermons and inspiring friendships. It is the beginning of the painful and arduous process of interior spiritual transformation in God.

She warns that we will feel uncomfortable and vulnerable in this dangerous dwelling place. We can be making great efforts to turn around towards God, and may be beginning to taste moments of God's Presence, but the longing for God and the sense of exile and separation from Him can begin to feel much more acute and painful.

She seems to be referring to the teasing and perilous state of the inner world, of the transparent walls in the castle, where we can see the deceptively visible centre but do not know how to reach it: where it is impossible to orientate ourselves without spiritual guidance and discernment.

Teresa says that here the soul is actually in less danger than in the first mansion, as there is a growing understanding of our progress in our journey towards, and in, God, and we can increasingly expect to penetrate more deeply into our interior castle. We suffer more at this second dwelling place simply because we have fewer defences. The more our soul is turning towards Him and reaching out to the Divine Spouse, the more He is reaching out and eagerly beckoning us towards Him.

She writes about the cacophony of temptations, distractions and conflicts that can occur when our spiritual life deepens. In this place, we are less able to deceive ourselves. We become more aware of our evasions and self-delusions and our interior and exterior conflicts can seem, paradoxically, to intensify.

It is important to understand that the increased conflict is a sign of increasing clarity of understanding. As we see more of what our peace and wholeness *could be,* we sense and see more plainly our own lack of it. A fuller consciousness begins to dawn of what our efforts can and, more importantly, cannot achieve. The heart of Teresa's call to prayer is a radical spiritual transformation, nothing less than the alignment of our will with God's Will.

For Teresa, spiritual life means active life in the world, using ongoing discernment about our spiritual work and destiny. It means an awakening of charity; a deepening capacity for suffering in the performance of deeds of charity, and an enkindling spiritual fire to sustain these actions.

The third mansion is an extended meditation on Matthew 19. This is the story where a (rich) man asks Jesus what he must do to possess eternal life, in addition to keeping all the commandments, and Jesus responds by commanding total surrender: 'If you wish to be perfect, go, sell your posessions, and give money to the poor, and you will have treasure in heaven; then come, follow me' (Mt 19:21).

Here we are called to a life of deeper spirituality and

love for, and in, Christ, and surrender to His will. In this dwelling place, our human personality and will are very much still in control. This is what is being so severely tested – our psychological and spiritual maturity, our spiritual sincerity and increasing willingness to surrender, let go and trust to God's Will. Teresa talks about the increasing need for spiritual discernment and discrimination at this stage, as it is not possible to judge from outward appearances what is happening deeper within the soul.

Like Jesus admonishing the young man, Teresa directly challenges those times in our lives when we might be feeling complacent, or safe, or content that we are doing 'all the right things'. It is a call to more radical change, awakening and transformation in the love of God. The problem she is emphasising here is that the soul has not yet fully surrendered to God – our own will and efforts have brought us to this place.

Although we might be doing all the right and virtuous things in the eyes of the world, internally we might still be maintaining a fearful and anxious regard about ourselves; we can still be locked, to some extent, within ourselves. She says tartly that this stage is very characteristic of persons who are so extremely correct that they are often shocked at everything they see!

Here, we are called to give up, however reluctantly, those things and aspects of our lives which are the nearest and dearest, particularly those with which we are the most identified. The giving up may be what is necessary to bring us closer to God. The loss of things we are close to, and the enormous pain and suffering this can cause are themes that Teresa returns to time and again, particularly in the dark night of the soul in the latter mansions. She emphasises that there is a need to understand and to proceed from a deeper humility, a humility that now possesses a kind of holy abandonment of ourselves into the possibilities of a deeper spiritual life.

The fourth dwelling place is the place of spiritual

transition and transformation, where the inner landscape begins to change qualitatively. Up to this point all we have done is prepare ourselves for surrender in our readiness and ability to accept our inner incompleteness and total dependency on God. From here on infused grace begins to operate more fully – our progress is up to God alone.

This is the place where the natural and the supernatural combine. In prayer we are beginning to experience something very different, as if being more and more effortlessly absorbed into a state of grace. It is a deeper level of conversion and abandonment of our own will. Teresa says the rational faculties must be decreasing as our capacity to love and be loved is increasing.

Some of Teresa's most sublime descriptions of deep prayer are here, and some of the subtle experiences of deep silence. In this dwelling place she writes of consolations and spiritual delights, two particular spiritual experiences. The Spanish *contentos* is translated as 'consolations', which are experiences of joy, peace, and satisfaction, happiness… similar to those derived from ordinary everyday events.

The Spanish *gustos* are experiences described as spiritual delights of 'infused', 'supernatural' or 'mystical prayer'. Often there is a sense of deep joy and ecstasy, which is more powerful than anything experienced before, or a sense of intoxication and complete awe in contemplating the grandeur and mysteries of God.

In this dwelling place, there is a deeper and more profound level of surrender to God. We are being asked to let go even more of our own agenda, and when these moments of infused prayer or gusto or spiritual delight come, our task is to surrender to them.

Teresa speaks here about an increasing sense of deep joy, of an intense ecstasy, of the gradual indwelling of an indescribable Love. In this place of deeper quiet, the human will and the divine will are in stages of deeper absorption, in preparation for the more permanent and established state of union.

Teresa is always mindful of the constant need to test the sincerity and genuineness of all spiritual development and experiences. Her spiritual guidance as to the wise discernment of these different states of prayer and absorption shows how to distinguish between genuine absorption in the divine, and states of stupor.

From the fifth dwelling place to the end of the text she is concerned with describing the perils and delights of the union of the soul with God. She stresses time after time that 'the devil', or destructive powers, can be as active as ever. Humility, which has been essential throughout, from now on becomes imperative, and she shows how to be on guard against false spiritual pride. The soul is beginning to undergo a deeper state of interior spiritual transformation, where the heart is surrendering even more to being infused and penetrated by the Holy Spirit and God's Love.

She describes a deepening prayer of quiet that becomes a prayer of union. There can be a sense of such stillness that the body scarcely moves and that distractions of ordinary consciousness – thoughts, memories and imagination – cannot disturb the profound inner silence. The distinctive prayer of the fifth mansion is a brief spell, lasting up to half an hour, of increasing absorption in God, and often very little identifiable awareness of our physical state and surroundings.

This is the beginning of the union of human and divine will and she emphasises that it is not possible to enter these more interior dwelling places by personal effort alone, but only by the grace of God. The fifth mansion is explicitly associated by Teresa with the text from Colossians 3:3: 'For you have died and your life is hidden with Christ in God', hiddenness being the keynote.

The metamorphosis of a silkworm into a butterfly is her main symbol to describe the transformation of the soul towards union with God. This also echoes the central feature of hiddenness. The soul at this stage is akin to a silkworm. The dark cocoon that is being spun around us is our prayer, waiting and stillness. By emptying the self we build Christ around us, for the emergence of the butterfly, the transformed soul, fragile and restless, but beautiful.

Teresa's description of the cocoon-like stage – becoming dead to the world, enveloped in its cocoon – is a description of the stage of the dark night of the soul. Her symbolic representation refers to experiences and states of pain, suffering, often intense alienation and sense of loss, despair, darkness and depression, which, for Teresa, were essential preludes to the more unitive spiritual states of the most interior mansions. Teresa seems to accept this type of suffering as an inevitable consequence of deepening surrender.

Our spiritual development and transformation in God is about the re-enactment, over and over again, of this story of the death of the worm and the birth of a butterfly. It describes our passages, crises, depressions, difficulties, our transitions and turning points. They nearly always, in large or small measure, entail a process of dying and rebirth into a different sense or experience of who we are, of our relationship to God and others, in our service and vocation in the world.

In this dwelling place, Teresa writes that the Beloved is giving the grace of the Holy Spirit as a token of His impending betrothal to the soul, in preparation for becoming His Bride. The soul cannot understand the mystery of spiritual union – it is inexplicable and paradoxical to the rational faculties. Teresa, being such a practical woman, emphasises the importance of weaving this focus of deep prayer and mystical silence into the praxis of daily life, and notes that the test of the authenticity of our prayer life is whether our love for our neighbour is growing in response.

The sixth mansion occupies nearly a third of the text, and deals with interior states of prayer and the intensification of the spiritual life, covering both the nature of the suffering and the various ecstasies of prayer that can occur. She emphasises the importance of the ongoing process of spiritual discernment, since this is the stage of the greatest disorientation of the soul. She discusses the increasing strength and subtlety of internal and external tests, trials, obstacles and opposition that can develop in response to a deepening spiritual life in this dwelling place.

This can be exacerbated by the tender and exquisite love that the soul is experiencing in times of intimacy with God – a type of oscillation between a sense of Divine Presence and Divine Absence. The butterfly, which has come to birth in the preceding stage, is vulnerable, restless and confused. There are acute trials ahead, including an intensification of the dark night, such as the onset of illness or persecution.

In this dwelling place, Teresa introduces the new experiences that the soul receives, and gives guidelines to help discern whether the soul is on the right path. Teresa speaks at length, passionately, of the Divine Love of God for the soul, and of the need for renunciation by the soul into that great Love that God has for his Bride. The soul is betrothed to her Beloved, Christ, and this shows in many different ways. His Divine Love is awakening the soul through the interior senses, either by interior vision or sight. Or the soul may begin to hear His Divine call, or smell the sweet perfume of the Holy Spirit.

Teresa is famous for her unusual and intense spiritual experiences, but in the text her instructions and guidelines for dealing with such interior states are particularly down to earth, full of common sense and extremely wise. The main events that she concentrates on in this mansion are locutions or interior words that seem to be spoken by God, wordless prayer, flight of the spirit, interior visions, raptures and ecstasies.

She emphasises the importance of looking at the effects of such experiences and how they have been integrated into life, advising prudence and patience until time reveals their fruits. All true spiritual phenomena will lead to a greater awareness of God and His Love, to a greater sense of humility, and a deepening awareness and compassion for others and their suffering.

The seventh and innermost mansion, Teresa writes, is different from all the others. For her, the interior marriage occurred through a vision of the Holy Trinity, and her inward conviction that the union of her will with God's will had taken place. She describes the seventh mansion as where:

> **this secret union takes place in the innermost centre of the soul, where God Himself must dwell.** (VII, Chapter 2, 2)

quite independent of the physical senses or faculties. In this interior state, in the core of our heart, there is no separation between soul and God.

Teresa says that spiritual marriage: 'might also be compared to water falling from the sky into a river or fountain, where the waters are united, and it would be no longer possible to divide them, or to separate the water of the river from that which has fallen from the heavens. Or it may be likened to a tiny stream, which falls into the sea; there is no possibility of separating them'.[4]

She emphasises that this union has nothing to do with the sensory world or the physical senses – that it takes place deep, deep within the heart. Although this union is happening in the centre of the heart, in the outer mansions there can still be difficulties, conflicts and pain. Mystical union is totally effortless and occurs in silence: 'the understanding need not stir nor seek for anything more; the Lord who created it, wishes it now to be at rest, and only through a little chink to survey what is passing in the soul.'[5]

In this innermost mansion, it is interesting that Teresa gives little attention to interior experiences, looking instead to the effects of this union in our relationship to others and the world. The purpose is the birth of good works, and a call to action and a life of active love in the world, with the confidence that it is possible to maintain an indwelling Presence of God in the innermost recesses of our heart.

ST TERESA TODAY

Teresa's life and Reform responded to the spiritual needs of her own times to turn away from material living in order to return to the essence of our Christian tradition. A similar rebirth has begun in our own time in response to similar needs even more urgent than before. The possibility of a great transformation within the heart of each soul is underway.

We are on the cusp of new times, when the Heavenly Waters are being poured upon humanity. A new era is rapidly approaching, and the unprecedented availability of spiritual knowledge is feeding the tremendous spiritual awakening that is occurring globally.

Perhaps we are in the final preparatory stages of the Parousia, the coming of the celestial Jerusalem on earth. Perhaps we are anticipating the definitive victory over death and the transfiguration of the cosmos that will happen at the Parousia.[6] For those with dawning awareness of this, who see the tiny 'window open to Eternity' slowly widening, the wisdom and teaching of the Christian contemplative journey provided by Teresa, and others among our spiritual forebears, are vitally necessary.

NOTES

1.   Melloni, J. *The Exercises of St Ignatius Loyola in the Western Tradition*, Gracewing, UK, 2000, p.38

2.   Ibid, p.38
3.   Ibid, pp.40-41
4.   Teresa of Avila, *The Interior Castle*, trans. Dis Carmelite, Sands
      & Co. London, 1945, p.109
5.   Ibid, p.114
6.   Clement, *op.cit.* p.266.

THE FIRST MANSION

Toward Awakening to Love

Do not let your hearts be troubled; believe in God, believe also in me. In my Father's house are many rooms; if it were not so, would I have told you that I go to prepare a place for you? And when I go and prepare a place for you, I will come again and will take you to myself, and where I am you may be also. And you know the way where I am going.

John 14:1-4 (RSV)

THE BEAUTY AND DIGNITY
OF THE SOUL

Towards the end of her life, Teresa travelled the length and breadth of Spain, founding new convents and ministering to her many 'spiritual daughters' in the various foundations already established. In the latter months of 1579, whilst travelling with three of her nuns through a heavy snowstorm, Teresa sought refuge in an inn in the town of Arevalo, where she met her old friend and former confessor, Fray Diego de Yepes.

He wrote in a letter many years later how they talked 'about their Divine Master a very great part of the night', and how the next evening Teresa had 'recounted to him the story of how she came to write *The Interior Castle.*' Nine years later he wrote what Teresa had told him that evening in a letter to Fray Luis de Leon:

> This holy mother had been desirous of obtaining some insight into the beauty of a soul in grace. Just at that time she was commanded to write a treatise of prayer, about which she knew a great deal from experience. On the eve of the festival of the Most Holy Trinity she was thinking what subject she should choose for this treatise, when God, who disposes all things in due form and order, granted this desire of hers, and gave her a subject.
>
> He showed her a most beautiful crystal globe, made in the shape of a castle, and containing seven mansions, in the seventh and innermost of which was the King of glory, in the greatest splendour, illumining and beautifying them all. The nearer one got to the centre, the stronger was the Light, outside the palace limits everything was foul, dark and infested with adders, vipers and other venomous creatures.
>
> While she was wondering at this beauty, which by God's grace can dwell in the human soul, the light suddenly vanished. Although the King of Glory did not leave the mansions, the crystal globe was plunged into darkness, became as black as coal and emitted an insufferable colour, and the venomous creatures outside the palace boundaries were permitted to enter the castle.

This was the vision which the holy Mother wished that
everyone might see, for it seemed to her that no mortal
seeing the beauty and splendour of grace, which sin destroys
and changes into such hideousness and misery, could possibly
have the temerity to offend God.

It was about this vision that she told me on that day and
she spoke so freely both of this and of other things that she
realised herself that she had done so and on the next morning
remarked to me: 'How I forgot myself last night! I cannot
think how it happened. These desires and this love of mine
made me lose all sense of proportion. Please God they may
have done me some good!' I promised her not to repeat what
she had said to anyone during her lifetime.[1]

Teresa likens the Christian contemplative path of the soul
towards sacred union with God to an ever-deepening
interior journey through many mansions of a magnificent
castle. Her imagery and metaphors represent, in symbolic
form, the slow interior transformation of the soul in God.

At the beginning of the text, she describes the essential
nature of our soul:

> **I thought of the soul as resembling a castle, formed of a
> single diamond or of very clear crystal, and containing
> many rooms, just as in heaven there are many mansions.
> And, well considered, Sisters, the soul of the just is nothing
> less than a paradise, in which, God tells us, He takes His
> delight.**
>
> **What, do you imagine, must that dwelling be in which a
> King so mighty, so wise and so pure, containing in Himself
> all good, can delight to rest? Nothing can be compared to
> the great beauty and capabilities of a soul; however keen
> our intellects may be, they are as unable to comprehend
> them as to comprehend God, for, as He has told us, He
> created us *in His own image and likeness*.** (I, Chapter 1, 2)

The spiritual path is the interior movement from the outer
reaches of the castle towards the innermost centre where
the Light and Glory of God dwells:

> **You must not think of these mansions as being placed one
> after the other, as things in a row, but fix your eyes on the
> centre, which is the dwelling or palace where the King is,**

and consider how a palmito tree has many layers of bark, which surround the savoury pith, and must be removed before it can be eaten. However large, magnificent and spacious you imagine this castle to be, you cannot exaggerate it; the capacity of the soul is beyond all our understanding, and the Sun within this palace enlightens every part of it.
(I, Chapter 2, 8)

Let us imagine that there are many rooms in this castle, of which some are above, some below, others at the side; in the centre, in the very midst of them all, is the principal chamber in which God and the soul hold their most secret intercourse.
(I, Chapter 1, 4)

Teresa's dominant symbol representing the soul as a 'most beautiful crystal globe made in the shape of a castle' is fascinating. The symbol of a castle, or house, with interior dwelling places or rooms has a long history. The biblical reference is to John's Gospel, 14:2: 'In my father's house there are many dwelling places.'

The Spanish for mansions, 'moradas', is derived from *morar*, which means to dwell. Dwelling places rather than mansions seems to more accurately describe the stations of the heart, or states of mystical prayer.

It is an intriguing symbol, and is original within the Christian tradition. Scholars have been unable to find any comparative documentation relating to the soul and the spiritual life in this way anywhere else in the Christian European mystical literature which antedates Teresa. However, interestingly, this is a well-known symbol in both Jewish and Muslim mystical texts, where equating the soul to a castle is virtually universal.[2]

The castle with seven interior mansions is made of a single diamond or very clear crystal. It is a powerful and dynamic symbol that, in a mandala-like way, contains, integrates and unifies many of the dimensions of the spiritual life that Teresa is attempting to articulate in such detail throughout the text.

By using this symbol of an interior castle Teresa is saying that the soul is a place of immeasurable beauty, capacity and spiritual depth. She sees spiritual growth as a constant 'journey inwards' to the depths where the most secret things pass between God and the soul.

It is a living, dynamic, multidimensional symbol that carries a great deal of meaning and spiritual teaching. She is trying to convey the meaning that our interior castle, and the various mansions or dwelling places on our spiritual journey, do not *automatically* exist and that, in this first mansion, the more interior dwelling places have not yet come into existence.

She is describing a spiritual potentiality, a great possibility, open to everyone to partake in or not, as we choose. Each soul has the capacity for God. We are, in effect, not fully human until the possibility for which we are created is finally realised.

The idea is that we have not arrived yet. We are in a constant process of 'becoming in God'. This is reflected in the whole sense of the possibility, of the promise and the hope of being born anew, of becoming a new creation in the Spirit, of allowing to come into existence a spiritual life and reality which is wholly new and other.

The symbol is also very important because the vision of an interior castle was given to her when she had *already been dwelling* in the seventh mansion for some time. She had reached full spiritual growth and had been longing for some insight into the beauty of a soul in grace.

This profound symbol of the soul which, at the outset, is only a possibility and a potentiality had, for Teresa, become total reality under the constant action of God and her own long and arduous surrender to His action in her life. This is truly the beauty of a soul in a state of grace.

It reflects Teresa's long experience in the prayer of union, and the nature of her relationship to God in that state. Her sense of her relationship to God had been so profoundly altered by the five years of spiritual marriage and a longer period of unitive experiences (which began around 1554–1556) that a change in the symbol occurred spontaneously when it came to her again at the beginning of writing *The Interior Castle*. Teresa chose the imagery of a diamond for the castle because of its qualities of indestructability, hardness, brilliance and beauty.[3]

The castle symbol also has a dual aspect – describing a fortress-like space as well as having the strength of diamond or crystal. This symbolic welding of castle and crystal attempts to unite different essential aspects of the spiritual journey – both the need for strong boundaries and containment to protect the delicate spiritual transformation process, as well as the recognition that the soul is precious in God's sight, jewel-like.

In the earlier mansions, Teresa describes the difficulties, obstacles, conflicts, pain, and problems in each one, with constant emphasis on and movement towards a luminous Divine centre. The spiritual ideal and hope of integrating the most difficult trials and conflicts of the start with God's Light, Presence and Silence in the innermost mansions is described, contained and constantly woven throughout the text by the use of the crystal castle symbol.

What is remarkable about Teresa's symbol is that it depicts the mystery that *God is both in us, and we are in God or comprehended by God*. She uses the diamond image to show the extent of God's penetration of the world such that nothing is outside God. It illustrates the state of the soul where it is no longer separate from God. This is what Teresa is trying to describe with her images of a crystal globe or clear diamond – in Unity, God penetrates through the soul and dwells there, yet the soul does not fully comprehend God – it is, as it were, a transfusion of our own self by His Self.[4]

It is fascinating to see that other great Christian mystics have used images remarkably close to Teresa's own vision and symbol to describe the experience of spiritual unity. The blessed Jan van Ruysbroec, writing in the thirteenth century, exclaims:

> Thus the Unity is ever drawing to itself and inviting to itself
> everything that has been born of it, either by nature or by
> grace. And therefore, too, such enlightened men are, with a
> free spirit, lifted up above reason into a bare and imageless
> vision, wherein lives the eternal indrawn summons of the
> Divine Unity, and with an imageless and bare understanding,
> they pass through all works, and all exercises, and all things,
> until they reach the summit of their spirits.
>
> There, their bare understanding is drenched through by
> the Eternal Brightness, even as the air is drenched through
> by the sunshine, And the bare, uplifted will is transformed
> and drenched through by abysmal love, even as iron is by
> fire. And the bare uplifted memory feels itself enwrapped
> and established in an abysmal Absence of Image.[5]

The genius of the castle symbol is that it holds together the
mystery that so often confuses and divides religious people
– the simultaneous immanence and transcendence of God.
God is known immanently in the bridal chamber of the
soul, where the soul knows it is comprehended in God as
transcendent.

Since divine union is in the innermost centre of our
soul, it does not take us out of the world to an exclusively
transcendent reality. But the union itself is transcendent,
as God is, so the goal of the inner journey is infinitely more
than simply relating to our inner, private subjectivity. The
symbol encompasses both the infinite, transcendent aspects
of God and the personal and immanent.[5a]

AWAKENING TO LIFE IN THE SPIRIT

What does Teresa tell us about the awakening of the soul
in the first mansion? She says that it is a matter of how to
'*be*' in a place, and that the first mansion represents the
awakening of our spiritual life through devotion and our
constant, ardent longing for God:

> **Now let us return to our beautiful and charming castle and**
> **discover how to enter it. This appears incongruous; if this**

castle is the soul, clearly no one can have to enter it, for it is
the person himself – one might as well tell someone to *go
into a room he is already in!*

There are, however, *very different ways of being* in this
castle; many souls live in the courtyard of the building
where the sentinels stand, neither caring to enter farther,
nor to know who dwells in that most delightful place, what
is in it and what rooms it contains. (I, Chapter 1, 7)

She is insistent that the way of initial development of our
state of being, the door of entry into our castle, is through
prayer, meditation and reflection. All religious traditions
speak of the importance of cultivating the necessary
devotional feeling in the heart in order to begin to awaken
the soul and her longing for God. Our devotion and
longing is the inner purifying fire that must burn and burn
for a very long time in the depths of our heart, being the
essential fuel that propels us on our spiritual journey
towards, and in, God.

Teresa is emphatic on the importance of prayer and
meditation in these early stages:

> Souls without prayer are like bodies, palsied and lame,
> having hands and feet they cannot use. Just so, there are
> souls so infirm and accustomed to think of nothing but
> earthly matters, that there seems no cure for them.
>
> It seems impossible for them to retire into their own
> hearts; accustomed as they are to be with the reptiles and
> other creatures, which live outside the castle, they have
> come at last to imitate their habits. (I, Chapter 1, 8)

> As far as I can understand, the gate by which to enter this
> castle is prayer and meditation. I do not allude more to
> mental than to vocal prayer, for if it is prayer at all, the
> mind must take part in it. (I, Chapter 1, 9)

She describes three types of meditative prayer experience
throughout the text, which represent deepening degrees of
penetration into the mystery of God. Teresa refers to the
predominant prayer in the earliest mansions as *the prayer of
recollection*, where our mind is quite active and methods
and techniques of prayer and contemplation are important
at these stages.

The prayer of quiet begins to develop in the fourth and fifth mansions, where a quality and depth of inner stillness and quiet begins to 'take root' and grow. This growing stillness moves towards *the prayer of union* in the innermost mansion, which ends in profound silence and solitude, where we are able to become utterly receptive to God's action, within and through us.

Teresa likens our spiritual development to the cultivation of a garden, and uses metaphors of how a garden is watered to describe various kinds of prayer, in a fourfold deepening of interior silence and stillness.

The Lord is the gardener; we are the assistants or 'tenants', the plants are the virtues and the water is that experience of God in prayer that we call 'consolation':

> A beginner must look on himself or herself as one setting out to make a garden for his Lord's pleasure, on most unfruitful soil, which abounds in weeds. His Majesty roots up the weeds and will put in good plants instead. Let us reckon that this is already done when a soul decides to practise prayer and has begun to do so.
>
> We have then, as good gardeners, with God's help, to make these plants grow, and to water them carefully so that they do not die, but produce flowers, which give out a good smell, to delight this Lord of ours. Then He will often come to take His pleasure in this garden and enjoy these virtues.
>
> Now, let us see how this garden is to be watered, so that we may understand what we have to do, and what labour it will cost us, also whether the gain will outweigh the effort, or how long it will take. It seems to me that the garden may be watered in four different ways. Either the water must be drawn from a well, which is very laborious; or by a water wheel and buckets, worked by a windlass. I have sometimes drawn it in this way, which is less laborious than the other, and brings up more water.
>
> Or it may flow from a stream or spring, which waters the ground much better, for the soul then retains more moisture and needs watering less often, which entails far less work for the gardener. Or by heavy rain, when the Lord waters it Himself without any labour of ours, and this is an incomparably better method than the rest.[6]

There are four different ways of drawing water for the garden, and they provide the framework for her discussion of the stages of the life of prayer. This four-fold metaphor relates to the threefold pattern of prayer of recollection, prayer of quiet and prayer of union. In using this metaphor, Teresa emphasises the cultivation and development of virtues. We do no seek the experience of God in prayer merely for its own sake, but in order that the good in our lives may thrive and grow.

The Christian virtues that Teresa frequently refers to in her writings include faith, hope and love, humility, self forgetfulness, sensitivity to the needs of others, and enthusiasm for the kingdom and glory of God. If these are growing in us, our prayer life is genuine and fruitful, no matter how 'dry' it may be.

If we cannot see any real growth in these virtues, something is wrong, no matter how abundant the water of consolation may be. It is, in fact, our growth in the virtues that attracts the Lord to us after He has first planted them in us.[7]

The first way of getting water for the garden, echoing the prayer of recollection, is by laboriously drawing it from the well by hand. This is very hard work, takes a great deal of personal effort, and we can obtain little water for the amount of labour that we put into it. What does this mean in practice?

The laborious drawing and carrying of the water corresponds to our efforts, using our understanding and imagination, to get to know the Lord. The small amount of water is the occasional moment of 'contact with the Lord' that such labour brings.

There are other reasons why the beginning of prayer is very laborious. All good prayer is based on an honest, even ruthless, knowledge of ourselves, which is very difficult in the early stages. It is also a real effort to know Christ, our Lord. We cannot begin to love what we do not know.

To love the Lord we need to come to know Him in Jesus Christ; and to love ourselves properly we need to come to know ourselves as we truly are. This is the very arduous labour of the first way of drawing water, and is the task with which we begin our tenancy of the garden that the Lord has entrusted to us.[8]

The prayer of recollection is the term that Teresa uses for meditative and contemplative prayer involving some form of technique or method, and it covers a wide range of meditation and prayer practices. However, for Teresa, the prayer of recollection is intensely relational, her primary intent being the experience of the living relationship of His Divine Presence within our soul.

She describes several ways in which we can approach Him in this type of prayer, which is the gateway to entering more deeply within ourselves to rest in Him:

> Speak with Him as with a Father, a Brother, a Lord, and a Spouse – and; sometimes in one way and sometimes in another; He will teach you what you must do to please Him. Do not be foolish; ask Him to let you speak to Him, and, as He is your spouse, to treat you as His brides…
>
> If one prays in this way, the prayer may be only vocal, but the mind will be recollected much sooner; and this is a prayer, which brings with it many blessings. It is called recollection because the soul collects together all the faculties and enters within itself to be with its God.'[9]

She is insistent that God only begins to become accessible to us through the practice of the prayer of recollection:

> You know that God is everywhere; and this is a great truth, for, of course, wherever the king is, the court is too; that is to say, wherever God is, there is Heaven. No doubt you can believe that, in any place where His Majesty is, there is fullness of glory. Remember how St Augustine tells us about his seeking God in many places and eventually finding Him within himself.
>
> Do you suppose it is of little importance that a soul which is often distracted should come to understand this truth and to find that, in order to speak to its Eternal Father and to take delight in Him, it has no need to go to Heaven or to speak in a loud voice?

> However quietly we speak, He is so near that He will hear us; we need no wings to go in search of Him but have only to find a place where we can be alone and look upon Him present within us. Nor need we feel strange in the presence of so kind a Guest: we must talk to Him very humbly, as we should to our father, asking Him for things as we should ask our father.[10]

She speaks about the importance of meditating on scripture, meditating on images of Christ or other holy persons, meditating on sacred words or phrases, or on certain deep symbolic images, such as the interior castle, that arise spontaneously from our own psyche that can be helpful in recollecting ourselves in God.

The traditional method of recollection that has been the mainstay of monastic life for centuries is the *lectio divina.* Teresa would certainly have been familiar with it. Lectio divina means 'study of the divine word' or study of scripture, and has four parts: reading a text of scripture, meditating on the text, praying over concerns and anxieties we may have, and contemplation – entering into the intimate and transforming experience of the Presence of God.[11]

It is clear from her writings that the primary method of recollective prayer for Teresa was the visual imagination of Scripture, which was especially directed toward her relationship with Christ. In her autobiography, she writes of a time when she was greatly distressed, and found comfort in imagining Christ in times of similar distress: 'I strove to picture Christ within me, and it did me greater good – in my opinion – to picture Him in those scenes where I saw Him more alone. It seemed to me that being alone and afflicted, as a person in need, He had to accept me.'

Meditative prayer, which enters into the stories of scripture with imagination, has been identified with the spiritual exercises of St Ignatius, which is a masterly description of the method widely used by spiritual directors and retreat leaders. St Ignatius was a contemporary of Teresa, and this particular method of prayer was widely practised during the sixteenth century.[12]

By 'faculties' Teresa means all the human attributes through which we engage with the world, which are the senses, reason, imagination and feelings. They are intended to be the guardians of the interior of our soul, but when we begin to turn inwards and become more aware of our self, our history and background and our unconscious life and motivations, we usually find internal conflict, splitting, denial, distortion and many unresolved difficulties and issues.

The term 'recollection' means the process of re-collecting, remembering, eventually bringing back to conscious awareness all the disparate, separated, parts of ourselves into unity of being, into a semblance of order, into a sense of wholeness.

As we are able to recollect ourselves inwardly, there can begin a new capacity for stillness, serenity and interior co-operation. It is only when we become aware of fresh possibilities within ourselves, and of the desire and the will to realise them, that further training and exercise in the contemplative life can be more effectively undertaken.

In these earliest mansions, any sense that we have of fresh spiritual possibilities is floating, amorphous and without coherence and direction, so the various methods and techniques of meditation and prayer are particularly important to ground them.

It is important also to remember not to judge our spiritual state at this early stage in purely subjective terms, as it is part of a growing objective discernment. At the same time that we become aware of new possibilities, we are also able to see what must be done in order to change, and work towards their realisation.

This dawning of a new life brings an awareness of its counterpart in the idea of a life which has been lost, despoiled, forsaken; the idea of a fall from paradise. At this stage we live 'in the beginning' of our spiritual life, and relationship to God, being only able to perceive things of the spirit through the senses, the faculties and the intellect.

This lack of spiritual vision, and the vitality and experience that go with it, leave us in an abnormal and deformed state in comparison to *what we can become*. Our normal pristine state is the one that we have lost, and our initial task consists of trying to recover our spiritual vision and the perception of spiritual realities that have been obscured from us.

Communion with God is what we have been created for, and at these early stages, through prayer and meditation, we are able to begin to turn inwards in order to awaken, cultivate and nurture our heart in her longing and love for God. It is beginning to reverse the customary direction of what our heart longs and craves for – turning from the outer world to the inner world.

The natural order of seeking to satisfy the senses and faculties with earthly pleasures begins to reverse. Our heart slowly turns to spiritual realities and the things of God. This is where we begin to discover and understand the inner order of things, and begin to carry in ourselves the knowledge and vision of the divine realities, of God in whose image we were created.

The beginning of the stage of spiritual awakening can occur in other more spontaneous ways, and generally has the effect of challenging our normal, rational, ordinary reasoning and perception of the world according to our senses and faculties. The blessings and grace of God touch everyone at some point in their lives, for it is freely given and offered by Him.

Not everyone responds with a free conversion of their self-will, and a desire to purify their inner life and conscience. What distinguishes those who continue on the spiritual path from those who do not is the depth of sincerity with which they greet such experiences and awakening, and the disciplined intensity with which they set about arranging their whole life and being around it.

If we persevere patiently, the time comes when our hope is realised, when the water of the experience of God begins to flow freely and with relatively little meditative labour, which is the second way of drawing water by means of a water wheel and aqueducts. The use of the crank to turn the water wheel represents the first degree of the prayer of quiet in the fourth mansion.

How does the image of the pump apply to prayer? When we are beginning to draw the waters of prayer in this second way, we are still going to the well of meditation and contemplation, and are still using our own faculties, reasoning and imagination to seek the experience of God. But now less labour of our faculties is producing more water.

The water is beginning to flow more freely, and comparatively little effort on the part of our reasoning and imagination is producing much more consolation. The Lord has provided a pump to multiply the results of our efforts. Perhaps for the first time, we are beginning to realise the meaning and joy of prayer as an encounter with God in Love.[13]

This is the first breakthrough in the interior life, and we are beginning to realise what it means to say that prayer is loving and not thinking. Teresa calls this the prayer of quiet, which begins at the fourth mansion:

> Let us speak now of the second manner, ordained by the Lord of the garden, for getting water; that is, by turning the crank of a water wheel and by aqueducts, the gardener obtains more water and with less labour; and he can rest without having to work constantly. Well, this method applied to what they call the prayer of quiet is what I now want to discuss.
>
> Here the soul begins to be recollected and comes upon something supernatural because in no way can it acquire this prayer through any efforts it may make. True, at one time it seemingly got tired turning the crank, and working with the intellect, and filling the aqueducts. But here the water is higher, and so the labour is much less than that required in pulling it up from the well. I mean that the water is closer because the grace is more clearly manifest to the soul.[14]

The pump is a great improvement on the labour of drawing water from the well by hand. But it still involves labour, with our mind and imagination, and there remain many obstacles, difficulties and distractions in recollecting.

So, this second way of drawing water is not the best there is. The third and fourth ways of drawing the waters of the Holy Spirit are purely gifts of God, which we can do nothing to bring about, and normally will come only after many years of a deepening life of prayer. Teresa says in her autobiography, referring to the third way: 'It is now, I believe, some five, or perhaps six years, since the Lord first granted me frequent and abundant experience of this sort of prayer' (Chapter 16), when she was over 50, and nearly thirty years after her enclosure as a Carmelite nun! [15]

The third way of drawing the water of prayer for the garden of the Lord is from a river or a stream – the garden is watered much better by this means because the ground is more fully soaked, and there is no need to water so frequently. This is the prayer of quiet, which Teresa describes at some length in the fourth mansion.

The fourth water, or way, is by a great deal of rain, where the Lord waters the garden without any work on our part. Our garden is simply watered by rain falling from the sky on its own, and Teresa calls this the prayer of union of the sixth and seventh mansions.

Teresa's prayer teaches an interior mode of surrender and listening for His Divine Guidance, which begins with methods and techniques and ends in the abandonment of our personal will and selves into the Divine 'arms of love'. She is very clear about the spiritual progression that the image of the four waters is seeking to convey – at each succeeding stage of the interior journey, God is doing more of the work and we are doing less.

She is also clear that, no matter which stage we are in, we need to direct the water. The water of prayer is not to be drunk for its own sake, but it is 'for the flowers', that is, to water and cultivate the virtues. In the fourth water, which appears without any effort on our part, the primary labour of the tenants is to be able to irrigate the land wisely and humbly. The water of God's love is now flowing and pulsating through us on its own, but we need continually to cooperate in making this water a source of life for the virtues in His Garden.

METANOIA

For Teresa, outside the castle are those who feel no attraction to God or the spiritual life, who are entirely satisfied with the sensations, attachments and identifications related to the exterior life and the gratification of personal needs, desires, wishes and passions. This state is characterised by egotism, which predominately emphasises and focuses on 'as much as possible for me and what I can take and own' often without consideration for others.

This attitude or state of mind can also be reflected in a pattern of personal relationships that become destructive or disordered. Here, others can be treated as a means to an end, or as objects to be manipulated for the satisfaction of personal desires, such as career advancement, emotional security, self-esteem or sexual needs. Often, other people tend to be used and abused, often unconsciously or without embarrassment.

It is a major life transition when we begin to turn inwardly towards God and the spiritual life with genuine longing and searching, and start to question ourselves, our direction and purpose in life – Who am I? What am I doing with my life? Where have I come from? Where am I going? The interior search begins in earnest when we take these first sincere steps on the way, and really want to grapple with our issues, struggle against our habits and make conscious efforts to remember and recollect ourselves, and try to begin to remember God and enter the prayer of recollection.

In order to find those places, people, books, and

influences that will begin to fuel our journey, we begin to become aware of the hunger 'for those things which are not of this world' in the depths of our heart. These interior movements and more exact discernment and discrimination between the different influences become increasingly important. They can either feed our soul, or leave us just as hungry and empty as before.

We begin to become conscious of our psychological and spiritual state of confusion, fragmentation, and alienation, which is typical of the normal unconscious inner world. It is the state where there is no inner centre, as yet, where we are racked with conflicts, dissociation, negative emotions, compulsions and behaviour over which we have no control. In fact, at this stage, these disparate negative drives control us.

From a spiritual perspective, at these early stages, there is often very little sense that 'I am', or 'I exist' as a whole person, let alone a living sense of being 'made in the image of God'. More often than not, we feel as if many of life's events and influences are passively 'happening to us', outside of our immediate control. Our thoughts, feelings, opinions and habits seem to be caused by external influences and impressions.

It is a state of mind and soul where responding to life's events and impressions can happen in a mechanical, machine-like way. It has been described as the false-self part of ourselves – it is what has been acquired and learnt from life in general and, in fact, does not belong to our true self at all.

Teresa vividly describes the spiritual state of the soul at these early stages on the path:

Let us speak no more of those crippled souls, who are in a most miserable and dangerous state, unless our Lord bid them rise, as He did the palsied man who had waited more than thirty years at the pool of Bethsaida. We will not think of the others who are last to enter the precincts of the castle; they are still very worldly, yet have some desire to do right,

and at times, though rarely, commend themselves to God's care.

They think about their souls every now and then; although very busy, they pray a few times a month, with minds generally filled with a thousand other matters, for where their treasure is, there is their heart also. Still, occasionally, they cast aside these cares; it is a great boon for them to realise to some extent the state of their souls, and to see that they will never reach the gate by the road they are following. (I, Chapter 1, 10)

If this was so in the sixteenth century, how much more difficult is it to enter one's interior castle in our modern twenty-first century! The inner lives of the majority of people in our Western culture are neglected, ignored, trivialised or consciously or unconsciously suppressed, like overgrown gardens whose owners are too busy to care for them.

All too often the 'life hidden with God within us' is generally lost to view, so easily forgotten or even erased by a torrent of outer activity and distractions. Of course, to rediscover it, as Teresa advises, we have to enter into ourselves again, and the early steps are the most difficult, because our inner spiritual life is in so much darkness and obscurity at this stage.

She describes the state of the soul 'outside the castle', in stark and vivid metaphors, as having withdrawn from the 'River of Life', of growing beside a 'black and fetid pool', as having a 'thick black cloth' thrown over it:

In a state of grace, the soul is like a well of limpid water, from which flow only streams of clearest crystal. Its works are pleasing both to God and man, rising from the River of Life, beside which it is rooted like a tree.

Otherwise it would produce neither leaves nor fruit, for the waters of grace nourish it, keep it from withering from drought, and cause it to bring forth good fruit. But the soul, by sinning, withdraws from this stream of life, and growing beside a black and fetid pool, can produce nothing but disgusting and unwholesome fruit.

Notice that it is not the fountain and the brilliant sun which lose their splendour and beauty, for they are placed in the very centre of the soul, and cannot be deprived of

> their lustre. **The soul is like a crystal in the sunshine over which a thick black cloth has been thrown, so however brightly the sun may shine, the crystal can never reflect it.**
> (I, Chapter 2, 3)

Following the radiant vision of the soul in a 'state of grace', Teresa's description of the state of the soul in mortal sin is truly challenging and shocking:

> **I wish you to consider the state to which mortal sin brings this magnificent and beautiful castle, this pearl of the East, this tree of life, planted beside the living waters of life which symbolise God Himself. No night can be so dark, neither gloom nor blackness can compare to its obscurity.**
> **Suffice to say that the sun in the centre of the soul, which gave it such splendour and beauty, is totally eclipsed, though the spirit is as fitted to enjoy God's presence as is the crystal to reflect the sun… While the soul is in mortal sin, nothing can profit it; none of its good works merit an eternal reward, since they do not proceed from God as their first principle, and by Him alone is our virtue real virtue.**
> (I, Chapter 2, 1-2)

The essence of sin is our refusal to respond to the call, the summons of God to *become*, to receive and be bathed in His life-giving spiritual waters, which He constantly wishes to bestow on us. Sin is essentially that part of us which refuses to change, to grow spiritually, to turn around towards God, to transform. It wishes to stay only 'in the flesh', so to speak, and denies the spiritual dimension and the reality of God.

Teresa's view of sin is different to the usual theological and legalistic categories and interpretations. Teresa's union with God for much of the latter part of her life means she views sin overridingly from a place of love, of the soul's love for God and His ever-present Love for the soul.

The reality of sin is essentially not being conscious of our spiritual nature. It is not waking up to what it is possible to become conformed to and be transformed in – the image and likeness of God, through Christ. By our unconsciousness, egotism and inattention, we have forgotten, hidden and obscured His Divine Image within the depths of our soul. Sin, 'the black and fetid pool within', makes us forget the essence of our soul, of our heart, which is the same as forgetting His Divine image within.

Sin, then, is when we are in denial of, and unconscious of, how fragmented, disconnected, atrophied and alienated our interior life is, and, in essence, how we are rejecting, refusing or ignoring any inner possibilities of change and spiritual transformation.

It is where we have not yet attained that 'great understanding', whereby we know that Love is ultimately victorious. It is where we have not yet undergone that 'change of mind', which is the essence of metanoia, of repentance, that consists in saying, 'I am accepted by God, and what is asked of me is to accept the fact that I have been accepted.'[16]

So, what is meant by repentance? What does it mean to turn away from growing beside a 'black and fetid pool', towards the 'River of Life, from which flow only streams of clearest crystal'? It is normally regarded as sorrow for sin, a feeling of guilt, a sense of grief and horror at the wounds we have inflicted on others and on ourselves.

But it is much more than this. The literal sense of the Greek term for repentance, metanoia, is 'a change of mind' – it is not just regret for the past, but a fundamental transformation of our outlook, a new way of looking at ourselves, at others and at God.

It is not a paroxysm of remorse and self-pity, but a fundamental conversion, the recentring of our life on God, in Christ. It is not self-hatred but the affirmation of our true self as made in God's Image and Likeness.

It is the beginning of the real growth of our interior life, of awakening to life in the Spirit, and is anchored in prayer, faith and virtue, and a deepening development of self-awareness, self-examination and self-appropriation. As a 'new mind', repentance is positive, not negative. It is not despondency, but eager anticipation; it is not to feel that one has reached an impasse, but to take the way out of spiritual death.

To repent is to look, not downward at our shortcomings, but upward at God's Love; not backward with self-reproach, but forward with hope and trustfulness. It is essentially to see, not what we have failed to be, but what, by the grace of Christ, we can yet become. Repentance is an illumination; a transition from darkness to Light. To repent is to open our eyes to His Divine Radiance – not to sit dolefully but to greet the new dawn of His Love in the depths of our heart.

The essence of repentance is also eschatological, openness to the Last Things that are not merely in the future but already present. To repent is to recognise that the Kingdom of Heaven is in our midst, continually at work among us, and if we accept the coming of this Kingdom, all things will be made new for us.[17]

The connection between repentance and the advent of the great Light is significant. Until we have seen the Light of Christ, we cannot really see our own darkness. So long as the room is in darkness we do not notice the dirt, but when we bring a powerful Light into the room – that is, when we stand before the Lord, naked within our heart, every speck of dust can be distinguished.

So it is in the earliest mansions of the interior castle of our soul. The sequence is not to repent first, and then to become aware of Christ; for it is only when the Light of Christ has already in some measure entered our life that we begin to truly understand and see our sinfulness.

St John of Kronstadt said that to repent is to know that there is a lie in our heart, but how can we detect the presence of a lie unless we have already some sense of the truth? In the words of Watkin, in an article on the mysticism of Augustine, 'Sin… is the shadow cast by the light of God intercepted by any attachment of the will which prevents it illuminating the soul. Thus knowledge of God gives rise to the sense of sin, not vice versa.' The Desert Fathers knew this, citing Isaiah seeing the Lord on His Throne and hearing the seraphim crying, 'Holy, Holy, Holy'. It is only after this vision that he exclaims: 'Woe is me! For I am lost, for I am a man of unclean lips' (Is 6:1-5).[18]

Metanoia, or repentance, signifies a return to the source of life, a turning back, the journey of return to Love. Except in exceptional circumstances, it does not begin in a single moment of conversion, a flash of insight that immediately and forever transforms our lives; nor is it no more than an occasional impulse or change in direction. It is a continual, and sometimes almost impossible, struggle to perceive the truth about our condition and ourselves, to turn away from the past and keep journeying towards God's Love, which He is constantly radiating from His Heart directly to ours.

This is most often symbolised by the parable of the prodigal son in Luke 15, which identifies certain stages in the spiritual journey, with repentance playing the central role. The son self-indulgently loses his birthright in a 'far-away country', and as a result, over time, feels an acute lack.

He takes employment with a citizen of that country, wanting even the coarsest food of that country, which nobody gives to him. At a certain moment in his life, he comes to himself, wakes up, recognises his situation and remembers the alternative of his Father's household. As a result of this metanoia, there is a complete change in direction of his life.

He forms the resolution to return home, accepts his humiliation, and begins the journey. On arriving home, his Father comes out to meet him with great compassion. As a result of his new attitude, he confesses his fault and enters into a new life in his Father's house. His Father does not punish him, but instead immediately gives him all the good things that have been lacking.[19]

Teresa understands the nature of the many distractions, obstacles, unnecessary cares and difficulties in this first dwelling place of prayer:

> **So worldly and preoccupied with earthly riches, honours and affairs, that as I have said, even if it sincerely wishes to enter into itself and enjoy the beauties of the castle, it is prevented by these distractions and seems unable to overcome so many obstacles. It is most important to withdraw from all unnecessary cares and business, as far as is compatible with the duties of one's state in life, in order to enter the second mansion.**
>
> **This is so essential, that unless done immediately I think it impossible for anyone ever to reach the principal room, or even to remain where he is without great risk of losing what is already gained; otherwise, although he is inside the castle, he will find it impossible to avoid being bitten some time or other by some of the very venomous creatures surrounding him.** (I, Chapter 2,16)

Metanoia is essentially the result of the very difficult struggle to achieve a true change of heart, the move from being head-centred to being heart-centred. It is fundamentally a change of the core of our being, the shift from a self-centred, anthropocentric life, driven by the spirit of the world, to a God-centred life, focused upon the Holy Spirit of God, where tasting and dwelling within the Living Presence of God becomes the core and goal of our being.

Metanoia involves a great deal more than radical change in the quality of our consciousness of God and ourselves and in the content of our mind and heart. It means going beyond the boundaries of our ordinary human reason, thought and faculties.

It is a total transformation of the seat of our heart and soul, an actual change in the 'centre of gravity' of the intelligence, 'putting off the old nature with its practices and putting on the new nature', which is being renewed in knowledge after the image of its creator.' (Col 3:9-10) (RSV).[20]

One modern commentator described the massive change in the psychology of the individual during the process of repentance, and detailed the kind of change necessary in a particularly poignant manner:

No one can continue to justify himself in the way he has always done and expect to become another and a new man. His feeling of his own righteousness must change, for as long as he feels that he is righteous as he is, he cannot change... the extraordinarily harsh teaching of the Gospels is to break this feeling of merit and complacency that everyone openly or secretly rests upon... in the light of the idea of the kingdom of heaven, in view of this possible inner evolution, a man must come to realise that he is almost nothing as he is, and that all his vanity, merit, conceit, self-esteem, self-liking, self-satisfaction and self-love, and all his imagination of himself is practically an illusion.

It is indeed only possible to understand that harsh teaching of Christ in view of its aim, which is to break up a man's whole psychology, the man as life has made him, the man as he regards himself as, and make him think and feel and act in a new way, so that he begins to move towards a higher level, towards another state of himself that exists within himself as a possibility. For to pass from one level to another, from the state of an acorn to the state of a tree, everything must be rearranged and altered. All a man's ordinary relations with different sides of himself must alter. The whole setting of his being must change. The whole man must change.[21]

SELF-KNOWLEDGE

In these early stages of the spiritual life, Teresa specifically counsels 'perseverance, humility and self-knowledge' in equal measure. *The Interior Castle* is a profound document of the psyche as well as of the soul, and her understanding of depth psychological dynamics, as well as God's movement within the soul, is expressed interchangeably throughout the text.

Her use of soul includes what we would refer to today as psyche, and her basic assumption throughout is that spiritual growth is generally accompanied by psychological growth and maturity. Scholastic theology spoke of faculties within the soul in an attempt psychologically to nuance interior reality. Teresa attempts to overcome the lack of psychological categories through her use of symbols and imagery.[22]

It is interesting that Teresa's special emphasis on the importance of self-knowledge in these earliest mansions is generally in accord with the modern depth psychological approach. For Teresa, knowing ourselves is about growing familiar with, and accepting of, our fallibility, our needs, our shadow, with the places where we are most vulnerable and unloved, our blocks, psychic and emotional pain, the limitations of what we can do on our own. Ultimately, it's about knowing our total dependence on God and His Love to hold and heal us.

These first steps on the spiritual journey entail waking up to the interior life, often with long periods of crisis, searching and aloneness and a growing perception of the limitations and frailty of our own human constructs, perspectives and defences. A powerful inner longing for God, even crying and lamenting from the depths of our heart for a very long time, is often what is necessary to break our psychological and emotional barriers to life in the Spirit, barriers of resistance, ignorance, egotism and spiritual slumber.

In the earliest mansions, the soul needs to learn to '*enter itself*' and to understand how important self-knowledge is to our whole spiritual journey:

> **A soul, which gives itself to prayer, either much or little, should on no account be kept within narrow bounds. Since God has given it [the soul] such great dignity, permit it to wander at will through the rooms of the castle, from the lowest to the highest. Let it not force itself to remain for very long in the same mansion, even that of self-knowledge.**
>
> **Mark well, however, that self-knowledge is indispensable, even for those whom God takes to dwell in the same mansion with Himself. Nothing else, however elevated, perfects the soul which must never seek to forget its own nothingness.**
> (I, Chapter 2, 9)

Unfortunately, however, spiritual progress and psychological maturity do not always go hand in hand. There are

individuals who have been, for example, severely abused or
tortured, either physically or emotionally, and have
responded quite heroically to the power of prayer and the
action of God in their lives, and, in rare instances, the Holy
Spirit can spontaneously heal severe wounding and trauma.
However, this need not signify psychological growth.

I believe there is little substitute for the patient, slow
psychological and psychotherapeutic work of exploring
and learning to accept ourselves the way we are. Here,
knowledge of God presupposes, and is intimately connected
to, knowledge of self. All things being equal, a deepening
union with God is generally accompanied by an increasingly
more integrated life and a greater focus of energy in the
service of God.

Teresa keeps returning to the importance of self-knowledge in several sections of her writings on the first mansion:

> **We need not tire ourselves by trying to realise all the beauty
> of this castle, although, being His creature, there is all
> the difference between the soul and God that there is
> between the creature and the Creator: the fact that it is
> made in God's image teaches us how great are its dignity
> and loveliness.**
>
> **It is no small fortune and disgrace that, through our
> own fault, we neither understand our nature nor our origin.
> Would it not be gross ignorance, my daughters, if, when a
> man was questioned about his name, or country, or parents,
> he could not answer? Stupid as this would be, it is unspeak-
> ably more foolish to care to learn nothing of our nature
> except that we possess bodies, and only to realise vaguely
> that we have souls, because people say so and it is a doctrine
> of faith.** (I, Chapter 1, 3)

A great deal has been discovered about the workings of the
human psyche and the nature of unconscious processes
over the past century, through the work of Freud and Jung
in their schools of psychoanalysis and depth, or analytical,
psychology. Jung, in particular, tried to look for the action
of the Spirit both in his clinical work and also in areas such
as literature and the arts.

The psychological and the spiritual constantly inter-penetrate – informing, relating to and nourishing each other. The Holy Spirit touches us *intimately* in our dreams, in myths and fairy tales, in our bodies, in our sexuality, in our emotional life, in our relationships, and in every area of our private and shared experiences. The worlds of depth psychology and spirituality lie very close together and must constantly seek to learn from each other.

Self-knowledge is even more important and necessary in our own day. As well as discerning the movement of the Holy Spirit in our lives, or inviting Him into the depths of our heart, we have to be acquainted with our own nature and origin, both conscious and unconscious. Any real depth of spiritual or moral conversion must necessarily be complemented by psychological development and maturity.

The yearning and desire to move towards deepening states of contemplative prayer and meditation must be augmented by the ongoing struggle to develop an in-depth understanding of ourselves. We need an increasing ability to reflect on, sense, articulate and adequately respond to what is going on within our psyche, both from the conscious and the unconscious levels. Spiritual transformation today is not only a matter of moving towards the innermost dwelling places, but also of ever more precise and technical self-knowledge on the path toward the mystery of union.

Christian mystical tradition has always emphasised the importance of psychological exploration and maturation. In his concept of the self, Jung shares the belief that God's Presence lies within the centre of the soul, expressed from a psychological, rather than a mystical, perspective. Hence, his writings on the psyche contain much of the teaching of spiritual direction and guidance from past centuries in the idiom of modern depth psychology. Obscure teachings from the past regarding the workings of the psyche are now well known.[23]

The foundation of self-knowledge depends on the establishment of a relatively well-developed personality –

that is, on a realistic sense of our strengths, weaknesses and competence in the many arenas of life. In this regard, the function of a healthy personality revolves around the development of sufficient identity, determination and willingness to adapt to life's demands and, through these experiences, to be able to integrate and internalise an adequate sense of self-worth and self-esteem.

Essentially, healthy self-regard is a normal part of our maturation, and is the foundation of adequate self-preservation, without which it becomes impossible to care for, and defend, what we feel is right and true. The process of ongoing self observation and attention to the workings of our body, emotions, and mind will slowly bring understanding and knowledge of the inner guiding centre that orders, organises and connects all the disparate parts of our psyche.

Teresa's spiritual perspective recognises the problem of the 'isolated personality', which is a state that ultimately leads to stasis, disconnection and stagnation when no further interior work is undertaken. She knows that rigid and inappropriate self-control usually only heightens our sense of alienation and isolation and reinforces our imprisoning defences.

As a wise spiritual director, she constantly encourages the letting go of our 'tight and defensive' control of life, in order that we learn to trust and explore the unknown world of the Holy Spirit. The process of healing through His Love happens to the surrendered and courageous heart. We need sufficient trust and faith, particularly at these early stages, to consciously open up and work on the isolated, traumatised and defended parts of our personality. Any ongoing regression and denial can lead to states of instability, disintegration and collapse.

Teresa warns that the spiritual journey into what is real and true, once begun, demands courage and perseverance to continue. It's a case of entering into the life of the Holy Spirit freely, willingly or being reluctantly dragged into it.

In fact, we can become dragged down, or under, by the struggle if our resistance to surrendering to the spiritual life is strong enough.[24]

Jung emphasised the role of dreams in understanding the depth and complexity of unconscious processes. Dreams and their interpretation are amongst the oldest phenomena of humanity. Antiquity records them as one of the prime expressions of revelation and prophecy. There are numerous references to dream interpretation throughout Scripture.

Jung understood them as autonomous self-representations of the psyche that generally stand in compensatory relationship to the dominant conscious perspective, and function as essential parts of the self-regulation of psychological processes. Dreams bring to a conscious course of action or attitude a compensating or complementing emphasis from the unconscious. Thus the psyche uses the function of dreaming to check its own excesses by balancing opposing conflicts, tensions and tendencies.

Writers in the Judeo-Christian tradition, on the whole, were remarkably sensitive to the dangers in taking dreams too seriously and viewing their kind of revelation as rivalling Scripture. This ancient temptation presents itself in modern dress in those 'disciples' who make a new religion out of modern psychology, psychoanalysis and analytical psychology, who forget, in making an idol of the unconscious, that it is only a part, not the whole, of the interior life.[25]

The real function of dreams is to keep us continually focusing on the unknown processes and workings of our unconscious. They are direct expressions of the way the unconscious is constantly responding to the demands, decisions and fluctuations of conscious life. They urge us to be aware of, and responsive to, the presence of other unseen and unknown interior processes within the psyche.

Dreaming is usually one of the main ways that the unconscious makes human interiority available to itself. Dreams present the unknown realm of our interior life through symbol, image, story, and narrative. This realm is organised and structured from the self, and so has its own unique language, meaning and structure.

Taking account of the unconscious in our spiritual life will rearrange not only how the Holy Spirit moves in us, but also every experience we are likely to have of the unconscious. Teresa's text demonstrates that our life in the Spirit deepens and darkens as it progresses, reaching down into our deepest pre verbal, pre-rational fantasies, instinctive drives, bodily passions and impulses as well as growing to transcendent realms. Our spiritual journey will open the depths of our unconscious, in all the darkest and most terrifying places, and dreams provide meaning and connection to the inner guiding principle through the unconscious.

Not only does Jung's account of the structure of the psyche match the teaching of the mystical tradition, but the general depth psychotherapeutic method is similar too. Although there are important differences between spiritual direction and modern psychotherapeutic practice, there are also similarities.

In modern forms of psychotherapy, what is going on below the level of our conscious thinking and agenda is carefully explored. Instead of ignoring the signs and signals from the unconscious, we are encouraged to pay serious attention to our dreams, to waking fantasies and daydreams, and to our thoughts and impulses. We are encouraged to look at them consciously, to try to understand the unconscious wishes, drives, impulses and unknown parts of ourselves, to become aware of ourselves in depth.

This very closely resembles the ancient injunction of spiritual direction to dwell in the cell of self-knowledge, in order to direct our surface attention constantly to the hidden motives underlying our conscious aims and actions. This is precisely what Teresa is referring to in emphasising the room of self-knowledge.[26]

The image of transparency can be found in the inter-relation of depth psychology and Christian faith, both worlds finding their fullest expression in this image. In any serious life of the soul we are made more permeable to God's Presence and purposes in our lives. In any focused concentration on the life of the psyche, our consciousness necessarily becomes more and more permeable and transparent to the presence and motives of the unconscious.

Touching the deep unconscious dimensions of our own personal problems introduces us to that level of association that is really communal and unites us with every other psyche. Jung talked about an objective layer of the psyche existing beneath what he called the 'personal unconscious', which is our most autobiographical interior place, composed of entirely personal materials – repressions, old dreams, early childhood memories.

This objective layer of the psyche, the 'collective', employs archetypal images that refer to elemental human experiences such as birth, transformation, suffering, death, and renewal. When we go through these experiences we connect with the collective unconscious.

Real self-knowledge does not mean a theoretical or intellectual knowledge of our human nature, but a real self-awareness, a heart knowledge of ourselves from a perspective of inner unity. To really know ourselves means to be intimately familiar with, and continually study and observe, the structure of our being, its many functions and different parts, and the manifold conditions which govern how these functions work, interact and respond to the myriad life influences, demands and expectations.

Crucially, an essential part of this interior growth is to slowly learn to be able to discriminate between the different functions and parts as impartially as possible, remembering, at the same time, the many possibilities of interior growth that are *potentially* available as we progress.

So we study and observe our human faculties and functions – our thinking, or intellectual capacities; our feelings or emotions, both negative and positive; our intuitive and sensation functions, as well as our conscious and unconscious motives; our raw, primitive instincts, body and sexuality as well as our rational and irrational nature.

We look at them in directly experiential ways, constantly observing, seeking to understand and discriminating between the many unknown parts of ourselves. True self-knowledge is learning not what I am but what is in me, knowing what does and does not belong to me, in this inward sense.

Often, ordinary waking consciousness is a world of many separate selves, of identification with transient moods, thoughts, feelings, and ideas of the moment, which are constantly in motion and usually only of brief duration. Without any real sense of inner stillness, the mind is unable to penetrate into itself to establish a more permanent inner sense of unity and stability.

Either the many different parts of ourselves, the often conflicting thoughts, feelings, actions, imagination, physical sensations and perceptions, are in control and are making our choices, or, with the formation of a more permanent magnetic centre, an inner unity is developing.

With such an inner unity beginning to grow, the capacity and free will to choose and act consciously will develop, as the different parts of our being and personality begin to come under the authority of this inner unity. This is a type of self-consciousness that watches and feels all of our experiences, and when released from other experience for a moment, is able to experience itself.

This is real self-knowledge – knowing myself, being self-aware, when all mundane knowing based on the senses and ordinary experience has become quiet. This can only happen when an inner witness or observer has developed the capacity to observe, *without identification or possession,* the 'field of consciousness' – thoughts, feelings, and actions. This observer is purely awareness in and of itself.

The emphasis on self-knowledge on the spiritual journey has been part of the Christian mystical tradition since the early centuries. Gregory of Nyssa, a well-known Orthodox saint and theologian of the Cappadocian school of the second century, wrote:

> Our greatest protection is self-knowledge. We must avoid the delusion that we are seeing ourselves when we are in reality looking at something else. This is what happens to those who do not observe themselves. They see strength, beauty, reputation, political power, abundant wealth, self-importance, bodily stature, a certain grace of form and the like, and they think that this is what they are.
>
> Such people are very bad at watching over themselves; because of their absorption in something else, they overlook what is really their own and leave it unguarded. How can a person protect something if he does not know it? The most secure protection for our treasure is to know ourselves; each of us must know himself as he is, and must distinguish himself from what is not himself, so that he does not unconsciously protect something else while thinking he is watching himself.
>
> Anyone who has any regard for the life of this world, or who thinks that worldly honour is worth protecting, does not know how to distinguish himself from what he is not. No passing thing is strictly ours.[27]

A permanent sense of self-awareness, or in Teresa's symbolic language, the strong protective walls of the interior castle, within which the 'journey in God' takes place, are beginning to be developed at these early stages. The Christian mystical tradition has used a variety of images and symbols for this stage – the development of a magnetic centre, or the formation of a psychological inner equivalent of the monk's or hermit's cell, into which we are able to withdraw from the outer distractions of the world.

Another ancient biblical image is that of an ark of the Covenant, based on the story of Moses and of the escape of the Israelites from the hands of the Egyptians. This has been seen, since the earliest days of the church, as a parable for the escape of the soul from the 'Egypt of worldly life'. If understood as a parable for an interior process, it tells of the development of an artificial inner centre that has the capacity to slowly integrate, balance and stabilise our previously unstable psyche.

It is about the growth of an inner temple, not made by human hands, which is able to begin to hold God's Presence within our soul, allowing a gradual shift of our centre of gravity so that we eventually revolve not around ourselves but around God. We achieve the slow move from being self-centred to becoming God-centred.

When this happens, such a magnetic centre can lead to a state of magnetisation to God in the latter mansions. This was most clearly described by St Theophan the Recluse. Through metanoia, and being able to become wholehearted in our search for God, our inner realignment, or inner gravitational pull, fundamentally changes from being centred on ourselves, to beginning to revolve around the things of God.[28]

Teresa notes that for as many entrances as there are to the first mansion, there are as many self-deceptions, lies, confusion, vanity, cruelty, ignorance and doubts to be battled with and conquered. The personal ego, or the personality, often believes that it is the true master of the house, being inflated and identified with its own personal ambitions, achievements and pleasures. She is fairly explicit about the particular difficulties in the earlier mansion:

> From personal experience I could give you much information as to what happens in these first mansions. I will only say that you must not imagine there are only a few, but a number of rooms, for souls enter them by many different ways, and always with a good intention. The devil is so angry at this, that he keeps legions of evil spirits hidden in each room to stop the progress of Christians, whom, being ignorant of this, he entraps in a thousand ways.
>
> He cannot so easily deceive souls which dwell nearer to the King as he can beginners still absorbed in the world, immersed in its pleasures and eager for its honours and distinctions. As the vassals of their souls, the senses and powers bestowed on them by God, are weak, such people

are easily vanquished, although desirous not to offend God.
(I, Chapter 2, 13)

How sad a sight must be a soul deprived of light! What a terrible state the chambers of this castle are in! How disorderly must be the senses – the inhabitants of the castle – the powers of the soul – its magistrates, governors and stewards – blind and uncontrolled as they are. (I, Chapter 2, 4)

Teresa is highlighting the manifold obstacles and difficulties in these early stages of spiritual progress. The main obstacles are the profound ignorance of who and what we are, of what our real possibilities for development are, and of what is necessary to achieve them. The fragmented condition of our self-understanding and motivation and the unconscious habits that make us carry on living as we have always done also stand in our way.

Embryonic self-consciousness shows us that there are many different groupings of inner and outer sensations that can profoundly disturb our attention and ability to maintain inner quiet and stillness. Pain, fatigue, stress, inactivity, illness, chemical imbalance with uncontrolled imagination, strong negative emotions and actions, artificial desires, excessive sentimentality, intellectual formulations unrelated to feelings or actions, constant over-activity – all of these interfere with our attention. Teresa observes that the senses, in these earliest mansions, can be completely out of order, blind and uncontrolled.

HUMILITY

Teresa emphasises the central role of deepening humility as one of the vital character ingredients on the spiritual journey in many of her writings, particularly in *The Way of Perfection* and *The Interior Castle*.

She sets down the three prerequisites of true peace in
The Way of Perfection and says of them:

> It is essential that we should understand how very important
> they are to us in helping us to preserve that peace, both
> inward and outward, which the Lord so earnestly recom-
> mended to us. One of these is love for each other; the second,
> detachment from all created things; the third, true humility,
> which although I put it last, is the most important of the
> three and embraces all the rest. (*The Way of Perfection*, IV)

Humility is essentially the absence of self-regard and
self-concern. It is spontaneous unselfconsciousness, without
which there can be no true love of God, or of our neighbour.
She is clear in her writings that the cultivation of deepening
humility is a surer test of holiness than any enjoyment of
mystical visions and favours:

> **Not only a good way, but the best of all ways, is to endeavour
> to enter first by the room where humility is practised, which
> is far better than at once rushing on to the others. This is
> the right road – if we know how easy and safe it is to walk
> by it, why ask for wings with which to fly.** (I, Chapter 2, 10)

Humility is usually described as a quality of being
'unassuming, unpretentious', of having a 'broken and
contrite heart', or even 'having a lowly opinion of oneself'.
The virtue of real humility is usually regarded as the honest
and contrite recognition of one's own shortcomings and
weaknesses, together with a focus on the mercy of God.

In the *Ladder of Divine Ascent*, St John Climacus refers
to humility as the 'constant forgetfulness of one's achievements.' This is quite different from having low self-esteem
or a general sense of inferiority – indeed, in Christ-like love
there is no false humility and no inferiority complex.[29] In
contrast to the view of humility as characteristic of the
weak and impotent, it is actually a source of immense
power and spiritual strength, as it is only through humility
that the debilitating power of pride can possibly be abated.

Self-knowledge, the point of departure for humility,

makes it possible for us to come to terms with our smallness and unworthiness in the Presence of God, and see that our ultimate reliance and dependence is on the mercy and love of God. Real humility can only come about as a result of self-knowledge, and is, in fact, a test of true self-knowledge.

Having true humility means that we are not troubled, anxious, worried or disturbed in our deepest centre. It leads to dwelling within peace and stillness, even in the midst of great inner trials and turmoil, and enables us to listen and serve God more honestly with the freedom, understanding and knowledge that humility brings.

An increasingly humble perspective allows us to put others before ourselves, and to see those virtues in others that we ourselves lack. From the profound acceptance of this springs an unwillingness to criticise others, or project onto them, which is not only a virtue in itself, but builds up the atmosphere in which Love can flourish.

Teresa is at pains to warn of the subtle and insidious dangers of pride and false humility. She says in her autobiography: 'I believe the devil is very successful in preventing people who pray, from advancing further by giving them false notions of humility. He persuades us that it is pride that gives us such great aims, and that makes us wish to imitate the saints.' (Chapter 13)

False humility causes a basic unrest, or dissonance, in the heart, because this type of humility tries to possess, grasp or devour something in order to nourish false pride, and can have a superficial, controlling, manipulative tone to it. It is humility with hooks to go with it, so to speak.

She warns sincere seekers who are advanced in this first mansion that it is easy to get caught up in their newly found journey and go into a hectic round of spiritual activities, which can often be an expression of false humility, as, at these early stages, the motivation for such activities can still be self-gratification.

At these early stages, although we have turned and awakened towards God and the spiritual life, and can be

especially pious and sincere about our longings and desire
for God, yet we may not be sure how to relate to Him, the
self, the world and other people. At this point in our
journey, we can still be mainly driven by a desire for
personal gratification, and this often spills over into our
religious activities as well.

Because this has been our habitual mode of relating and
being, we will unconsciously expect God to act as a spiritual
equivalent of the sensual satisfaction that has previously
been the focus of our life. We can be enmeshed in a form
of spiritual narcissism, from which it is difficult to escape.
We may still wish to make God an object, a means to
satisfy our own sensual desires, yet another being who is
obliged to give us satisfaction and pleasure.[30]

Because we are being called, beckoned, towards a
direction wholly other than what the world and personal
gratification can offer, there is usually increasing resistance
to this activity of the Holy Spirit in our hearts and lives.
Our defence mechanisms can kick in ruthlessly – we can
deny, rationalise or intellectualise our old destructive
attitudes and behaviours. We can convince ourselves that
they are acceptable, but this only makes it more difficult to
face the truth about ourselves and the type of life we are
leading, and turn around towards God.

Such conflicting desires can provoke strong states of
emotional distress, confusion, fear, anxiety and resistance.
As our desire for God becomes more real, it begins to clash
with the old pattern of experiences, attitudes and actions
which are self-serving and self-seeking and based on personal
power, aggrandisement and gratification. They will not
lead to any sort of deepening spiritual life.

If this conflicting interior reality becomes particularly
strong, destructive and hostile attitudes, such as rage,
inability or unwillingness to assume personal responsibility,
increasing forms of manipulation, lying, acting out,
resistance to any form of spiritual direction, or even forms
of psychological breakdown can develop. If the sense of

feeling threatened is strong, the person can resort to any and every means to maintain the disordered and self-defeating defences of the psyche.[31]

The honest and sincere cultivation of humility is the necessary antidote to this type of paralysis of the soul. The various forms of destructiveness and resistance to spiritual growth and development have their roots in excessive egocentricity. Delusions of personal omnipotence, inflation, grandiosity or the dangers of spiritual pride or possessiveness may develop.

True humility engages in the spiritual struggle against false pride, which includes excessive, or obsessive self-love, self-interest and egotism. These faults entirely enclose us within ourselves, in direct opposition to the will of God, and to the needs of others, and lead to inner conflict with our own true self.

Excessive expressions of self-love occur in a form of what is known as narcissistic relatedness, where there is an overpowering need for acute self-admiration, whether of physical, intellectual or even spiritual attributes. In relationships with others, the person is essentially indifferent to, or incapable of empathising with, the needs of those around them.

In narcissistic forms of relating, there is usually a deep-seated problem with the development of personal identity, as these defensive patterns of relating are actually protection against injury to an already very poor, or undeveloped, sense of identity and self-esteem.

The subjective experience of narcissistic woundedness arises from internally distorted perceptions of our own self-image and worth. These perceptions are usually incongruent, dissonant and unrealistic when mirrored by the outside world. There is essentially an inability to experience reciprocal mirroring with significant others, which is so vital in learning to develop an undistorted sense of identity and self-worth.

Some of the common features of narcissism are

depression, grandiosity, acute vulnerability, inability to empathise with others and very poor self-esteem.[32] The usually strong grandiose power drives in narcissistic relatedness are usually a compensation for acute states of vulnerability, neediness and a poor sense of identity.

The point here is that false humility can actually be a type of defensive pattern, which can hide all sorts of psychological problems, difficulties and lack of healthy, normal psychological development. Jung considered that very high, or very low self-esteem are essentially defence mechanisms, compensating for a sense of inferiority and low self-worth:

> If we now consider the fact that, as a result of psychic compensation, great humility stands very close to pride, and that 'pride goeth before a fall', we can easily discover behind the haughtiness certain traits of an anxious sense of inferiority. In fact, we shall see clearly how his uncertainty forces the enthusiast to puff up his truths, of which he feels none too sure, and to win proselytes to his side in order that his followers may prove to himself the value and trustworthiness of his own convictions.[33]

At these early stages of the spiritual life, many of these hidden patterns will be slowly revealed, and should be worked with either in psychotherapy or under spiritual direction.

True humility is not easily acquired, neither is it something that is attained once and for all and then requires no effort. To acquire humility is a continuous and lifelong struggle. Even the saints, as described in their hagiographies, feel they have not yet acquired real humility! As St Silouan on his deathbed confessed: 'I have not yet learned humility.'[34]

Continuous self-examination and self-reflection, maintaining a low opinion of oneself before God, will overcome excessive spiritual pride and promote a truly humble spirit. Some of the stronger and more powerful methods, which are part of the more severe monastic vocation, are constant self-accusation and blaming of oneself for offences against God and others, and promoting a deep sense of self-abasement and worthlessness before God.[35] All of these methods should be discussed and supervised under the most careful and sensitive spiritual direction.

When the taste and the presence of Divine Love begin to touch our heart, mind and body, it is the egotism, hate, fear and envy within us that hinder this Love entering and taking root deep within. Usually only some form of deep humiliation, suffering, pain or self-abasement has the capacity to break the power of these negative bonds and liberate us from the prison of our own making.

Of course, the gospel story of Jesus, from the Trans-figuration on, is concerned with His humiliation and total abasement, which was utterly necessary before His res-urrection. Christ-like humility is, first and foremost, a 'kenosis' – an emptying or denial of our self in order for His Life and Love to enter, and become united, in the depths of our soul.

True perfection lies in the capacity to love God with all our heart, mind and soul, and to love others, and all else serves as a means of protecting this love. When we truly love, real humility is always at work. Teresa says that humility works the way a bee works making honey in the beehive.

When a bee is making honey in the beehive, it is doing that for which it was made. It is not bothered, disturbed, anxious or troubled. It does not work to make honey in order to receive love and attention, nor is it driven by compulsions or competition, nor does it use work as a distraction from other life necessities.

It is doing what it was destined to do by God:

Let humility always be at work, like the bee to the honeycomb, or all will be lost. But, remember, the bee leaves its hive to fly in search of flowers and the soul should sometimes cease thinking of itself to rise in meditation on the grandeur and majesty of its God. It will learn its own

> **baseness better thus than by self-contemplation, and will be freer from the reptiles which enter the first room where self-knowledge is acquired.** (I, Chapter 2, 9)

To understand her teaching concerning humility is to sense a deep interior peace and contentment. Further on in the fourth mansion, she continues to emphasise that the practice of humility is the 'chief exercise' for those who wish to pray:

> **We are his, sisters, let Him do what He will with us, and lead us where He will. If we are really humble and annihilate ourselves, not only in our imagination (which often deceives us) but if we truly detach ourselves from all things, our Lord will not only grant us these favours but many others that we do not even know how to wish for.** (IV, Chapter 2, 8)

THE LIZARDS AND THE SNAKES

The first mansion is fraught with difficulties, blocks, distractions and obstacles that seem to constantly pull us away from God. One of the main tests in this early stage concerns spiritual sincerity in our search for God. Whether we are *really* turning away from external material pursuits, passions and pleasures, and trying to develop the necessary one-pointed interior concentration in prayer, meditation and reflection. As soon as we turn towards the interior world in prayer and reflection, we usually encounter whole dimensions of ourselves that have previously been unconscious, hidden and unknown.

The neglected or dark side of ourselves is usually encountered fairly quickly. Teresa symbolises these more negative, broken parts as the 'lizards and the snakes' in the moat outside the castle. These symbols are the chief negative motifs in *The Interior Castle,* and represent all of those forces and dynamics that attack, block and distract us from outside, and hinder and disturb us from within.

From an interior perspective, the 'lizards and the snakes'

symbolise all the neglected parts of our life and psyche. Throughout our spiritual journey, they will need to be constantly recognised, accepted, made conscious, assimilated and ultimately dissolved, changed and transformed – 'made new' – in God's Love.

In modern psychological parlance, these are the shadow parts of the psyche, encompassing all the psychic contents that have been driven back into the unconscious, all the neglected, undeveloped, unacknowledged parts of our personality. Jung described the shadow as the 'negative side of the personality, the sum of all those unpleasant qualities we like to hide, together with the insufficiently developed functions and the content of the personal unconscious.'[36] The 'lizards and the snakes' represent our inner darkness and all the preoccupations and internal distractions that pull us away from the deeper contemplative 'journey towards, and in, God'.

In the first mansion, these are predominantly our over-involvement in, identification with and attachment to worldly matters and concerns, our perceived status, self-image and identity. Teresa introduces these potentially negative and debilitating parts of our psyche in evocative symbolic language to warn of the insidious and powerful nature of unconscious forces that can have destructive and inhibiting effects on the natural processes of psychological and spiritual growth.

It is not possible to escape confrontation with the neglected, broken, darker parts of ourselves. Sooner or later we will encounter the multitude of 'snakes, vipers and venomous creatures' that populate our inner world when we start to turn within, particularly in these earliest mansions. From a spiritual perspective, Teresa warns that the shadow parts of our psyche and personality can still be dominant here, since this dimension is usually so hidden, dormant, unknown and unconscious at these early stages: 'these inhabitants see scarcely anything, these fierce and wild beasts blind the eyes of the beginner.'

Spiritual directors affirm how difficult it is to become aware and conscious of our shadow side, with its pride, manipulation, hunger for power, jealousy, envy, need for revenge, desire for possession, sexual temptations and the like. In these early stages, our shadow side is just beginning to reveal itself, and this gathers momentum in the second mansion where 'confronting and battling with the lizards and snakes' becomes necessary. This process, interior ascesis or purification, is required in these early mansions, in order to journey further within the castle.

Teresa is fairly adamant about how hard it is in these early stages to 'enter within ourselves', especially if we are accustomed to only thinking about, and being preoccupied with, external and worldly matters. She knows how difficult it is for us to enter the castle, to 'retire into our own heart', because we have become so used to dealing with the 'insects and reptiles', the distractions, our broken, wounded parts and such, in the walls surrounding the castle that we have become over-identified and over-attached to them:

> Just so, there are souls so infirm and accustomed to think of nothing but earthly matters, that there seems no cure for them. It appears impossible for them to retire into their own hearts; accustomed as they are to be with the reptiles and other creatures that live outside the castle, they have come at last to imitate their habits. (I, Chapter I, 8)

It is only through the Presence of the light and truth of God, through prayer and reflection, can we gradually begin to penetrate the 'lizards and the snakes' dimension of our psyche. Then it is possible for this part of ourselves, the shadow, to be slowly reintegrated and transformed in Love:

> You must notice that the light that comes from the King's palace hardly shines at all in these first mansions; although not as gloomy and black as the soul in mortal sin, yet they are in semi-darkness, and their inhabitants see scarcely anything.
>
> I cannot explain myself; I do not mean that this is the fault of the mansions themselves, but that the number of

snakes, vipers and venomous reptiles from outside the castle prevent souls entering them from seeing the light.

They resemble a person entering a chamber full of brilliant sunshine, with eyes clogged and half closed with dust. Though the room itself is light, he cannot see because of his self-imposed impediment. In the same way, these fierce and wild beasts blind the eyes of the beginner, so that he sees nothing but them.

Such, it appears to me, is the soul which, though not in a state of mortal sin, is so worldly and preoccupied with earthly riches, honours and affairs, that as I said, even if it sincerely wishes to enter into itself and enjoy the beauties of the castle, it is prevented by these distractions and seems unable to overcome so many obstacles. It is most important to withdraw from all unnecessary cares and business, as far as is compatible with the duties of one's state of life, in order to enter the second mansion. (I, Chapter 2, 15,16)

Teresa is clear that the obstacles and difficulties with the 'lizards and the snakes' continue throughout our spiritual journey, even to the innermost mansions – albeit in more subtle forms. In the second dwelling place, where, through our continual efforts and ascesis, we are facing up to the neglected, unconscious dimensions of our psyche in a deeper and more honest way, she tells us that this is an ongoing, continuous struggle and that preventing failure is not always possible:

These beasts are so poisonous and their presence so dangerous and noisy that it would be a wonder if we kept from stumbling and falling over them. (I, Chapter 2, 1,2)

She explains that not even in the very last dwelling place can anyone count on an end to these psychological and spiritual dangers. Although it is rare, she says that sometimes the Lord allows such attacks so that we will appreciate the tremendous favours we are receiving, and develop great fortitude in trials and adversity.[37]

Even in the seventh mansion, Teresa explains:

I told you that in most cases our Lord occasionally leaves such persons to the weakness of their nature. The venomous creatures from the moat round the castle and the other mansions at once join together to revenge themselves for the time when they were deprived of their power.

True, this lasts but a short time – a day perhaps, or a little longer – but during this disturbance, which generally arises from some passing event, these persons learn what benefits they derive from the holy company they are in.

Our Lord gives them great fortitude, so that they never desert His service nor the good resolutions they have made, which only seem to gather strength by trial. (VII, Chapter 4, 1, 2)

As Teresa wisely advises, unless we are able to accept these parts of ourselves, and begin to communicate with our hidden underground depths at these early stages on our journey, these realms will certainly disrupt our spiritual journey. If they are not faced, owned and ultimately transformed our 'lizards and serpents', almost certainly, will turn around and bite, poison and generally wreak havoc in our interior life.

It takes a tremendous amount of humility, integrity, self-honesty and the action of charity and virtue to acknowledge our shadow, and begin the long, arduous work of its transformation. Up until this stage, most of the shadow parts have been repressed and hidden – now these traits come up to full consciousness for acknowledgement, healing and transformation through acceptance and love.

Teresa also talks about the other forces of evil in the castle – the devils. Behind the serpents in the castle stand the devils, which personify all the threats to our spiritual journey. It is really the devils that are waging the war inside the castle, and she explains that they will not ignore a single one of the multitude of rooms in this first dwelling place:[38]

I will only say that you must not imagine there are only a few, but a number of rooms, for souls enter them by many different ways, and always with good intention. The devil is so angry at this, that he keeps legions of evil spirits hidden in each room to stop the progress of Christians, whom, being ignorant of this, he entraps in a thousand ways.

He cannot so easily deceive souls which dwell nearer to

the King as he can beginners still absorbed in the world, immersed in its pleasures, and eager for its honours and distinctions. (I, Chapter 2, 13)

The devils are even more active in the second mansion, and can continue right up to the innermost mansions. Not even souls in union with God may relax against the devil:

No enclosure can be too strict for Satan to enter, nor any desert too remote for him to visit. God may permit him to tempt the soul to prove its virtue; for as He intends it to enlighten others, it is better for it to fail in the beginning than when it might do them great harm. (V, Chapter 4, 7)

The devil is the traditional figure used to indicate the source of evil, the tempter who leads us into destructiveness. From a psychological perspective, this figure is one of many used by the psyche in its personification of the neglected, negative parts of the personality, that we are ashamed of, or will not recognise, because they are unacceptable and clash with the more acceptable, known self-image.

The shadow often represents the past, and the primitive, undeveloped, and what we feel are the inferior parts of ourselves which have not been given the chance to be accepted, healed and fully integrated into the whole of our being. These 'reptiles and the serpents' are usually encountered as powerful forces within the psyche as soon as we begin to explore the unknown and descend into the unconscious.

These undifferentiated, undeveloped, primitive and childish contents of our psyche are often experienced as autonomous and sometimes overwhelming. This is the wounded inner child – where huge parts of ourselves have been relegated to the unconscious after childhood trauma.

If psychological wounds from childhood are not attended to and healed, especially if they are sustained and reinforced into adulthood, they feed the repressed, shadow side of our personality. The effect of repression is to cut off access to that part of ourselves. We may repress feelings, or a character trait, or a talent, or a way of thinking for fear of disapproval or rejection by a teacher, a parent or an authority. When those parts of ourselves are cut off, all the rest of our potential and creativity is also cut off and repressed.

Some of these ideas may be difficult to grasp on a practical or theoretical level, and rather than referring to the shadow as a thing, it is better to think of psychological traits or qualities that are in the shadow i.e. hidden, behind one's back in the dark, or shadowy. Psychological or emotional traumas sustained during childhood, caused primarily by cruel or negative programming, are injured areas that need to be healed and brought back into full awareness, and integration if possible.

The image evoked by the term 'shadow' as first used by Jung and later taken up by his followers presents all the repressed material of our unconscious organised into a counterpart to the conscious parts of our lives. A person's shadow contains psychic material that has been crystallised in the unconscious to compensate for (often) one-dimensional development of ourselves.

As in the case of light, the conscious self produces an unconscious dark area – the shadow. There are some common everyday expressions that illustrate this – when someone is plagued by fear and anxiety they are 'afraid of their own shadow', when someone has fallen under the spell of another person, they are 'following them around like their shadow'. It is classified according to the environment that has produced it, such as the family shadow, institutional shadow, and national shadow.[39]

If our conscious willing, choosing and intending are tracked deeply enough, we will come to realms of darkness, coldness and heartlessness, where it becomes apparent that we have the capacity to be extremely selfish, wilful, unfeeling and controlling. In our natural condition, before the action of the Holy Spirit and God's Love in our lives, human desire usually strives for purely egoistic purposes, and the predominant intent is to fulfil personal desires for power and pleasure at any cost.

Up until we become conscious of our shadow areas, most people do not know how self-centred and egotistical they can be. We try to hide such traits from others and ourselves behind facades and masks that show us to be considerate, thoughtful, empathic, reflective and genial. We want to appear unselfish, and in control of our appetites and pleasures as much as possible.

Generally, the shadow has an immoral or at least a disreputable quality, containing features of a person's nature that are contrary to the customs and moral conventions of society. In terms of becoming conscious of our shadow, Jung writes of how much integrity, honesty and sincerity is required to become aware of our shadow, and how linked it is to self-knowledge:

> The shadow is a moral problem that challenges the whole ego-personality, for no one can become conscious of the shadow without considerable moral effort. To become conscious of it involves recognising the dark aspects as present and real. This act is the essential condition for any kind of self-knowledge, and it therefore, as a rule, meets with considerable resistance. Indeed, self knowledge as a psycho-therapeutic measure frequently requires much painstaking work extending over a long period.[40]

The shadow part of our personality contains painful memories, experiences and personal qualities all of which have been forgotten, repressed or denied, rejected and hidden, both from ourselves as well as others. It is an ever-bleeding wound, and so confrontation with our shadow is no easy task. Locked in the dark basement of the unconscious, out of sight from the world, the shadow carries with it great pain and vulnerability, suffering, sadness, deep despair, anger, alienation and resentment.

Why is this area so important? There are many reasons. Working on our repressed, wounded parts is an integral part of knowing ourselves in any depth capacity. Acknowledging and reintegrating these rejected parts lets us recover them.

Usually much of our individual creativity and capacity to surrender reside here. The shadow contains not only negative and destructive elements, but also tremendous potential for deeper spiritual growth and development. Jung found that the shadow, in metaphorical terms, contains ninety percent gold.

So, what is in the shadow is our unloved and undeveloped potential for deeper growth and development. We have to reconnect and reintegrate all those parts before we can enter more fully and completely the further mansions of our castle.

The positive aspects of the shadow represent all the unlived and untapped potential for expression and creativity. So, although the shadow areas often act negatively, they are capable of being brought to the light for the healing and enrichment of the whole personality. This positive aspect of the shadow represents all that potential which could be tapped, but for pressures, anxieties, fears, or the amount of work it would take to own and integrate these parts.

Another important reason for befriending and integrating our shadow parts is that doing so is fundamental to authentic self-esteem. How can we truly love ourselves or have confidence in ourselves if a part of us is ignored and works against our own best interests? Also, our shadow parts tend to be projected onto different types of relationships if we do not acknowledge and work with them, and so this is essential for maintaining healthy social and personal relationships.

The root cause of many interpersonal conflicts and professional burnout can be found in shadow projections. Vulnerabilities, weaknesses or shortcomings get projected onto other people and situations. It is vital to understand this process. Becoming aware of our projections onto others, and then being able to take back what we have projected vastly improves interpersonal relations.[41]

It is a mysterious paradox that the place of our greatest pain, vulnerability and powerlessness is the door through which our heart can be so broken that it forces us to turn away from the outer world and trace the thread of our own darkness back to our source in God. It is only by fully acknowledging, experiencing and surrendering our inner darkness, pain and exile to the Light and endless Love of God, that it is possible to journey further within the interior castle. We can do nothing by our own efforts and our own will in the place of our greatest wounds.

These are the hidden interior places where we can only gradually accept ourselves in our most naked and vulnerable human state and offer ourselves up to be healed by His Love. It is our wounds that take us home to God. During this journey, we have to accept and integrate what we find within us – all the pain, anger and hurt – the many forms that our darkness has taken. We will find the prostitute, the thief and the beggar within us. We will see the hurt we have caused others and the hurt we have caused ourselves.

To handle and reintegrate our shadow parts is very delicate psycho-spiritual work. Great patience is required. Exposing too much unconscious material too quickly can have disabling and counterproductive effects. To illustrate this danger, Jung uses the metaphor of the fisherman who didn't load his boat (the conscious ego identity) properly.

If he overloads it, it is in danger of sinking. If, on the other hand, he doesn't pack in a heavy enough load, he is wasting time and energy.[42] It is vital to respect the (often long) incubation period necessary for reintegrating our shadow. It takes a long time to break up and form new links to the conscious parts of ourselves.

There are many strategies that can help us recognise our shadow parts. Our honest response to questions like those that follow can facilitate our self knowledge and awareness of these hidden parts of ourselves: What topics of discussion do I tend to avoid in my conversations with people? Sexuality, aggression, faith, ambition, incompetence? In what kinds of situations do I find myself becoming nervous, oversensitive and defensive?

What type of remark would startle me? In what situations do I feel inferior, lacking in self-confidence or embarrassed? In what field do I panic at the idea of allowing someone to see my weakness or vulnerability? Do I feel embarrassed if someone asks me point blank to carry out an activity like speaking or singing in public? Am I inclined to be offended when someone criticises me?

Other self-revelatory questions relate to the social image we wish to convey, and to what may lie in the shadow area. What are the most flattering aspects of my social ego, those traits that I would like others to recognise? And what opposite qualities or traits have I had to repress to highlight the positive ones? Other questions relate to our attempts to conceal particular weaknesses and vulnerabilities. Where do I feel upset or dissatisfied with myself? For example, am I unhappy with my physical appearance or a particular character trait?[43]

Further equally effective strategies for becoming aware of our vulnerable and shadow areas include analysing our dreams, becoming attentive to fantasies and daydreams, being able to examine closely the nature and content of our humour, and most importantly, being able to examine and become conscious of what we project onto others. To handle the shadow areas of human experience requires particularly sensitive and patient care. It is possible for the shadow parts to change and be redirected to become positive sources of creativity and talent, but first they need to be admitted, accepted and acknowledged.

Projection is a common defence against being in touch with our wounded shadow parts. Projection is the unconscious, unperceived and unintentional, transfer of subjective, repressed psychic elements onto an outer object. In other words, projection enables us to see, hear and feel emotions, qualities and traits that lie repressed within us, through how they resonate outside us. It is the mechanism that enables us to see in others what we cannot see in ourselves. It is the externalising of our own unacceptable feelings and then attributing them to others.

So one of the main ways that we can be aware of our shadow parts is to examine our projections and try to become aware of them. We alienate ourselves from the elements of our shadow that we project onto others and deprive ourselves of knowing and using our full resources. Those things that we cannot abide in ourselves we will tend to project upon others.

If I do not admit my shadow side I will unconsciously find another who will carry my shadow for me. Once this projection is made then I need not be upset with myself. My problems are now outside and I can fight them out there rather than within the real arena that is myself and my own neglected dark areas.[44]

Positive capacities also tend to be projected when they are felt to be under attack, or if we are unable to accept our creative, positive qualities. When unacknowledged or disowned contents of the psyche are projected or pushed onto another person or situation, relief can often result because the other has been forced to carry the rejected and disowned parts of ourselves.

Projections are not made at random. They often have some basis in reality, because usually, in some way, 'the cap fits' the person or situation on whom the projection is being made. This makes projection a powerful and cogent defence and one that is hard to recognise and own because it is so split off, disowned or unconscious. The recipients of projections often act as convenient hooks, making the owning and recognition of the defence more difficult.

It is important to emphasise that when we send projections, we are almost always unconscious of both the act of projecting onto others and the nature of the projections. We are aware only that we are caught up in strong, intriguing feelings whose object might be either fascinating or repulsive. We experience attraction if we consider the projected qualities or character traits desirable, and we experience repulsion if we find what we have projected problematic or threatening.

It is the presence of strong emotion that often points to projected material. In general, extreme or inappropriate emotion accompanies an unconscious projection. Rage, fear, even admiration can be signs that projection is taking place, and in those instances we are giving away parts of ourselves.

Projections usually give us excuses to treat others badly, and tend to justify aggressive or violent attitudes or behaviour because the 'evil' is clearly in the other, not in ourselves. Jung commented on this difficulty:

> While some traits peculiar to the shadow can be recognised without too much difficulty as one's own personal qualities, in this case both insight and goodwill are unavailing because the cause of the motion appears to lie, beyond all possibility of doubt, in the other person. No matter how obvious it may be to the neutral observer that it is a matter of projections, there is little hope that the subject will perceive this himself. He must be convinced that he throws a very long shadow before he is willing to withdraw his emotionally toned projections from their object.[45]

If we do not engage in the difficult conscious work to become aware of our shadow, we will attribute those unacknowledged and rejected parts to others, who usually become the source of numerous problems and conflicts in our human relationships. If, for example, I can't stand a gentle, calm and reserved person, there is no doubt that I am lacking these qualities which I need to balance my over-aggressive personality, my agitated manner and my desire to make an impression.

Certain aspects of the shadow resist any conscious assimilation, and can be particularly resistant to reintegration unless there is a great deal of suffering and purgation. Jung emphasises the tremendous psychological and spiritual dangers of this:

Let us suppose that a certain individual shows no inclination whatever to recognise his projections. The projection-making factor then has a free hand and can realise its object – if it has one – or bring about some other situation characteristic of its power. As we know, it is not the conscious subject but the unconscious, which does the projecting. Hence, one meets with projections, one does not make them. The effect of projection is to isolate the subject from his environment, since instead of a real relation to it there is now only an illusory one. Projections change the world into the replica of one's own unknown face.[46]

Teresa has great insight into the nature of the shadow, and warns against projecting our shadow upon others. She admits that others may have their faults and corrections may have to be made, but that the primary responsibility for each individual is to attend to our inner journey that will reveal our own neglected areas.

She is particularly sensitive to what can be learned when the shadow is projected:

> **Let us look at our own faults, and not at other people's. People who are extremely correct themselves are often shocked at everything they see; however, *we might learn a great deal that is essential from the very persons whom we censure...* We ought not to insist on everyone following in our footsteps, nor to take it upon ourselves to give instructions in spirituality, when, perhaps we do not even know what it is.** (III, Chapter 2, 19)

So, these are the many and varied types of 'lizards and the snakes' that keep on attacking and disabling us in our spiritual journey. It is very important that pilgrims, certainly by this stage, are under some form of spiritual direction and, where necessary, in counselling or psychotherapy. It is not really possible to do this depth of work on ourselves, without the necessary specialised guidance and help, both psychological and spiritual. Shadow integration at these early stages takes very slow, sensitive care.

We are moving towards the capacity to accept ourselves exactly as we really are, in all our nakedness and exposure.

It is only then that our naked self can become a chalice into which His Wine and Love are poured. Teresa says that while our understanding is becoming more alert and attuned, our inner delusions, false imagination and temptations often become much stronger.

It can be experienced as an inner war, which requires steadfast discrimination, discernment and great ethical and moral courage. All the attachments and identifications of our personality, which keep our heart spiritually chained, are beginning to be more and more consciously revealed, to be purified and surrendered in the fires of our longing for God.

In these early dwelling places the very foundations of our interior castle are beginning to be firmly tested for their steadfastness, endurance, perseverance and self-knowledge. The more we begin to turn around, awaken to return home to God, the more we will suffer and must endure personal and collective torment both from within and sometimes, as Teresa did, from others and the wider community.

Teresa describes the spiritual effect of turning away from the journey towards God, and remaining in 'mortal sin' in vivid imagery:

> **In a state of grace, the soul is like a well of limpid water, from which flow only streams of clearest crystal. Its works are pleasing both to God and man, rising from the River of Life, beside which it is rooted like a tree.**
>
> **Otherwise it would produce neither leaves nor fruit, for the waters of grace nourish it, keep it from withering from drought, and cause it to bring forth good fruit. But the soul, by sinning, withdraws from this stream of life, and growing beside a black and fetid pool, can produce nothing but disgusting and unwholesome fruit.**
>
> **Notice that it is not the fountain and the brilliant sun which lose their splendour and beauty, for they are placed in the very centre of the soul, and cannot be deprived of their lustre. The soul is like a crystal in the sunshine over which a thick black cloth has been thrown, so however brightly the sun may shine, the crystal can never reflect it.**

(I, Chapter 2, 3)

NOTES: FIRST MANSION

1. Allison Peers, E. (trans). *The Interior Castle,* in *The Complete Works of Saint Teresa of Jesus,* Volume 2, Sheed and Ward, London, 1946, p.187

2. See Lopez Baralt, E. *Islam in Spanish Literature: From the Middle Ages to the Present,* E.J. Brill, Leiden, 1992

3. Coelho, M. *St Teresa of Avila's Transformation of the Symbol of the Interior Castle,* Teresianum Ephemeredes Carmeliticae, 1987, I, pp.116/123

4. Ibid, p.119

5. Underhill, E. *op. cit.* p.422

5a Coelho, M. *op.cit.* p.125

6. Teresa of Avila, *The Life of St Teresa by herself, op.cit.* p.78

7. Green, T. *When the Well Runs Dry – Prayer beyond the Beginnings,* Ave Maria Press, Notre Dame, Indiana, 1998, p.41

8. Ibid, p.46

9. Allison Peers, E. (trans). The *Way of Perfection* in *The Complete Works of Saint Teresa of Jesus,* Volume 2, Sheed and Ward, London, 1946, p.115

10. Ibid, p.114

11. Dwight, J. *Embracing God,* Abingdon Press, Nashville, 1996, p.79.

12. Melloni, J. *op.cit.* p.21

13. Green, T. *op.cit.* p.49

14. Teresa of Avila, *The Life of St Teresa by herself, op.cit.* Chapter 14.

15. Green, T. *op.cit.* p.57

16. Bishop Kallistos Ware. *The Inner Kingdom,* St Vladimir's Seminary Press, Crestwood, New York, 2000, p.48

17. Ibid, pp.45-46

18. Ibid, p.47

19. Amis, R. *op.cit.* pp.187-188

20. Ibid, pp.205-210

21. Nicoll, M. *The New Man,* Watkins, London, 1950 p.62

22. Welch, J. *Spiritual Pilgrims: Carl Jung and Teresa of Avila,* Paulist Press, New York/Mahwah, 1982, p.66

23. Bryant, C. *Jung and the Christian Way,* Darton Longman and Todd, London, 1983, p. 48.

24. Welch, J. *op.cit.* p.208

25. Ulanov, A. *Dreams and the Paradoxes of the Spirit,* in *Picturing God,* Cowley Press, Cambridge, Mass, 1986, p.77

26. Bryant, C. *op.cit.* p.50

27. Gregory of Nyssa, *From Glory to Glory,* St Vladimir's Seminary Press, Crestwood, NY, 1979

28. Amis. R. *op.cit.* pp.291-294

29. Boosalis, H. *Orthodox Spiritual Life,* St Tikhons Seminary Press, Pennsylvania, 2000, pp.101-102

30. Houdek, F. *op.cit.* pp.20-21

31. Ibid, pp.22-23
32. Jacobi, M. *Individuation and Narcissism*, pp.150-171
33. Ibid, pp.88
34. Boosalis, H. *op.cit.* p.117
35. Ibid, pp.121-125
36. C.G. Jung, *Two Essays on Analytical Psychology*, Collected works 7, trans R.F.C. Hull, Routledge, Kegan Paul, London, 1953/1966, para 103n
37. Welch, J. *op.cit.* p.113
38. Ibid, p.119
39. Monbourquette, J. *How to Befriend your Shadow*, DLT, Ottowa, 2001, pp.28-35
40. C.G.Jung, *Aion*, Collected works 9ii, trans. R.F.C. Hull, Routledge, Kegan Paul, London, 1959, para 14
41. Monbourquette, J. *op.cit.* chapter 6
42. Ibid, p.108
43. Ibid, chapter 7
44. Welch, J. *op.cit.* p.121
45. Jung, C.G. *Aion*, *op.cit.* para 16
46. Ibid, para 17.

THE SECOND MANSION

Entering and Purifying

The will inclines to love our Lord and longs to make some return to Him Who is so amiable, and Who has given so many proofs of His love, especially by His constant presence with the soul, which this faithful Lover never quits, ever accompanying it and giving it life and being.

St Teresa, Second Mansion

DECISION, DISCIPLINE, EFFORT

The interior journey has now begun, and Teresa says that the entrance to the castle proper, the doorway into our heart, is through prayer. The second mansion is a critical stage on the interior journey as it is the beginning of the often very painful and arduous process of interior transformation, purgation, and purification towards, and in, God. She describes this mansion as a dangerous, uncomfortable dwelling place.

We can be making efforts to turn around towards God in prayer and meditation and may be beginning to taste moments of God's Presence, but the sense of exile and separation from God can also begin to feel more acute and painful. Here, we are entering the teasing and perilous state of the inner world, where, in the early stages, it is very difficult, if not impossible, to orientate ourselves without spiritual guidance and discernment.

Interior trials and tests are becoming increasingly painful and we are beginning to undergo more serious testing of our deeper spiritual intentions and motivations. Teresa cautions:

> **In this part of the castle are found souls which have begun to practise prayer; they realise the importance of their not remaining in the first mansions, yet often lack determination to quit their present condition by avoiding occasions of sin, which is a very perilous state to be in.** (II, 2)

Prayer is becoming central in our life, as we begin to experience it more deeply. The focus of our attention is beginning to turn around from preoccupation with the outside world, with all its concerns, anxieties, competitiveness and emphasis on personal survival, towards the spiritual life.

In these beginning stages of prayer, much of what we learn about and experience comes through the mind and the senses. We read and talk about it, learning, hearing and experimenting with different forms and types of prayer, all of which begin to focus our mind and attention on the things of God. We are slowly becoming aware of the first stages of mental prayer, where there is a gradual movement from an emphasis on reasoning and analysis to prayer that comes from the heart.

Much of this early stimulus and guidance can come from outside sources, whether from workshops, retreats, spiritual directors or from our own study and reading. Teresa writes that God's voice may be heard:

> **Through the conversations of good people, or from sermons, or from reading good books, or in many other ways. Sometimes he calls souls by means of sickness or troubles, or by some truth He teaches them during prayer, for tepid as they may be in seeking Him, God holds them very dear.** (II, 5)

We are attracted to various methods and techniques that place our mind on God and we may go to workshops, seminars, retreats and conferences in order to nurture the growth and deepening of our spiritual life. We can start to experience an insatiable hunger for prayer, as it can begin to be so stimulating and delightful in this dwelling place, but it can lead to inflated and over-ambitious desires.

There can be danger in the impatient and ambitious spiritual hopes and wishes that can develop in these earlier mansions. Misguided romanticising about how wonderful prayer is can happen, and can fuel tendencies to inflation and omnipotence. We can feel very special and unique and desire the most mystical, contemplative prayer possible at this early stage. We can journey into flights of fancy through an overactive imagination and think ourselves the greatest of mystics. Not recommended!

We are really only at the beginning, in the second mansion, which is very much on the periphery of the castle. We need to be content and very patient with the slow growth of our interior life in God. Teresa tartly comments here:

> What a farce it is! Here are we, with a thousand obstacles,
> drawbacks, and imperfections within ourselves, our virtues
> so newly born that they have scarcely the strength to act
> (and God grant that they exist at all!) yet we are not ashamed
> to expect sweetness in prayer and to complain of feeling
> dryness. (II, 14)

There are no quick and easy routes, no magic formulae on
the road of prayer. The secret is to remain, as much as
possible, in the present moment of prayer and meditation,
allowing our mind and body to become quiet and still and
let go into being held and contained within the growing
cocoon of the Love and Presence of God.

The pilgrimage on the path of prayer can prove to be
long and arduous. The passage of time always brings us
face to face with harsh realities, both inner and outer. This
is the honeymoon stage of prayer, where everything is
wonderful and fascinating, where we revel in the beauty of
prayer and take pleasure in the many new delights that it is
bringing. We will discover, in time, that prayer has other
aspects and is certainly not all sweetness and light.[1]

God can speak to us in many ways once we have begun
to cultivate the art of prayer and silent watchfulness. We
can be astounded at the number of ways in which God
continually communicates and teaches us. We need to be
open and receptive to all the small hints and subtle signs
that are given. Slowly, there is an interior movement from
analysis, reasoning and discursive methods of prayer to
prayer that comes from deeper layers of the heart. We are
beginning to allow more time and space to pray and 'be
with God'.

Our sense of prayerfulness, mindfulness and attentiveness
is slowly improving. We grow increasingly aware of the
presence and action of God's Love in the centre of our life.
He will gradually imprint His Love and Truth onto us, if
we are quiet and receptive enough in moments of silence.
There is a true awakening in us and a new coming into life
that was not there before. God, through the Holy Spirit, is

becoming a real and viable part of our daily life, and this spiritual regeneration resembles a second birth.

As our spiritual life is becoming more apparent, there is a gradual shift in our priorities which indicates that new values are emerging. Matters of the spirit become more real and vital and what we value and perceive as important undergoes a fundamental change.

We may begin to realise that our sense of self-worth has tended to be based on what we own, produce, earn, or achieve, and that our new attitudes reflecting our spiritual life are beginning to be at odds with, or very different to, those with a more worldly perspective. Many things we felt comfortable with before we now see to be opposed to the spiritual life.

The second dwelling place represents a state of being where there is, as yet, no spiritual 'depth' for God to touch directly; He can only communicate with what is already there and He does so indirectly. Through our growing prayer and emphasis on the things of God, we are beginning to plant the essential seeds of our spiritual life in the soil of our psyche to germinate.

Growth will come if we continue in determination and patience. The warm energy of the Sun, of His Light and Love, cannot be felt or seen at its full intensity because the seeds of our new interior life have only just been sown and are not ready. The warm energy from the Sun that is absorbed by the soil will give the spiritual seeds strength to grow and persevere during the trials and difficulties ahead.

Other Christian saints have emphasised the difficulties of the trials and torments at these stages on the way, and tell of how crucial it is to have commitment to the new life that is beginning to awaken within. In her *Treatise on Purgatory*, Catherine of Genoa put it in this way:

> God created the soul, pure, simple, clean from all stain of sin, and with a kind of instinct which draws it towards him as its beatific end... when a soul returns to its first purity and to the cleanness of its first creation, this instinct, which

impels it towards God as to its beatific end, is awakened within it.

Increasing every moment, this instinct reacts on the soul with terrifying impetuousness; and the fire of charity impresses it with an irresistible impulse towards its last end, so that it regards this feeling within of an obstacle that stops this impulse towards God as an intolerable suffering; and the more light it receives, the more intense the torment.'[2]

THE CALL OF LOVE

We are beginning to experience our spiritual exile from the Beloved more acutely in these mansions. We are just that little step closer to Him. We can begin to hear His Voice in the silence, and begin to smell the holy fragrance of His Breath that much closer to our heart. Teresa says that here, paradoxically, since we are in such distress, the soul is actually in less danger than in the first mansions.

Now we understand something of the stages of progress on our spiritual journey. We hope to penetrate more deeply within the castle. We are painfully and consciously aware of our spiritual exile and separation from Him in these mansions. Teresa explains:

> **In some ways, these souls suffer a great deal more than those in the first mansions, although not in such danger, as they begin to understand their peril and there are great hopes of their entering farther into the castle. I say that they suffer a great deal more, for those in an earlier stage are like deaf-mutes and are not so distressed at being unable to speak, while the others, who can hear but cannot talk, find it much harder. (II, 3)**

We suffer more in this dwelling place simply because we have fewer defences against the reality of God penetrating our soul. The more we begin to turn around towards Him and respond to His call to become His bride, the more He is reaching out and beckoning the soul towards Him:

These souls hear our Lord calling them, for as they approach nearer to where His Majesty dwells He proves a loving neighbour, though they may still be engaged in the amusements and business, and pleasures and vanities of this world... Yet such are the pity and compassion of this Lord of ours, so desirous is He that we should seek Him and enjoy His company, that in one way or another He never ceases calling us to Him. So sweet is His voice, that the poor soul is disconsolate at being unable to follow His bidding at once, and therefore, as I said, suffers more than if it could not hear Him. (II, 4)

The further we penetrate within the castle and open our heart and surrender to God, the more His Majesty is constantly reaching out to us from the innermost mansion. He is continually calling us, time after time after time, to approach His Kingdom.

He is so anxious that we should love and desire Him, and Him alone, and ceaselessly strive after His companionship, that He is continually calling us, as our Friend and Lover, to approach his Kingdom:

The will inclines to love our Lord and longs to make some return to Him Who is so amiable, and Who has given so many proofs of His Love, especially by His constant presence within the soul, which this faithful Lover never quits, ever accompanying it and giving it life and being. The understanding aids by showing that however many years life might last, no one could ever wish for a better friend than God. (II, 9)

We are becoming more aware that love, to be loved and to love, is a choice, and that the cultivation of love requires conscious decisions if it is to be nurtured to full strength. Here, love of God and for others is becoming much less subjective and more objective – it is far more than a delightful mood, a happy sensation, a feeling of contentment, or an inner warm glow that is transitory, based on changing contexts and experiences.

Love is now coming from a sense of conscience that is conscious, accurate, educated and directed, and not based on self-love and 'what I can get in return'. Loving God is becoming a conscious choice directed toward Him even when the attraction to love Him, others or ourselves is still quite weak.

Of course, we still have many attachments and attractions to the pleasures of the here and now that are not of God in these early dwelling places. Choosing love becomes easier when it is not simply an ideal, hope, wish or intent, centred in the mind, but when it arises from His love for us that is becoming merged within our heart. Teresa says that in this mansion we are becoming servants of Love – we are finding out more of what this *really means*.[3]

It is in the second mansion, through this love, that we are given the strength to make the sincere effort to wean ourselves away from attachments to the things of the world. As we journey towards the end of this mansion, the sincerity of our intent is manifested when we start to live as if everything comes from a radiance of this love. We are able to become more faithful and charitable; there is a kindness and gentleness, an honesty, openness and courage in the face of life. We can choose to rise above self-love, discouragement, failure and see beyond the attraction to the transitory and appearances.

ASCESIS

In a large house there are utensils not only of gold and silver, but also of wood and clay, some for special use, some for ordinary. All who cleanse themselves of the things I have mentioned will become special utensils, dedicated and useful to the owner of the house, ready for every good work. Shun youthful passions and pursue righteousness, faith, love and peace, along with those who call on the Lord from a pure heart.

2 Timothy 2:20-22

Teresa says that in the second dwelling place the real temptations, trials and deeper processes of inner ascesis are just beginning. This is the stage where the foundations of our interior castle are slowly being built and fortified, as they have to be stable and strong all the way into the innermost mansions. It is the beginning of the growth of the new interior chariot that will transport our soul to heavenly places, echoing Elijah's chariot of fire taking him into Heaven. (cf 2 Kings 2:11)

Such spiritual foundations are usually firmly tested over a long period of time. Very painful betrayal, sometimes by our nearest and dearest, persecution, major crises, long agonising periods of breakdown, collapse and aridity are common. Anything that has the capacity to test our sincere aim to journey towards union with our Beloved may be used.

Ascesis means exercise, training, and, by extension combat. As free human beings with a capacity to create positively, we are challenged to keep faith with the great transformation in Christ, and change the relationship that we necessarily have with material things – our genetic inheritance, psychological and social background – so that we finally transform the materials themselves.

The purpose of ascesis is to divest oneself of surplus weight, of spiritual fat. It is to dissolve in the waters of baptism, in the water of tears, all the hardness of the heart, so that it may become an antenna of exquisite sensitivity, infinitely vulnerable to the beauty of the world and to the sufferings of human beings, and to God, the Love who has conquered by the wood of the cross.[4]

So, this is the primary dwelling place of ongoing and deepening ascesis, the place of physical, psychological and spiritual disciplines and efforts, aimed at cleansing, purifying and healing ourselves to overcome the effects of our past. This is where we work to restore ourselves to the possibilities of receiving the fullness of God's love in our heart. There are various levels and types of ascetical exercise and discipline, all of which are conscious efforts aimed at healing and cleansing different parts of our being.

Physical ascesis, involving fasting, exercise, particular care with diet and abstinence, is a training that strengthens the body while keeping it controlled in order to purify it. These practices help to conserve energy and also develop an acceptance of physical restrictions that teaches us to deny ourselves excessive gratification and indulgence.

The accepted wisdom on physical ascesis is that without other more psychological and spiritual practices it can certainly become unbalanced and one-sided. Conscious modification of the expression of negative states of mind, and making efforts to choose to behave in a loving, caring, hospitable manner to others, are examples of ascetical practice of the conscious control of our behaviour and how we relate to others.[5]

Of course, as Teresa says, prayer and meditation are the primary forms of spiritual ascesis or the 'cure of the soul'. These practices begin to lay the foundations of a different, transformed way of life, opening our heart towards God. Sincere long-term ascetical practices are essential in order to purify and enlighten the mind and heart. To be effective, the desire and will to do them must emerge from the heart by our conscious assent.

We need to understand it to be essentially necessary. Assent is the real test, here. When our desire to cleanse and purify our mind comes from the most sincere and genuine intention of the heart, we have true assent. If it comes from pride, or as a discipline imposed on us by others, these practices cannot be effective in the long term.[6]

Teresa describes the nature of the inner war and increased conflict that begins to be waged more seriously in this dwelling place and warns that the shadow parts of our personality, and the 'devils', are more active than ever:

> **These souls suffer a great deal more than those in the first mansions... For now the devils set on us the reptiles, that is to say, thoughts about the world and its joys which they**

> **picture as unending... beware of the poisonous reptiles,
> that is to say the bad thoughts and aridities which are often
> permitted by God to assail and torment us so that we cannot
> repel them... I implore those who have not yet begun to
> enter into themselves, to stop this warfare; I beg those already
> started in the right path, not to let the combat turn them
> back from it.** (II, 3, 7, 16, 17)

We become more aware of our contradictions, insecurities, discord, conflicts and shadow in this mansion. We are beginning to experience more dryness, negative thoughts and other distractions in prayer. There are many new snakes and reptiles to contend with, which will pursue us relentlessly through our spiritual journey. Teresa assures us that they are certainly to be considered as part of God's plan for us. She advises not to be alarmed or disturbed by these increased wanderings of the mind, as distractions will always come and go. Our aim and intent is to remain still and quiet within.

Teresa warns against concentrating on the faults of others and not confronting the darkness within ourselves. She shows great insight into the nature of the shadow and is adamant that everyone has faults, problem areas, 'blind spots' and aspects of character that need to grow into greater maturity. She wisely counsels that the primary responsibility for every individual is to attend to our own interior journey, which will reveal our own neglected shadow areas.

She is particularly sensitive to what can be learned when the shadow is projected onto others:

> **Let us look at our own faults and not at other people's.
> People who are extremely correct themselves are often
> shocked at everything they see; however, we might often
> learn a great deal that is essential from the very persons
> whom we censure. Our exterior comportment and manners
> may be better – this is well enough, but not of the first
> importance.** (III, Chapter 2, 19)

Teresa's call for insight into oneself rather than for criticism of others is a call to endure the conflict in one's own psyche that is being stirred up by the action of the Holy Spirit and by our deepening commitment to Him. The increasing inner turmoil in our heart and life is very difficult, but is very necessary and even helpful. Since the shadow side of life is an inescapable part of the human condition, it constantly calls for our attention and integration.

The spiritual and psychological consequences of not engaging in this ongoing, often very painful and difficult, process can be catastrophic. What will happen is that the shadow, both personal and collective, will become split off, rejected, disowned and projected onto others and into the world. Then the *other* person, race, group or country carries our shadow – the *others* become sinful, bad, wrong, full of hate, inferior and the like.

If we are unable to take responsibility for the darker parts of ourselves, unable to stay, consciously and compassionately, in touch with the most difficult parts of ourselves – sexual issues, envy, jealousy, anger, aggression, sickness and death – then others and the world will be shrouded in darkness through our splitting and projection. We make the other and the world our enemy, rather than confronting and exploring the enemy (the shadow) within.

Teresa mentions the usefulness of all tests and temptations, as constant reminders to be vigilant, awake to the hidden and unknown movements of God:

He even allows these reptiles to bite us, so that we may learn better how to be on our guard in the future and see if we are really grieving at having offended Him.

Our shadow side is the open wound of the conscious personality. It is where we are the most vulnerable and in pain, the most powerless, hurt, and 'out of control'. But, from a spiritual perspective, it is that place through which His Light can enter into our soul. It is the only door within that cannot be locked and barred. It is where we have the fewest defences and are the most transparent. It is the place where we have no conscious choice any longer but to be open, to give up, give over and surrender to His action and purposes in our soul. The place of our shadow is the inner doorway to God.

Only by fully acknowledging, experiencing and surrendering our inner darkness, helplessness and vulnerability to the Light of God, is it possible to journey further within the castle. Where we hurt most, we can do the least – we can do nothing but surrender and allow His Light to enter and heal. We are forced to accept ourselves in our most naked and vulnerable human state and willingly offer ourselves up to Love.

PATIENCE AND PERSEVERANCE

By your endurance you will gain your souls.

Luke 21:19

In this dwelling place, interior trials and tests start to become increasingly painful and acute. Teresa writes about the cacophony of temptations, distractions and conflicts that can begin to occur when our spiritual life is deepening. In this dwelling place, we are less able to deceive ourselves and can become more aware of our evasions, self-delusions and conflicts. This can make them seem to intensify.

It is important to understand that the increased conflict can be a sign of increasing self-knowledge and clarity of understanding. We sense more directly what our peace and wholeness in God could be as we see more plainly our lack of it.

Teresa is firm that steadfast discrimination, spiritual discernment and great ethical and moral courage are required as the inner war in the soul becomes more intense. The assault, both inner and outer, is very real but the reward, ultimately, is entry into the Kingdom of Heaven. At the deeper stages, it really becomes all or nothing as the King of Glory wants to infuse and unite the whole of our being with His Love and Light, not just the parts that we choose to give to Him.

All the thousands of attachments and identifications that keep our soul spiritually trapped and chained are more and more consciously revealed, to be purged, purified and surrendered in the furnace of Love. There is certainly no short cut, no easy route on this path. More and more subtle levels of what had previously been unconscious within us begin to emerge to be faced, owned, and healed.

Teresa says here:

> Perseverance is the first essential; and with this we are sure to profit greatly. However, the devils now fiercely assault the soul in a thousand different ways; it suffers more than ever, because formerly it was mute and deaf, or at least could hear very little, and offered but feeble resistance, like one who has almost lost all hope of victory.
>
> Here, however, the understanding being more vigilant and the powers more alert, we cannot avoid hearing the fighting and cannonading around us. (II, 6,7)

There is real confusion, disorientation and often the sense of loss, death, aridity, desolation, emptiness, agony and distress at this stage, where we shout the heart-rending cries of our soul – 'What is this all for? Why? Why is it becoming so much more difficult and painful? It makes no rational sense at all. What is happening to me?'

Our outer attachments and identifications are beginning to fall away and we are not, as yet, fully anchored on the staircase to God within. The stepping-stones of memory, faith, will and understanding are the main places of refuge for our new and faltering steps:

> Oh Jesus, what turmoil the devils cause in the poor soul! How unhappy it feels, not knowing whether to go forward or to return to the first mansion. On the other hand, reason shows it the delusion of overrating worldly things, while faith teaches what alone can satisfy its craving.
>
> Memory reminds the soul how all earthly joys end, recalling the death of those who lived at ease; how some died suddenly and were soon forgotten, how others, once so

> **prosperous, are now buried beneath the ground and men pass by the graves where they lie, the prey of worms, while the mind recalls many other such incidents.** (II, 8)

The vital attitudes that the pilgrim needs to hold onto are the central importance of the inner work of the transformation of the shadow, the necessity of constant inner labour and the necessary growth of humility and moral integrity that is entailed in such a momentous interior struggle for God.

The soul must hold onto our longing for the Divine with great tenacity over a long time. In silence and dignity, and through all the testing, trials and purgation of our own particular life, character and predispositions, we must persevere.

In times of long interior desolation and aridity, Teresa is particularly consoling in terms of keeping a sense of the bigger spiritual picture of the journey:

> **His Majesty knows best what is good for us; it is not for us to advise Him how to treat us, for He has the right to tell us that we know not what we ask. Remember, it is of the greatest importance – the sole aim of one beginning to practise prayer should be to endure trials, and to resolve and strive to the utmost of her power to conform her own will to the will of God. Be certain that in this consists all the greatest perfection to be attained in the spiritual life.** (II, 15)

If we really want the spiritual treasures He is longing to bestow on the soul, patience gives us the contentment to be exactly where we are in our spiritual development. Virtues in the second mansion are just beginning to grow – and we have to contend with a thousand faults and failings within ourselves.

All the snakes and reptiles are still very active on the journey! The seeds of our spiritual journey are just beginning to grow in the soil of our soul. It is still early days. The idea of slow growing seeds gives us the patience and courage to continue in these times of trials, conflicts, confusion and pain.

Resistance to turning away from the things of the world is still strong and present in this dwelling place, but now we have more faith and understanding. Memory reminds us that all earthly gains will one day come to an abrupt end. Death always ends temporal pursuits, and often comes unexpectedly, as a thief in the night. We hear the cries of a Godless world acutely, but our steadfast persistence and patience in pursuing the spiritual life urges us on.

The most refined and accurate descriptions of the necessary purgation of the soul in the fires of His Love are found in the remarkable poems and extended spiritual commentaries of St John of the Cross – *The Living Flame of Love* and *The Spiritual Canticle. The Living Flame of Love* is, in essence, a prolonged meditation on John 14:23: 'Those who love me will keep my word, and my Father will love them, and we will come to them and make our home with them.'

Here he compares the soul to a damp log that, when initially placed in the transforming fire of Divine Love, spits, crackles and exudes much smoke:

> Before the divine fire is introduced into and united to the substance of the soul through a person's perfect and complete purgation and purity, its flame, which is the Holy Spirit, wounds it by destroying and consuming the imperfections of its bad habits. And this is the work of the Holy Spirit, in which He disposes it for the divine union and transformation in God through love.
>
> The very fire of love which afterwards is united with the soul, glorifying it, is that which previously assails it by purging it, just as the fire that penetrates a log of wood is the same that first makes an assault upon it, wounding it with its flame, drying it out, and stripping it of its unsightly qualities until it is so disposed that it can be penetrated and transformed into the fire.
>
> Spiritual writers call this the purgative way. In it a person suffers great privation and feels heavy afflictions in his spirit, which ordinarily overflow into the senses, for this flame is extremely oppressive. In this preparatory purgation, the flame is not bright for the person, but dark... it is not gentle, but afflictive... neither is the flame refreshing and peaceful, but

it is consuming and contentious, making a person faint and suffer with self knowledge.

It is not glorious for the soul, but rather makes it feel wretched and distressed in the spiritual light of self-knowledge, which it bestows. As Jeremiah says, God sends fire into its bones and instructs it, and as David says, He tries it with fire.[7]

Everything in this dwelling place depends on the determination to move forward, inward and outward, no matter the difficulties and obstacles. In *The Way of Perfection*, Teresa urges us not to be swayed from our commitment to the way:

I say it is most important – all important indeed – that they should begin well by making an earnest and most determined resolve not to halt until they reach the goal or die on the road or have not the heart to confront the trials which they meet, whether the very world dissolves around them.

It is about striving for detachment from everything that is not of God. Every possible means must be taken to strengthen our resolve towards life in God and to maintain a relentless determination to persevere, for in no other way can we truly respond to the call of His Love which is always beckoning us.

It is essential to work patiently at cleansing the 'mirror of our heart', by prayer, meditation, contemplation and the steady, active practice of virtue and generosity in every way possible. Through humility, self-renunciation, purity and meekness of heart, hungering and thirsting after righteousness and justice, we must persevere with patience under inner and outer attack.

Teresa warns that things like spiritual favours tend to be reserved for the later mansions where grace will be granted when our desire to align ourselves with the will of God is stronger and more pure:

There is one thing so important that I will repeat it once more – it is that at the beginning one must not think of such things as spiritual favours, for that is a very poor way of starting to build such a large and beautiful edifice.

> **If it is begun upon sand, it will all collapse: souls, which build like that, will never be free from annoyances and temptations. For, it is not in these Mansions, but in those which are farther on, that it rains manna; once there, the soul has all that it desires, because it desires only what is the will of God.** (II, 13)

Patient endurance in the face of the many trials, difficulties and agonies on the way is, perhaps, one of the most important foundations of our deepening spiritual life. As the Greek Orthodox Fathers have wisely noted:

> Endurance is like an unshakeable rock in the winds and waves of life. However the tempest batters him, the patient man remains steadfast and doesn't turn back; and when he finds relief and joy, he is not carried away by self-glory. He is always the same, whether things are hard or easy, and for this reason he is proof against the snares of the enemy.
>
> When storms beset him, he endures them with joy, awaiting their end; and when the heavens smile on him, he expects temptation – until his last breath, as St Anthony has said. Such a person knows that nothing in life is unchangeable, and that all things pass. Thus he is not troubled or anxious about any of them, but leaves all things in the hands of God, for He has us in His care and to Him belong all glory, honour and dominion through the ages.[8]

So, for Teresa, the task of the contemplative life is ultimately active life in the world and the discerning of meaningful service for each individual, according to their vocation, gifts, talents and character. Aligning our will with the supernatural will, the will of God, unites all creatures and the universe in Love. Our task is to become consciously part of that force of Love.

SPIRITUAL COMPANIONSHIP

In these earliest mansions, Teresa writes of the fundamental necessity for spiritual direction and for increasingly keeping the company of like-minded friends and companions.

Spiritual companionship is indispensable, and being part of a church, community or religious group is essential.

She points out that real spiritual experience without wise guidance runs serious risks. It is so important, at these early stages, to associate with the companions of God – whether as guide, friend, spiritual director or priest. She advises:

> **It is of utmost importance for the beginner to associate with those who lead a spiritual life, and not only with those in the same mansion as herself, but with others who have travelled farther into the castle, who will aid her greatly and draw her to join them.** (II, 12)

Spiritual companionship provides the necessary checks and balances on this unknown and difficult journey and gives access to crucial spiritual advice and wisdom at times of pitfalls, obstacles, dangers and crises. Spiritual direction is usually regarded as a charismatic activity, carried out by those who are endowed with the gifts for it.

Throughout the Christian tradition, this unique relationship has been described in many ways – as soul friend,[9] midwife,[10] teacher, parent, companion and more. Spiritual companionship is regarded as one of the highest forms of human relationship. All religious traditions hold it as special. The ancient Celtic concept of *amchara* means 'father of my soul', and the Buddhist *lama*, means 'incomparable mother'. The Greek Orthodox call their monks *kaloiros*, which means 'beautiful elder', conveying the depth of warmth and wisdom of genuine spiritual companionship.[11]

Essentially, spiritual direction is a conversation, a dialogue between two people with a purpose. God is very much at the centre, as the 'third party' in the relationship. Focus, shape and direction come from constant attentiveness to the mystery of His action and presence. Spiritual direction is not a single conversation, nor a series of conversations, but a lifelong process. Nor is the spiritual companion the prime mover. Each makes themselves open to divine power working through them by way of the Word of God, of his Spirit and His overwhelming love.[12]

In such a conversation, one person enables another to express their experience of personal faith and the mystery of God in prayer, in worship and in life. Its immediate purpose is to encourage a deeper, more honest understanding which can lead us to make discerning choices.

Our growing understanding is the foundation from which we make our choices in line with God's presence and constant transforming action in our heart and life. This conversation also rests on the acceptance and understanding that life is constantly mediating God to us, that the created universe is the area of God's constant presence and action. It is a relationship that is bound to be quite challenging and provoking and often will profoundly change both parties.

More often than not, new insights and understandings emerge to challenge pre-existing, limited views. Through spiritual companionship, we learn to hear more clearly, to clarify more distinctly, to discover and interpret more honestly and to discern more acutely the varied voices of personal experience and different influences in our life. The process means that decisions and changes we make can be in greater harmony with our unique journey of faith and mystery in God.

It is important to emphasise that in spiritual direction, God is, of course, the ultimate foundation on which this conversation becomes possible. The inexhaustible love of God will manifest through the relationship with our spiritual companion or guide. Teresa shows this. To see this, and enter into such a relationship, will turn us upside down and profoundly change us.

Unthought-of, and unknown, depths are revealed and come to expression within us. We feel that, at last, we begin to truly know who we are and why we exist and what our purpose is – to conform to the will of God in our lives. We are being born anew, this time into our true life and heritage in the Kingdom of the Spirit.

The aims of spiritual direction are expressed in different ways. They have to do with, for example, living well; doing the truth in love; making choices in tune with the Holy Spirit; living in communion with God and others; growing in holiness and wholeness; discovering and living the truth of oneself; maintaining our authentic personal identity in relationship; promoting a transformation of consciousness, both personal and communal; engaging with God and with life in such a way that the Spirit of God animates and shapes all dimensions of life; and loving God and neighbour as a way to fullness of life.[13]

There are usually several elements involved in the process of spiritual direction. It is usually a personal encounter that is conversational, where both parties play a distinct role. The emphasis is on mutuality. This is essential if all of the life experience of each person, including faith, commitment, talents, disappointments, failures and losses, is to be actively at work in the conversation. Undergoing spiritual direction gives us an opportunity to raise our deepest experience to consciousness as we engage in the patient effort to recognise God's mysterious and loving Presence within all the levels of our being.[14]

Genuine spiritual companionship involves the mutual search for understanding and truth. It is not an exercise in influencing, persuading, controlling, manipulating or dominating another person, nor is it a battle with a view to conquest of any sort. The emergence of real understanding is usually very liberating. It represents a movement from illusion to reality, from falsehoods and lies to truth and honesty and thus can have a tremendous capacity to unblock energies, obstacles and resources.

The primary purpose of the conversation is to express faith and mystery. It is an opportunity to clarify and to objectify what is going on in our experience of the world, of God, of others and of ourselves. Through this conversation we assimilate the reality of our interior life as we struggle to express our experience in words, symbols, or images.[15]

The development of discernment is essential in the process of spiritual direction. The attempt to understand the origin, meaning and purpose of our experience enables us to make choices that are congruent with our growing life in the Spirit. Discernment lies at the heart of spiritual direction, enhancing our deepening life in God, if skilled, and destructive in its effect, if unskilled.

We examine the interior movements that result from God's personal involvement in our heart and soul and sift through them, distinguishing and separating, developing a discerning heart. We are attentive to these interior movements, choosing those that bring us into deeper union with God in the innermost mansions and rejecting those that draw us away.[16]

The Ignatian tradition distinguishes between two different kinds of affective responses to God that form the basis of discernment – the experience of spiritual consolation and spiritual desolation. These may be called spiritual, not because they exist in some area of our personal life that is nonmaterial nor because they are different in nature from the other feelings that we experience, but rather because they are associated with, or evoked by, God and things that have to do with God.[17]

Consolation refers to what we might consider to be positive or creative moods, desires or feelings. Desolation comprises the affective experiences that we would see as negative or destructive. However, there are two levels of meaning.

The more immediate level, the one more easily grasped, is that of our affective experience – the feelings, moods, or desires elicited by our experience of life and which can be easily named, such as anger, resentment, envy, guilt, peace, joy, happiness, confidence, love, longing for justice. There is also the fundamental level of being, of where we actually stand in relation to God and the level at which God knows and is constantly present in us through grace.[18]

Instances of consolation may include a sense of confidence in God and in His love for the world and any experience that leads to a strengthening of that confidence;

a sense that a person or an event in our life is a gift or an 'epiphany', or a place where we meet God; an attraction to the greater good; a movement of love or desire towards God; an awareness of having sinned and of needing and receiving God's forgiveness; an experience of inner, personal freedom or liberation; a desire and movement toward loving and serving others in the name of Jesus.

Desolation is an experience of the opposite of these and seems to set blocks and obstacles between us and God, leading us to close in on ourselves in a downward spiral. It can include such experiences as a sense that life is empty and meaningless; a state of self-disgust or self-hatred; a weakening or a loss of confidence in God and in His love; a movement of love or desire which takes us away from God; times when God seems to be absent; being trapped in a circle of remorse and guilt at one's own weakness and sinfulness; an attraction to what is less good; an inability to accept or trust in God's forgiveness; an experience of being not free, of being paralysed by fear, anxiety, attachments, addiction; a sense that God is absent from the world.[19]

There is a basic assumption that the main framework of understanding which grounds, shapes, guides and evaluates the practice of spiritual direction and which helps to distinguish between good and bad practice is primarily theological/spiritual and faith-based, rather than primarily psychological. Nowadays, spiritual direction often requires a good deal of psychological understanding and knowledge, but the emphasis is usually on the spiritual issues.

Spiritual direction focuses on discerning the action of the Holy Spirit, and the will of God, in our heart and lives. Insights originating in the fields of the arts, philosophy, and psychology usually have an invaluable, but often ancillary, part to play in informing good spiritual direction.

There are many similarities, but also profound dif-ferences, between spiritual direction, counselling and psychotherapy. A number of excellent sources discuss this area in some depth.[20] Spiritual direction is not primarily psychological counselling or psychotherapy, although they are similar in context, format and structure.

The psychological disciplines tend to concentrate on problem areas of life, and usually seek resolution through an emotional/cognitive understanding of personal history, or by modifying personal decision-making and behaviour from a psychodynamic perspective. This interpersonal relationship may lack any conscious reference to God, to the action of the Holy Spirit, to mystery or to faith.

In contrast, spiritual direction deals explicitly with the spiritual themes in our life, attempting to embrace the totality of our life and experience. Although problem-solving and decision-making, of course, occur during spiritual direction, they are not primary functions.

However, it is usually very difficult, if not impossible, to make a clear distinction between purely psychological realities and what could come only from the Holy Spirit, especially in these earliest mansions. Psychological balance is not a pre-condition for spiritual progress, and psychic weakness is never an insuperable obstacle. Everything depends on discerning how the dark sides and the light sides are employed, and in what direction the two develop, to the advantage or disadvantage of the inner person and, finally, of love. The emergence of 'the new person' in Christ is essentially interwoven with each person's psychology.[21]

NOTES: SECOND MANSION

1. Humphreys, C. *From Ash to Fire*, New City Press, NY, 1992, p.32
2. Harvey, A. *The Son of Man – the Mystical Path to Christ*, Jeremy Tarcher, NY, 1998, p.109
3. Humphreys, C. *op.cit.* pp.37-38
4. Clement, O. *op.cit.* pp.130-131
5. Amis, R. *op.cit.* p.138
6. Ibid, p.140

7. Kavanaugh, K. and Rodriguez, O. (trans) *Collected Works of St John of the Cross*, ICS Publications, 1979 p.586
8. Ware, Kallistos, (Bishop) (ed). *The Philokalia*, Vol 3, Faber and Faber, 1984, p.224
9. Leech, K. *Soul Friend: Spiritual direction in the modern world*, Darton, Longman and Todd, London, 1994
10. Guenther, M. *Holy Listening: the Art of Spiritual Direction*, Darton Longman and Todd, 1993
11. Louf, A. *Tuning in to Grace – the Quest for God*, Darton Longman and Todd, p.82
12. Ibid, p.95
13. Lonsdale, D. *What is Spiritual Direction – A Discussion Paper*, December 1998, p.3
14. Houdek, F. *op.cit.* pp.6-7
15. Ibid.
16. Conroy, M. *The Discerning Heart, Discovering a Personal God*, Loyola University Press, 1993
17. Lonsdale, D. *Listening to the Music of the Spirit*, Ave Maria Press, Notre Dame, Indiana, 1993, p.71
18. Ibid, p.72
19. Ibid, pp.74-76
20. See Barry, W.A. and Connolly, W.J. *The Practice of Spiritual Direction*, Harper Collins, San Francisco, 1991; May, G. *Care of Mind, Care of Spirit; Psychiatric dimensions of Spiritual Direction*, Harper and Row, San Francisco, 1982; Ruffing, J. *Spiritual Direction Beyond the Beginnings*, St Pauls Publishing, London, 2000
21. Louf, A. *op.cit.* p.85.

THE THIRD MANSION

What must I do to Acquire Eternal Life?

We all say we desire it, but there is need of more than that for the Lord to possess entire dominion over the soul… Enter, then, enter, my daughters, into your interior; pass beyond the thought of your own petty works, which are no more, nor even as much, as Christians are bound to perform; let it suffice that you are God's servants, do not pursue so much as to catch nothing.

Think of the saints, who have entered the Divine Presence, and you will see the difference between them and ourselves.

St Teresa, Third Mansion

SURRENDERING TO LOVE

This mansion is the call to a life of deeper spirituality and surrender to the will of God in our lives. Here, we are beginning to enter the deeper chambers of our heart. Spiritual testing and trials become more subtle and internal, out of sight of the outside world.

It is the crucial testing of our sincerity and willingness to surrender, in the cave of our heart, to being infused by the Holy Spirit. The human personality and will are very much still in control in this dwelling place. It is our psychological and spiritual maturity, our spiritual sincerity, and increasing willingness to surrender, let go and trust to God's Will and Providence which is being tested here.

This is between the soul and God on a deep intimate level in the heart where the soul is continually being called to and beckoned by Him. This deeper spiritual call is clear and unambiguous – Do you want the Heavenly King, and only Him? Do you want to enter the innermost sanctum of His Presence more than anything else?

If our response is anything less than complete surrender, then our spiritual commitment, trust and sincerity is fully tested in this mansion. Our deepest intentions in the heart are searched and exposed even further, testing whether we want God, and only God. Are we on this path to encounter and unite with Him, and Him alone, for no other motive, purpose or reason than our love, yearning and desire for Him?

The third dwelling place is an extended meditation on Matthew 19. It is the story where Jesus tells a man, when questioned as to what he must do to possess eternal life in addition to keeping all the commandments, responds by commanding total commitment and surrender – 'If you wish to be perfect, go, sell your possessions, and give money to the poor, and you will have treasure in heaven: then come, follow me' (Mt 19:21).

Teresa refers to this story several times as the main spiritual message in this mansion:

> **Since I began to speak of these dwelling rooms I have him constantly before my mind, for we are exactly like him; this very frequently produces the great dryness we feel in prayer, though sometimes it proceeds from other causes as well. Such souls know that nothing would induce them to commit a sin (many of them would not even commit a venial sin advertently), and that they employ their life and riches well. They cannot, therefore, patiently endure to be excluded from the presence of our King, Whose vassals they consider themselves, as indeed they are. An earthly king may have many subjects, yet all do not enter his court.**
> (III, Chapter 1, 9,10)

Teresa's comments are poignant and fruitful. She is challenging everything that appears exemplary and self-righteous in our lives and in our perception of ourselves. This is the state of our preconceived notions of God, of the making of God in our own image, and endeavouring to keep within the safe, tried and tested ways of what we 'think and feel' our spiritual life should be. From an interior perspective, those places where we are too secure, comfortable, self-satisfied, well-ordered and safe are under the spotlight.

She tells us that this dwelling place is the normal state of most 'good Christians'. Certain virtues have been developed and we are trying to 'do our best' to live a good and righteous life. We may be setting aside as much time in prayer and recollection as possible, we may be helping others as much as we can and may have overcome many of our difficulties, bad habits and problems. Often we can feel great satisfaction in doing as many good works and things for God as possible.

She summarises the general state of those who have entered this mansion:

> **To return to what I began to explain about the souls that have entered the third mansions. God has shown them no small favour, but a very great one, in enabling them to pass through the first difficulties. Thanks to His mercy I believe**

there are many such people in the world; they are very desirous not to offend His Majesty even by venial sins, they love penance and spend hours in meditation, they employ their time well, exercise themselves in works of charity to their neighbours, are well ordered in their conversation and dress, and those who own a household govern it well. (III, Chapter 1, 8)

This dwelling place is a very important transitional place in the ongoing interior action of the Holy Spirit in our soul. Our constant striving and surrendering is transforming us into what He wants us to become, which is conformed into His Image and Likeness. Teresa admonishes us – if we stay in this place, we will be excluded from entering into God's Presence, and will stay in the outermost court of the Heavenly King.

This dwelling place can become a place of spiritual stalemate, of impasse, because it is at the end of what our own efforts can do. Staying in this place means we are not continuing to spiritually grow, deepen and change within.

It can become too comfortable, settled, and cosy in this mansion, and there is the danger that we can feel that we have reached the end of our spiritual journey. Denial, resistance and pride act as stumbling blocks that stop us surrendering and opening our heart even more deeply to God's action.

Our awareness of how much we need to change within can grow dim, our sense of the need for deeper and more profound humility towards God can darken, and we can become too heavily reliant on what others and the world tell us, of how good, virtuous and important we are.

Our guilt, growing doubts and fear of God can become increasingly buried under layers of self-satisfaction and self-importance. We can become increasingly blind, asleep to our spiritual faults, bad habits and shortcomings, completely unaware of our deeper negative traits on a more subtle and unseen level.

Teresa talks about the danger of self-righteousness in this mansion, particularly when we are seen by others to be

pillars of virtue in the community and fountains of wisdom,
yet we can barely tolerate or learn from the smallest of trials
and temptations:

> **I have known some, in fact, I may say numerous souls, who
> have reached this state, and for many years lived, apparently,
> a regular and well ordered life, of both body and mind. It
> would seem that they must have gained the mastery over
> this world, or at least be extremely detached from it, yet if
> His Majesty sends very moderate trials they become so
> disturbed and disheartened as not only to astonish but to
> make me anxious about them. Advice is useless; they have
> practised virtue for so long they think themselves capable
> of teaching it, and believe that they have abundant reason
> to feel miserable.** (III, Chapter 2, 1)

She tells us that it is useless to give these people advice – we
can become so self-righteous that we think we know
everything there is to know already about the spiritual life!
We can find ourselves easily shocked by the faults of others
and we are more concerned about our own image than
about 'becoming' in the image of God.

This state of mind only calls for concern, understanding
and compassion. It is no good anyone contradicting us
because we see ourselves as so virtuous already:

> **they must not be argued with, for they are convinced that
> they suffer only for God's sake, and cannot be made to
> understand they are acting imperfectly.** (III, Chapter 2, 2)

Here, we cannot realise that our own disturbances are
really the opposite of what He, and the action of the Holy
Spirit, are all about. We need humility and a deepening
sense of our insignificance to guard against a false, inflated
sense of our own importance in this mansion.

One of the greatest dangers is that we can reduce God
to our cognitive and reasoned models of Him, which we
can then understand and which make Him safe and distant.
God is now being made *in our own image*, where He is
much easier to cope with in a conceptual box, compart-
mentalised for our own safety and need for control. We are
caught up in our own ways of looking at things.

We do not allow the action of God to create those deeper demands, trials or temptations that will test our spiritual sincerity and willingness to surrender our own self-will to His will. Teresa is pointing out that the roots of our basic egotism and selfishness are still untouched.

The sources of human selfishness and greed are subtly hidden, and at these deeper levels we will not experience the necessary humiliation, conscience and shame until we are exposed or challenged in spiritually fortuitous ways! Here, our motivation for virtuous behaviour can often be the expectation that God will, or should, give us His Love and Presence because we deserve it!

Teresa wants us to guard against thinking that we are more important than we really are, just because we have changed or eliminated some prominent negative traits. This surface level is not what is being challenged in this dwelling place – what is in the core of our heart is.

We can often be over-concerned about our image and appearance in the world. Our pride and the depth of our self-centredness is that much more difficult to recognise, own and change. After the first impulses of grace which have opened our heart to His Love and generosity, the first wonderful experiences and touches of spiritual awakening in the earlier mansions may have given way to a more lukewarm and routine spiritual life.

However, we can be putting too much trust and reliance on our own strengths and accomplishments and on what our own efforts have produced. All the good works that we are now involved in can begin to usurp the place of the strong love and intense longing we once had for God. A false sense of security can now develop from too narrow a focus on external activity.

Unless we are actively engaged in relentless and authentic self-examination with a more than ordinary degree of courage and integrity, we will eventually slacken off and fall back into our unconscious, sleep-inducing mechanical and destructive habits. Teresa is prompting us – Don't be so sure of yourself. Fear the Lord. Fear yourself, in the sense that our own human standards are utterly surpassed in the holy and sacred life, which is our true spiritual aim.

Teresa talks about the increasing need for spiritual discernment and discrimination at this stage. It is not always possible to judge from outward appearances and behaviour what is happening deeper within ourselves. Much more than this is required here. The true state of the soul and its intent are weighed by what is deep within the heart, not by doing the 'right thing in the eyes of the world'.

She says firmly:

> We all say we desire it, but there is need of more than that for the Lord to possess entire dominion over the soul... Enter, then, enter, my daughters, into your interior; pass beyond the thought of your own petty works, which are no more, nor even as much, as Christians are bound to perform; let it suffice that you are God's servants, do not pursue so much as to catch nothing.
>
> Think of the saints, who have entered the Divine Presence, and you will see the difference between them and ourselves. (III, Chapter 1, 9, 10)

What is needed and tested in this chamber is not anything that the world can see. Deep within this chamber of the heart, the sincerity and resoluteness of our will to surrender to Divine Providence is being tested. What is needed more and more in this mansion is humility and the surrendering of our personal will to God.

Here, the function of humility is to understand that God's action in our lives is not based on giving, or on doing great deeds for Him. It is ultimately grounded in seeing ourselves as an undeserving servant, awaiting His guidance and will in our lives.

From this position, we are less likely to feel that God is, in any way, obliged to grant us favours according to what we have to give, or according to our importance, our gifts or any of our achievements. That error is based on our own judgement, and shows an attitude of selfishness, identification and pride.

Promoting social justice, building hospitals and schools, or healing the sick are all essential and wonderful ministries for God. However, what Teresa is pointing out is that it is not the work itself that is the main concern – *it is what our heart is becoming through the work that is the most important thing.*

She implores:

> **Do not ask for what you do not deserve, nor should we ever think, however much we may have done for God, that we merit the reward of the saints, for we have offended Him. Oh, humility, humility! I know not why, but I am always tempted to think that persons who complain so much of aridities must be a little wanting in this virtue. However, I am not speaking of severe interior sufferings, which are far worse than a want of devotion.** (III, Chapter 1, 11)

The point here is that we have not yet fully surrendered to God in this mansion – our own efforts, our own striving and will have brought us to this place. Although we might be doing all the right things, internally we might still be fearful and anxious about ourselves, still very locked in our own image or idea about ourselves.

Like Jesus admonishing the young man, Teresa is directly challenging those times in our lives when we are feeling too complacent, too safe, or content with doing 'all the right things'. Teresa reminds us that:

> **People who are extremely correct themselves are often shocked at everything they see.** (III, Chapter 2, 19)

She reminds us emphatically that without complete self-renunciation to the Holy Spirit, the soul finds this mansion very arduous and oppressive. If we lack purity of heart, if we do not ask sincerely, or forget to ask often enough, or if we evade the sense of exile and guilt that comes from our awareness of the gap between what we are and what we might become, it can become a very difficult transitional dwelling place.

This heavy load needs to be lightened and transformed before we can enter His deeper dwelling places. We are becoming more porous and permeable to the action of the Holy Spirit, becoming lighter as feathers on the Breath of God.

One of the Fathers commented on the profound difference between appearances and what is really happening within the depth of the heart – the essence of Teresa's message in this dwelling place:

> It is therefore not in outward shape or form that the distinguishing characteristic of Christians consists. Many Christians believe that the difference does lie in some external sign. They are in mind and thought similar to those of the world. They undergo the same disturbing restlessness and instability of thoughts, lack of faith, confusion, agitation, and fear as other people do.
>
> They really do differ somewhat in external form and way of acting in a limited area, but in heart and mind they are shackled by earthly bonds. They do not have divine rest and heavenly peace of the spirit in their hearts because they never begged it of God nor did they ever believe that He would deign to grant these to them.[1]

DARK NIGHT OF THE SENSES

> One dark night,
> Fired with love's urgent longings
> – Ah, the sheer grace! –
> I went out unseen,
> My house being now all stilled.
>
> Stanza One, *Dark Night*

This night, which as we say is contemplation, causes two kinds of darkness or purgation in spiritual persons according to the two parts of the soul, the sensory and the spiritual. Hence one night of purgation is sensory, by which the senses are purged and accommodated to the spirit; and the other night or purgation is spiritual, by which the spirit is purged and denuded as well as accommodated and prepared for union with God through love.

The sensory night is common and happens to many;

these are the beginners of whom we shall treat first. The spiritual night is the lot of very few, those who have been tried and are proficient, and of whom we will speak afterward.

John of the Cross, *Dark Night*, I, 8:1

Constant themes that Teresa discusses throughout the early part of the text are the various stages of purification of the soul, and the necessary discernment, humility and wisdom required to be able to listen to and learn from what is beginning to change within the depths of our heart. She also gives specific spiritual guidance on the consolations and desolations encountered at this stage of the spiritual journey.

This mansion is the place of unavoidable suffering, of complete impasse, where our personal efforts are of no use any more, where we cannot 'do' any more except let go, surrender and die to our own personal desires and will, where we are called into deeper interior states of contemplative stillness and quiet.

However, the expert on this theme is Teresa's close friend and confessor, John of the Cross. In his most famous work, *Dark Night*, John presents a masterly analysis of the dark night of the senses and of the spirit. The sensory night is that which deals with the daily purification and purgation of unhealthy attachments, possessions and the like, which is very much part of the fabric and dealings of everyday life. The dark night of the spirit is rarer because of the depth of sacrifice, surrender and grace which is required in the latter dwelling places.

John calls the whole journey made by the soul to union with God, night, which he divides into three parts, twilight, midnight and dawn:

For the first part, which is that of the senses, is comparable to the beginning of the night, the point at which things begin to fade from sight. And the second part, which is faith, is comparable to midnight, which is total darkness. And the third part is like the close of night, which is God, the part which is now near to the light of day.

Twilight refers to the dark night of the senses in the second and third dwelling places. Midnight refers to the dark night of the spirit in the sixth dwelling place, which precedes divine union. Dawn is the time of union with God. This symbolic movement from twilight to midnight to dawn describes the progressive purification, surrender, and transformation of our human heart in the love of God and the grace of the Holy Spirit.

The dark night most affects us where we are deeply involved, committed, attached and identified. From a spiritual perspective, it melts and dissolves whatever separates our heart from truly becoming detached and empty enough to become infused and set on fire with Love.

Both Teresa and John are describing the gradual movement from personal desire and egotistical love, those possessive, entangled, complex, selfish and very limited emotions to more objective, selfless, purified and spiritual love and desire that are ultimately fulfilled in divine union. Our passions and desires are not being suppressed or destroyed but, through a process of active redemption, are gradually becoming transferred, transfigured, purified, transformed and set on fire through our love for Him.

It is also important to emphasise that, for John and Teresa, each stage of these very painful and difficult purgations and purifications is, of course, ultimately a sign of new spiritual life slowly emerging. From a spiritual perspective, the pain is *always* a sign of growth and movement in the deepening and purifying of our desire for, and relationship to, God, which we need to increasingly hold onto in naked faith and hope in these darker places within our soul. Love makes us very vulnerable, and it is Love itself and its growth and development that precipitate darkness in ourselves and in the 'other'.[2]

John inherited the categories and terminology which he uses in *Dark Night* from scholastic philosophy, so his term 'the senses' refers to the body, the imagination and the emotions or passions. In the first book of *Dark Night*, John describes the early stages on the spiritual journey when this part of our being is the most dominant, where we are essentially hostage to the needs and gratification of the senses and passions, being predominantly sensual beings at this stage.

Spirit refers to that part of our being that converges in choice, free will, conscience and self. In this third dwelling place, where significant inner 'reordering' is taking place and the movement from discursive meditation to contemplation is occurring, we are increasingly able to focus on and dwell within a more interior dimension.

We are becoming spiritual and with that, our sensuality and passions are becoming purified, connecting and integrating within that unity of soul and the spirit that is now being made possible – in effect, our sensuality is coming back home.[3] In the second book of *Dark Night*, John focuses on the deeper trials and purgations of the dark night of the spirit.

This is the spiritual journey, the surrender of sense to spirit, and of spirit to the Holy Spirit, and because this surrender is directly experienced as a process of interior dying, John calls it a 'night' journey. As well as sense and spirit, John distinguishes between active and passive, what we do and what is done to us. This yields a rather stocky four-fold pattern – the active night of the senses; the passive night of the senses; and the active night of the spirit; and passive night of the spirit, or dark night of the soul in the later mansions.[4]

In the active night of the senses, we are often called to, and feel drawn to give up, however reluctantly, those things and aspects of ourselves and our lives that are the nearest and dearest. Releasing those with which we are most identified may be what is necessary to bring us closer to God and His Presence. The loss of things we are closest to, and the enormous pain and suffering that it can cause are themes that Teresa returns to time and again, particularly in the stage of the dark night of the spirit in the sixth mansion.

So, in the night of the senses, John focuses on detachment. Essentially, attachments and identifications take away our ability to freely choose what is right and good for our soul. Holding on is destructive to the soul and deprives us of this freedom:

> We are calling this nakedness a night for the soul, for we are not discussing the mere lack of things; this lack will not divest the soul, if it craves for all these objects. We are dealing with the denudation of the soul's appetites and gratifications.
>
> This is what leaves it free and empty of all things, even though it possesses them. Since the things of the world cannot enter the soul, they are not in themselves an encumbrance or harm to it; rather it is the will and appetite dwelling within it that causes the damage when set on these things. (*Ascent of Mount Carmel*, I, 3:4)

John is fairly emphatic about the necessity of truly passing through this dark night of the senses in order to journey towards union with God:

> The necessity to pass through this dark night (the mortification of the appetites and denial of pleasure in all things) to attain divine union with God arises from the fact that all of a person's attachments to creatures are pure darkness in God's sight.
>
> Clothed in these affections, a person will be incapable of the enlightenment and dominating fullness of God's pure and simple light, unless he rejects them. There can be no concordance between light and darkness; as St John says: 'Tenebrae eam non comprehenderunt' [The darkness could not receive the light] (Jn 1:5). (*Ascent of Mount Carmel*, I, 4:1)

He was particularly scathing about spiritual avarice, that 'possessiveness of heart and attachment to the number, workmanship and over decoration of religious objects', commenting that:

> This attachment is contrary to poverty of spirit, which is intent only on the substance of the devotion, benefits by no more than what procures this sufficiently, and tires of all

other multiplicity and elaborate ornamentation. Since true devotion comes from the heart and looks only to the truth and substance represented by spiritual objects, and since everything else is imperfect attachment and possessiveness, any appetite for these things must be uprooted if some degree of perfection is to be reached. (*Dark Night*, I, 3:1)

He notes that any of these daily habitual imperfections and our attachments to them – all of our unsatisfied cravings and desires – are able to cause a great deal of harm. Particularly so the smallest and most unconscious attachments because these are the places whose existence and power over our soul we are the most blind to and self-rationalising about.

He gives examples of the types of attachments and compulsions that are particularly difficult to change, such as the need to talk all the time, and those:

small attachments one never really desires to conquer e.g. to a person, to clothing, to a book or a cell, or to the way food is prepared, and to other trifling conversations and little satisfactions in tasting, knowing and hearing things, etc. (*Ascent of Mount Carmel*, I, 11:4)

He points out how imprisoning even our smallest attachments and identifications are, from a spiritual perspective, and notes emphatically:

that as long as he continues this attachment it is impossible to make progress in perfection, even though the imperfection may be very small. (*Ascent of Mount Carmel*, I, 11:4)

He compares the soul to a bird tied to the ground by different types of attachments and identifications:

It makes little difference whether a bird is tied by a thin thread or by a cord. For even if tied by thread, the bird will be prevented from taking off just as surely as if it were tied by cord – that is, it will be impeded from flight as long as it does not break the thread.

Admittedly, the thread is easier to rend, but no matter how easily this may be done, the bird will not fly away without first doing so. This is the lot of a man who is attached to something; no matter how much virtue he has

> he will not reach the freedom of the divine union. (*Ascent of Mount Carmel*, I, 11:4)

Spiritual growth is always accompanied by the gradual lessening of our attachments to various desires and passions. In the early stages, we might be consciously aware of the types of identifications and motivations that come from some form of attachment.

Usually the loss of the things themselves, and the investment that we had in them, and the security, both conscious and unconscious, that they gave us need to be fully mourned. Whatever the loss or detachment, it can often be experienced as a bereavement, and, where necessary, needs to be recognised as such.

Over longer periods of time, underlying, previously unconscious, attachments usually come to our awareness as the more obvious ones are released. It is these deeper and more intractable attachments that are so difficult to get free from, as John says.

While this is going on, we can also experience long periods of distress, depression and anxiety related to the loss of confidence in the old assumptions that we may have held about ourselves, our accomplishments and desires, and about those values that society esteems in general.

Often there is tremendous sadness, grief, insecurity and uncertainty in this movement from the known, the secure, the tangible and what is controllable, to what we do not know, towards the 'unknowing' and the 'not known'.

This movement towards an experience of God is transcending any words, concepts or image of God. It is moving towards contemplatively 'resting' and 'being in God' alone. This is especially poignant and relevant in our age that so strongly values self-determination, self-will, achievement, success and accomplishment, and generally devalues 'not knowing', suffering and humility.[5]

The two most pervasive psychological maladjustments in spiritual growth are the 'cop-out' and narcissism. The spiritual cop-out is where spiritual insight or practice is used to avoid dealing with our daily responsibilities. It is where meditation constitutes an escape from the world rather than a way into it, where prayer is used as a tranquilliser, and what goes under the label of spiritual surrender may be nothing more than self-enforced, theologically rationalised passivity, or submission to one's own or someone else's ego.

Spiritual narcissism uses spiritual insights or practice to increase our self-importance rather than to deepen our humility. It fosters the 'holier-than-thou' attitude or the subtler feelings of pride or power. The intricacies of spiritual narcissism are complex and we can't escape the temptations to pride or power. We feel 'pleased' about our humility, or we think we have finally 'learned' how to pray, or we get the sense that we are now 'able' to surrender.

Essentially, spiritual narcissism involves the taking over of spiritual growth phenomena and the substituting of personal pride for humble gratitude. The misplaced and distorted surrenders associated with spiritual cop-outs and spiritual narcissism fail to meet the authentic criteria for legitimate spiritual surrender. These criteria require that the surrender be a conscious act, that it not be directed towards any delimitable fully known object, and that it be freely and intentionally chosen. It always involves the acceptance of full responsibility for the act of surrendering and all its consequences.[6]

This is why Teresa is keen to emphasise that there is now a need to understand and proceed from a much deeper humility about ourselves and about what is possible and not possible by our own efforts. She points to a type, a quality of surrender and humility that allows a kind of holy abandonment of ourselves into God and into the possibilities of a deeper spiritual life.

It is a fearful thing, putting ourselves into 'the hands of the living God'. It may now propel us into situations in life that we would never allow ourselves to get into willingly or consciously. It demands an increasing trust and freedom from concern about ourselves, neither of which are easily come by. The decision is made worse by our awareness that this is the path of sacrifice of our personal self-will and self-determination. At this stage, we must take up our own cross of sacrifice in order to participate more fully in the mystery of the divine life and love of Christ.

John focuses on the importance of order and discretion at this stage. He advises us to try to give preference to all those things that go against our attachments, in order to overcome the repugnance of our will towards doing them. He wants us to try to do the opposite of our natural dominant inclinations. This is very, very difficult from a worldly perspective, as *it is going against nature*, so to speak, and can only be accomplished by the grace of God working in our lives.

John gives specific counsel for the soul entering into the active night of the senses:

> Endeavour to be inclined always; not to the easiest, but to the most difficult; not to the most delightful, but to the most distasteful; not to the most gratifying, but to the less pleasant; not to what means rest for you, but to hard work: not to the consoling, but to the unconsoling; not to the most, but to the least; not to the highest and most precious, but to the lowest and most despised; not to wanting something, but to wanting nothing; do not go about looking for the best of temporal things, but for the worst, and, for Christ, desire to enter into complete nakedness, emptiness and poverty in everything in the world. (*Ascent of Mount Carmel*, I, 13:6)

In the passive night of the senses, John says that there is an increasing stillness of the senses and deepening silence and quiet. Our interior sensory faculties become engulfed in this night and we experience aridity, dryness and desolation in prayer. He is clear that as we are still very much at the beginning:

> Not too distant from love of pleasure and of self, God is now desiring to withdraw them from this base manner of loving and lead them on to a higher degree of divine love. (*Dark Night*, I, 8:3)

John clearly tells us that God now desires to liberate us from the lowly exercise of the senses and discursive meditation and to lead us into the experience of spirit. We become capable of a communion with God that is much more abundant, free and receptive to the action of the Holy Spirit in our heart.

So, it is when we:

> are going about our spiritual exercises with delight and satisfaction, when in our opinion the sun of divine favour is shining most brightly on us, that God darkens all this light and closes the door and spring of the sweet spiritual water they were tasting as often and as long as they desired… God now leaves them in such darkness that they do not know which way to turn in their discursive imaginings; they cannot advance a step in meditation, as they used to, now that the interior sense faculties are engulfed in this night. He leaves them in such dryness that they not only fail to receive satisfaction and pleasure from their spiritual exercises and works, as they formerly did, but also find these exercises distasteful and bitter… When God sees that they have grown a little, He weans them from the sweet breast so that they might be strengthened, lays aside their swaddling bands, and puts them down from His arms that they may grow accustomed to walking by themselves. This change is a surprise to them because everything seems to be functioning in reverse. (*Dark Night*, I, 8:3)

In *Ascent of Mount Carmel*, John gives further guidelines in the stages of prayer for those passing from meditation to contemplative prayer. If it is possible to let go without it being in any way forced, then deepening contemplation is certainly the next stage, but there should be no sense of pressure, of being pushed, manipulated:

> At the outset… a person will need to make use of meditation, and this need will continue until he acquires the habit of contemplation to a certain perfect degree. The indication of this will be that every time he intends to meditate, he will immediately notice this knowledge and peace as well as his own lack of power or desire to meditate. Until reaching this stage, a person will sometimes contemplate, and sometimes meditate. (*Ascent of Mount Carmel* II, 15:1)

A great range of different sensations and experiences, in which heart, mind and body all play a part, always characterises spiritual growth and development. Many are essentially psychological reactions to spiritual experiences. Some spiritual experiences are mistaken for primarily psychological changes and certain psychological phenomena can masquerade as spiritual experiences (as well as the classic spiritual consolations and desolations).

The genius of John of the Cross is in his guidelines for distinguishing the purgation of the sensory dark night from darkness due to 'some bad humour or indisposition of the body', such as a bout of depression, mental illness or neurosis, and in his outlining of the signs for discerning the genuineness of the dark night purification.

These are essentially the theological signs in prayer of the passage from discursive meditation towards contemplative prayer. The critical consideration in all of this is the discerning of the true source of the spiritual experience – *whether it essentially arises from within ourselves, or from God.*

John outlines two sets of signs, one in the second book of the *Ascent of Mount Carmel* and the other in the first book of the *Dark Night*. Although the perspective is different in each section, from the side of our faith response to the sensory dark night in the former, and from God's side in the latter, the signs correlate and are the same.

The sensory dark night basically has three qualities, or three principal signs for discernment. Firstly, even though there is a lack of satisfaction in prayer, nothing else will do instead. There is no compensation outside of God, and a great deal of dissatisfaction with all created things:

> Since these souls do not get satisfaction or consolation from the things of God; they do not get any from creatures either. Since God puts a soul in this dark night in order to dry up and purge its sensory appetite, He does not allow it to find sweetness or delight in anything.
>
> Through this sign it can in all likelihood be inferred that this dryness and distaste is not the outcome of newly committed sins and imperfections. If this were so, some

inclination or propensity to look for satisfaction in something other than the things of God would be felt in the sensory part. (*Dark Night*, I, 9:2)

Secondly, there is a growing interior capacity to remain alone and still without any particular knowledge or understanding, and it is the trusting and positive ability to be increasingly quiet in His Presence which determines whether it is right or not to abandon active meditation:

> The second sign for the discernment of this purgation is that the memory ordinarily turns to God solicitously and with painful care, and the soul thinks it is not serving God but turning back, because it is aware of this distaste for the things of God. Hence, it is obvious that this aversion and dryness is not the fruit of laxity and tepidity, for lukewarm people do not care much for the things of God nor are they inwardly solicitous about them.
>
> Those suffering from the purgative dryness are ordinarily solicitous, concerned and pained about not serving God. Even though the dryness may be furthered by melancholia or some other humour, as it often is, it does not thereby fail to produce its purgative effect on the appetite, for the soul will be deprived of every satisfaction and be concerned only about God. (*Dark Night*, I, 9:3)

Because our desires seem so passive at this stage, and we have very little inclination to do anything about the situation, the temptation to quit, to walk away, to forget, to lose courage and fortitude, to turn our back on further spiritual possibilities can become strong, even overpowering. Hopelessness, worthlessness, and despair can invade our perception and psyche.

By this time we are usually in the throes of a real crisis, both inwardly and outwardly, in our relationships to ourselves, to others and to our community. It is at this stage that people will abandon God, prayer, their relationships, their friends, their ministry, community, and even the spiritual life altogether.

This is undoubtedly a most difficult phase from a spiritual perspective. If we don't have the faith, courage,

fortitude, patience and hope to journey on through the
depths of darkness and dryness, we could forfeit and forestall
the possibility of the new vision. We risk losing the genuine
hope and maturity of love towards, and in God, that
begins to emerge as we are able to move into the deeper
dwelling places.

This is, of course, on the other side of the darkness,
despair and dryness and usually cannot be imagined this
side of the darkness. Essentially, darkness is the place where
our egotism is truly dying and real unselfish love for the
'other' is beginning to be set free.[7]

John then carefully explains the spiritual purpose of this
type of purgation in the sensory night:

> The reason for this dryness is that God transfers His goods
> and strength from sense to Spirit. Since the sensory part of
> the soul is incapable of the goods of the spirit, it remains
> deprived, dry and empty. Thus, while the spirit is tasting,
> the flesh tastes nothing at all and becomes weak in its work.
> But through this nourishment the spirit grows stronger and
> more alert, and becomes more solicitous than before about
> not failing God... Since its spiritual palate is neither purged
> nor accommodated for so subtle a taste, it [the soul] is unable
> to savour the spiritual savour and good until gradually
> prepared by means of this dark and obscure night. The soul
> instead experiences dryness and distaste because of a lack of
> the gratification it formerly enjoyed so readily. (*Dark Night*,
> I, 9:4)

The only way to break out of this place of impasse, of the
utter limit of our own efforts and self-will, is to surrender
more deeply in faith and trust. His unfathomable mysteries
of Love are beckoning us onward and inward, beyond our
personal control, limits, fears, anxieties and self-justification
that the sensory dark night is purging and purifying.

John explains that one of the main signs that we should
discontinue discursive meditation and pass on to the state
of contemplation is when we now:

> Like to remain alone in loving awareness of God, without
> particular considerations, in interior peace and quiet and

repose, and without the acts and exercises (at least discursive, those in which one progresses from point to point) of the intellect, memory and will; and that he prefers to remain only in the general, loving awareness and knowledge we mentioned, and that he, without any particular knowledge or understanding. (*Ascent of Mount Carmel*, II, 13:4)

Finally, there is an inability to meditate in any discursive manner. We have gained all we can through using our senses in prayer, and to continue would only mean 'staying in the same interior place'. As it is the stage when God is transferring his goods and strength from sense to spirit, it is time for the interior move from structured discourse with God to a more direct experience of formless contemplation:

> The third sign for the discernment of this purgation of the senses is the powerlessness, in spite of one's efforts, to meditate and make use of the imagination, the interior sense, as was one's previous custom.
>
> At this time, God does not communicate Himself through the senses as He did before, by means of the discursive analysis and synthesis of ideas, but begins to communicate Himself through pure spirit by an act of simple contemplation, in which there is no discursive succession of thought.
>
> The exterior and interior senses of the lower part of the soul cannot attain to this contemplation. As a result, the imaginative power and fantasy can no longer rest in any consideration or find support in it. (*Dark Night*, I, 9:8)

All our own efforts to meditate are basically not working anymore. John is clear that God is putting us in this state to conduct us along a very different path, and that any desire to work with the faculties and senses hinders rather than helps His work. What was formerly essential for growth and development now actively hinders any spiritual growth or change.

The real test here is the honest and ruthless exploration of what *is the real focus of our desire or longing*. John is constantly aware that religious movement toward God can emerge either from personal desires for satisfaction or from personal drives for reassurance or escape from life. In other words, John is very conscious of the tendency for religion to become projections, or a set of projective images or ideas, which are shaped and determined by our nature, history, personality, life experiences and culture.

If this is not essentially changed by the Holy Spirit of Jesus gradually permeating individual experiences and influencing patterns of development and growth, there is no possibility of the contemplation of anything but our own projections. John is at pains to show how our images of God and of ourselves are progressively changed and shattered by life experience. There is a change and a shattering of many of our old and outmoded images and concepts of God, which can cause great confusion, sense of loss and meaninglessness.[8] It is difficult to overestimate how painful this sensory purgation can be.

We are becoming more and more passive to the work of God on the soul. Our personal efforts have less and less purpose and effect, and actually become an obstacle to the interior spiritual transformation being wrought by God's action:

> He therefore binds the interior faculties and leaves no support in the intellect, nor satisfaction in the will, nor remembrance in the memory. At this time a person's own efforts are of no avail, but an obstacle to the interior peace and work God is producing in the spirit through that dryness of senses.
>
> Since this peace is something spiritual and delicate, its fruit is quiet, delicate, solitary, satisfying and peaceful, and far removed from all these other gratifications of beginners, which are very palpable and sensory. (*Dark Night*, I, 9:7)

NOTES: THIRD MANSION

1. Amis, R. *op.cit.* p.90
2. Fitzgerald, Constance, *Impasse and Dark Night*, in *Women's Spirituality*, Conn, J.W. (ed). Paulist Press, New Jersey, 1996, p.415

3. Matthew, I. *The Impact of God*, Hodder and Stoughton, London, 1995, p.59
4. Ibid, p.59
5. May, G. *Care of Mind, Care of Spirit*, Harper Collins, San Francisco, 1982, p.99
6. Ibid, pp.101-102
7. Fitzgerald, C. *op.cit.* p.419
8. Ibid, pp.417-418.

THE FOURTH MANSION

Infused by Love

Now that I commence writing about the fourth mansions, it is requisite… to commend myself to the Holy Spirit and to beg Him henceforth to speak for me, that I may be enabled to treat these matters intelligibly. Henceforth they begin to be supernatural and it will be most difficult to speak clearly about them, unless His Majesty undertakes it for me.

St Teresa, Fourth Mansion

TRANSITION AND TRANSFORMATION

The fourth dwelling place is the place of spiritual transformation and transition, where the inner landscape of our soul is beginning to qualitatively change. From the arduous, seemingly never-ending purification and purgation of the outer mansions, this interior dwelling place is becoming very different.

It is the place of a more profound level of letting go into the unknown, of surrendering into mystery and unknowing. Our relationship with God is now becoming a far deeper reliance on our naked faith, love, and dependence on Him, and Him alone – fundamentally moving towards a more direct encounter and absorption into His Presence, Majesty and Mystery.

This profound transition could be symbolised by flying, gliding or jumping off the edge of a high cliff, where the depths of our spiritual courage, steadfastness and faith in God – into His Hands, into His Divine Providence – will be tested to the very marrow of our bones.

The following dream accurately describes the type and level of inner trust that is required in such a transition:

> I am in a small cable car, and several of my closest spiritual companions start to board until it fills up completely, with no seats left. My spiritual director then enters the cable car, and sits at the helm. I get in and sit directly behind him. It is clear that the car is on the edge of a very high mountain, virtually on a precipice.
>
> The car is about to roll off the precipice and out into the atmosphere, as it has been designed to gently begin to fly towards an unknown destination. This stage appears to be integral to the journey I have embarked on.
>
> I have no fear, anxiety or concern, because I totally trust in my spiritual director, who is the driver of the cable car. We become ready, and the car begins to slide off, and glide out and over the precipice into the air, with no support or foundation other than my total trust in my spiritual guide.

The new type of prayer experiences that are now granted require an endurance and fortitude because there is now no possibility of returning to our former state of being. It can be like coming to a huge chasm in our journey, where we have to become lighter and lighter, throwing off as much inner baggage as possible in order to become like a feather on the Breath of God.

We are now entering a difficult and painful, yet truly illuminating and spiritually transforming dwelling place. We are being invited into the inner court of the castle, and something of His Light, of the Beauty and the Radiance of Christ, the Divine King, shining from the centremost mansion, is now able to touch our soul.

This fourth dwelling place involves the movement from the place of awakening, purification and purgation to the possibility of becoming more and more receptive to the action of God, and becoming more deeply spiritually transformed by the action of the Holy Spirit.

Now is the moment, the hour, the day, when the Lord begins to introduce us into His Inner Kingdom because we are now in the position to recognise, receive and welcome Him into our heart. This new life is intimately connected with Christ, the King, who dwells in the innermost sanctuary of the castle.

It is the momentous movement from the emphasis on our ascetical efforts of prayer, contemplation, and good works in the earlier mansions, to the more mystical stages and possibilities on our journey. Teresa says that we are unable to enter these more interior rooms unless we have lived for *a long time* in the outer ones, learning the ways, manners and etiquette of the Heavenly King's court.

The previous dwelling places have concerned our efforts in prayer and spiritual exercises, essentially the ascetical aspect of the Christian tradition. This dwelling place is stressing the mystical aspect of the tradition – the pneumatikos – or 'spiritual', having the sense of proceeding from the Holy Spirit. It is clear that the spiritual is what is open to the action of the Holy Spirit – essentially, what does not come from ourselves, but what is received.[1]

According to the usage established by St Paul, the realm of the spiritual is to be distinguished not from the bodily, but from what he calls the psyche:

> Now we have received not the spirit of the world, but the Spirit that is from God, so that we may understand the gifts bestowed on us by God. And we speak of these things in words not taught by human wisdom but taught by the Spirit, interpreting spiritual things to those who are spiritual.
>
> Those who are unspiritual do not receive the gifts of God's Spirit, for they are foolishness to them, and they are unable to understand them because they are discerned spiritually. Those who are spiritual discern all things, and they are themselves subject to no one else's scrutiny. (1 Corinthians 2:12-15)

Throughout the first three mansions, much information, learning, knowledge and experience has been gathered and integrated, all essential for developing and consolidating our psychological, emotional and physical foundation. In this dwelling place, however, we are now being asked to give up a good proportion of our rational understanding, and the many mental images of God that have been developed earlier.

For some individuals this is a very difficult transition – letting go of the endless workings of the mind, of the many ideas, concepts and thoughts that we have accumulated *about* God. At this stage, they will actually limit the action of the Holy Spirit. Many of our most cherished self-images and God-images can be in fact, psychological defensive manoeuvres designed to resist our truly letting go to the action of the Holy Spirit.

These mental and emotional defences arrest the soul's spiritual development by interfering with the possibility of our entering the innermost dwelling places, and can ultimately leave us dwelling only in the outer mansions. To the rational mind this part of the journey can appear quite terrifying.

It is always very painful and difficult to let go of our ego-centred sense of worth, spirituality, importance and dependence, but it is not possible to take these attitudes, our heavy loads and baggage, across the bridge, across the chasm, across the threshold. Our love, hunger and desire for God must now have 'no strings attached', because our love has to be a totally freely willed gift to Him. It is the only way to survive after we cross this important spiritual transition. We will be truly unable to measure God, or the Divine King, by any of our own human standards once we are on the other side of the bridge.

This dwelling place signifies a totally radical change, entailing a breakdown in the safety of our ideas and concepts about God. Here is the movement from faith based on law and belief to a faith based more wholly on love. Faith here goes beyond rational understanding. We have run out of endless questions and answers *about* God. We are beginning to know why there are essentially very few answers that can feed, contain and satisfy the growing sense and experience of the Immensity and Infinity of God.

We have a growing hunger and desire to rest more passively and silently *and be alone* in His Love and Presence. The biographer of St Silouan, the twentieth-century Orthodox saint from Mount Athos, expresses this transition beautifully:

> God is Light inaccessible. His Being exceeds not only all corporeal but also all mental images. Therefore, so long as man's mind is busied with reflection, with words, concepts and images, it has not attained perfection in prayer.
>
> The human mind and personality only reach the stillness of pure and perfect prayer when from the love of God all created things are left behind... when a man utterly forgets the world and his own body so that afterwards he no longer knows whether he was in or out of the body in the hour of prayer.
>
> Such superlatively pure prayer is a rare gift of God. It depends not on human effort but on the power of the Lord which with infinite care and tenderness transports man into

the world of Divine Light; or, as it would be better to say, Divine Light manifests itself and lovingly encompasses man's whole being so that he is no longer able either to meditate or remember anything.[2]

Now, like gliding off the alpine cliff, or taking a plane or boat to a completely unknown destination, there are no specific procedures, no precise definitions, and no road maps. It is as if we have to live, breathe and become more and more absorbed within the footsteps of Christ and His Saints. We must be very careful to faithfully trace the footsteps of the Master in order to cross this difficult threshold into the unknown.

The spiritual passage is becoming much more narrow. Jesus refers to this when he says – 'enter through the narrow gate; for the gate is wide and the road is easy that leads to destruction, and there are many who take it. For the gate is narrow and the road is hard that leads to life, and there are few who find it' (Mt 7:14).

It is crossing that great threshold between death and new spiritual life – the beginning of the new birth in Christ within the heart, into the native realm of the Holy Spirit – that denotes the way to resurrection and eternal life.

Here is where there is a change from thinking about God, with the emphasis on all our human efforts, towards *being* for, and living in, God. Up to this mansion, all we have done is prepare ourselves to surrender to, and be infused by, His Love and Presence, through our readiness and openness of heart and deepening ability to recognise the truth of our inner incompleteness and total dependency on God.

Now, *infused grace* is beginning to operate more fully. Teresa tells us that it is the dwelling place where the *natural and supernatural combine.* In prayer and contemplation, we are beginning to experience very different states of being in our love affair with God, and it is happening increasingly effortlessly.

What is called supernatural prayer, infused contemplation, or passive, mystical prayer, is where God is taking over in the centre of our heart. The difference between active and passive prayer depends on the quality of our attention and the nature of our action and emphasis. If we are engaging in any form of active participation in our communion with God, then the prayer is active prayer.

If we are becoming more still within, becoming quietly and more subtly aware of His Presence; or if we are beginning to feel more held, or absorbed, by Him; or suspended or immersed in Him – then the prayer is seemingly passive. This is first experienced here in the fourth mansion.

Our own efforts are ceasing and now there is a more direct contact and loving embrace with God. We begin to experience less of our own selves and are more and more absorbed in, and captivated by, the Divine Love and Presence of God. There are fewer images and concepts of Him, as the soul begins to listen and rest in His mysterious Presence.

Teresa expresses how different this mansion is from the previous ones by describing the spiritual sweetness of the earlier mansions, and the spiritual consolations of the innermost mansions:

> It appears to me that what we acquire for ourselves in meditation and petitions to our Lord may be termed 'sweetness in devotion'. It is natural, although ultimately aided by the grace of God. I must be understood to imply this in all I say, for we can do nothing without Him. This sweetness arises principally from the good work we perform, and appears to result from our labours; well may we feel happy at having thus spent our time.
>
> We shall find, on consideration, that many temporal matters give us the same pleasure – such as unexpectedly coming into a large fortune... I consider both these joys and those we feel in religious matters to be natural ones. Although there is nothing wrong about the former, yet those produced by devotion spring from a more noble source – in short, they begin in ourselves and end in God.
>
> Spiritual consolations, on the contrary, arise from God,

**and our nature feels them and rejoices as keenly in them,
and indeed far more keenly, than in the others I described.**
(IV, Chapter 1, 4)

In the former, what is experienced flows through the
ordinary channels of life experience, whereas in the latter,
the spiritual waters are flowing straight from their source,
the heavenly realms. Essentially Teresa is talking about
what happened in her own spiritual life.

She is clear that what had happened to her previously
did not come from her 'interior depths'. She realises that it
had been the natural activity of the outermost mansions –
her thoughts and feelings *about* God, her good works and
her grief over her sinfulness.

Now, the soul isn't doing any of the work. The work of
the Holy Spirit is happening effortlessly in her depths.
Teresa says that it is impossible to strive or push for spiritual
favours by our own efforts here, as they have very little
effect. Our heart is beginning to give way to becoming
absorbed into His Presence and the power of His Love,
which can only be granted by grace.

Furthermore, we are increasingly unable to comprehend
such bestowal of spiritual riches and blessings from the level
of our ordinary human reasoning. Divine Providence begins
to operate more actively and it requires a deepening level of
trust to be more open and surrendered to His Ways in our
heart and life, allowing the diminishing of our own ways.

Interestingly, she states quite firmly that for those who
have had no experience of the grace of God touching their
life in such profoundly intimate and transformative ways,
this stage can appear obscure, neurotic or even pathological!
In this dwelling place, it is not possible to understand what
is happening in the depth of our heart 'according to human
wisdom' (1 Cor 2:13), as St Paul writes, because such
things 'are discerned spiritually' (1 Cor 2:14).

The saint is clear that those who know, and have begun
to experience the grace and blessings of God, will
comprehend:

As these mansions are nearer the King's dwelling, they are very beautiful, and so subtle are the things seen and heard in them, that, as those tell us who have tried to do so, the mind cannot give a lucid idea of them to those inexperienced in the matter. People who have enjoyed these favours, especially if it was to any great extent, will easily comprehend me.

Apparently a person must have dwelt for a long time in the former mansions before entering these; although in ordinary cases the soul must have been in the last one spoken of, yet as you must often have heard, there is no fixed rule, for God gives when, how and to whom He wills – the goods are His own, and His choice wrongs no one. (IV, Chapter 1, 2, 3)

She tells us that we need to have lived in the earlier mansions for a long time before any sense of the indwelling Presence of the Lord can begin to be experienced, before any possibility of the transformation of the heart can occur. She notes that our inner struggle with the 'lizards and the snakes' in the outer courts of the castle can sometimes happen even here, and is actually very helpful if it does.

They are the constant reminders of our human frailty, weakness and vulnerability:

The poisonous reptiles rarely come into these rooms, and if they enter, they do more good than harm. I think it is far better for them to get in and make war on the soul in this state of prayer; were it not tempted, the devil might sometimes deceive it about divine consolations, thus injuring it far more.

Besides, the soul would benefit less, because all occasions of gaining merit would be withdrawn, were it left continually absorbed in God. I am not confident that this absorption is genuine when it always remains in the same state, nor does it appear to me possible for the Holy Ghost to dwell constantly within us, to the same extent during our earthly exile. (IV, Chapter 1, 3)

She recognises that it is essential to be continually facing our inner darkness and sinfulness, as a constant reminder of the reality of temptations and spiritual deception. Closing the castle door on outer preoccupations and journeying inwards towards union with our Spouse entails facing *even more deeply* the reality of our fragmented, dark and untransformed inner world, where the difficulties and struggles can intensify at this stage.

It can mean the agony of tearing apart all that is dear to us for the sake of the mysterious, the unknown. To consent with all our heart to be drawn beyond ourselves into the sphere of God, even though it is ultimately our sole fulfilment, is usually alien, frightening and painful to our limited understanding and corporeality.

Our struggle to surrender the power and supremacy of our egotism – all of the false habits, conditionings, beliefs, assumptions and dogmas that keep our heart bound and gagged – is a spiritual battle that cannot be overestimated.

Throughout her life, Teresa experienced the fact that the spiritual journey brings enormous interior struggles and difficulties, unique to itself. She wisely counsels:

> **We should not be distressed by reason of our thoughts, nor allow ourselves to be worried by them; if they come from the devil, he will let us alone if we take no notice of them; and if they are, as often happens, one of the many frailties entailed by Adam's sin, let us be patient and suffer them for the love of God.**
>
> **Likewise, since we must eat and sleep without being able to avoid it, much to our grief, let us acknowledge then we are human, and long to be where no one may despise us. Sometimes I recall these words, spoken by the Spouse in the Canticle; truly never in our lives have we better reason to say them, for I think no earthly scorn or suffering can try us so severely as these struggles within our souls.**
>
> **All uneasiness, or conflict can be borne while we have peace in ourselves, as I said; but if, while seeking for rest amidst the thoughts and trials of the world – knowing that God has prepared this rest for us – the obstacle is found in ourselves, the trial must needs prove painful and almost insufferable.** (IV, Chapter 1, 11)

Experiencing this spiritual terrain is a deeply disconcerting encounter for the person who mistakenly thinks or feels that we 'know ourselves'. What is important is our growing reliance on faith and love of God alone, as well as the development of discernment that separates spiritual truth from deception. This is vital in order to remain in an increasing state of watchfulness, expectancy and receptivity to the action of the Holy Spirit.

Teresa writes that the essential fuel on our contemplative journey towards God is to have our ordinary rational faculties decreasing, as our capacity to love and be loved is increasing:

> **I only wish to warn you that to make rapid progress and to reach the mansions we wish to enter, it is not so essential to *think* as much as to *love* much; therefore you must practise whatever most excites you to this... Love does not consist in great sweetness of devotion, but in a more fervent determination to strive to please God in all things.** (IV, Chapter 1, 7)

This is very difficult for many of us. Teresa is talking about the difference between the level of ordinary personal love, and an order of Love completely other – that very Great Love that God can bestow on the soul, which can only be experienced in the depths of our empty and surrendered heart, by becoming filled by His Love from the deepest dwelling place.

It is not possible to 'think' in ordinary rational terms about such things. It is an experience of another order, another level of spiritual being and mystery altogether. Our ordinary rational mind can be anxious, over-active or in torment, whilst in the innermost mansions, the heart is beginning to experience a sense of God's love and peace, quite beyond human understanding.

We can begin to touch, understand and experience a deeper sense of faith and assurance that our heart and being are intimately connected to, and are living, breathing parts of, that profound and awesome pattern of God's Mystery, Presence and Power, which is much greater, more profound and beneficent than the mind can understand or fathom.

What does all this mean for us in the midst of the hustle and bustle of everyday life, and the constant demands that we have to meet on a daily basis? The element that really distinguishes the person who has a more mystical and contemplative orientation is our very different perspective on what happens in life. We see and have faith in the constant miracles that occur. We have a sense of God's Presence and Being which permeates all of creation.

We have the ability to reflect on all the aspects of life, and see the work of God and His Light in all things – in the wonderful, in suffering, in the horrific and in the very ordinary. We can see and experience the awe and wonder of the work of God throughout creation, and have our feet firmly placed on the ground.

In a famous nineteenth-century devotional text, *The Way of the Pilgrim*, an anonymous Russian peasant wanderer beautifully describes the profound spiritual change in his perception of the world and others due to his constant prayer transfiguring his relationship with the material world, changing all things into a sacrament of God's Presence and rendering them transparent:

> When I began to pray with my heart, everything surrounding me took on a delightful form: the trees, the grass, the birds, the earth, the air, and the light. All things seemed to be saying to me that they existed for humanity's sake, that they were testifying to God's love for humankind, that they were all praying and singing the glory of God.
>
> And I understood from this what the Philokalia calls 'the knowledge of the speech of all creatures'… I felt love for Jesus Christ and all God's creation… Again, I went wandering from one place to the next, but I no longer walked with difficulties as before.
>
> The invocation of the Name of Jesus Christ cheered me on my way, and all people treated me rather well; it seemed as if they all loved me… If someone insults or injures me, I only recall how sweet is the Jesus Prayer, and then and there both insult and anger pass and I forget everything.[3]

THE TWO FOUNTAINS

Teresa is clear that in this dwelling place we begin to taste the Presence of God and smell the sweet perfume of the Holy Spirit, which are beginning gradually to permeate the inner senses of the soul through the surrender and abandonment of ourselves to His Being and Love. Here we find some of her most subtle writings on prayer and on the deepening silence and stillness in God that is now occurring.

There begins to be an intermingling of natural and supernatural prayer. Natural prayer is when we are actively communicating with God, when we are being directive and discursive, when we making efforts towards God. Supernatural prayer is where God takes over and begins to pour His Living Waters into our soul.

There is a deepening stillness and quietness within, the beginning of a greater awareness of the Presence of God and the sense of being absorbed, suspended or immersed in Him in an apparently passive way. Now, there is less and less of ourselves and more immersion and surrender in our heart to God's Presence.

Teresa is irresistibly drawn to the symbol of water, and uses it throughout her writings to describe the mystical life:

> I can find no simile more appropriate than water by which to explain spiritual things... I love this element so much that I have studied it more attentively than other things. God, Who is so great, so wise, has doubtless hidden secrets in all things He created, which we should greatly benefit by knowing. (IV, Chapter 2, 3)

She uses the water fountains to describe and understand the different experiences and states of prayer. She describes two types of conduits and fountains which carry the spiritual waters:

> To make the matter clearer, let us imagine we see two fountains with basins that fill with water... these two basins are filled in different ways; the one with water from a distance flowing into it through many pipes and waterworks, while

> the other basin is built near the source of the spring itself
> and fills quite noiselessly. If the fountain is plentiful, like
> the one we speak of, after the basin is full the water overflows
> in a great storm, which flows continually. No machinery is
> needed here, nor does the water run through aqueducts.
> (IV, Chapter 2, 3)

The first type of basin is analogous to *active prayer* where a
lot of effort is required in getting the water to the fountain.
Like the water source, God's Presence is also a long way
away, and often it is the inspiration from external sources –
such as liturgy, music, nature, an inspiring work of art,
special friendships or spiritual writings which stimulates
and initiates our prayer life. Like the water source, this type
of active prayer implies a distance, and here it is basically *us
doing all the work*.

This first basin, artificially filled, represents prayer that
begins with the person and ends in God. She emphasises
that this route is a long and difficult one and is being done
mainly through our own struggles, efforts, skills and human
faculties. In this basin:

> the water running through the aqueducts resembles sensible
> devotion, which is obtained by meditation. We gain it by
> our thoughts, by meditating on created things, by the labour
> of our own minds; in short, it is the result of our endeavours,
> and so makes the commotion I spoke of, while profiting
> the soul. (IV, Chapter 2, 4)

Teresa says that the other basin is *quite different*. The
second basin, where the water wells up spontaneously and
marvellously, is that which begins with God and ends in
the person. The water flowing into this fountain comes
from a spring right underneath the basin, in direct
connection to the Source of the Water. This is analogous
to passive prayer, where no energy, labour or technology is
used to bring the water to the fountain.

Here, we are becoming more aware of God being within
us, as His Presence, His Water, is filling us in mysterious
and inexplicable ways:

The other fountain, like divine consolations, receives the water from the source itself, which signifies God: as usual, when His Majesty wills to bestow on us any supernatural favours, we experience the greatest peace, calm, and sweetness in the inmost depths of our being; I know neither where nor how.

This joy is not, like earthly happiness, at once felt by the heart; after gradually filling it to the brim, the delight overflows throughout all the mansions and faculties, until at last it reaches the body. Therefore, I say it arises from God and ends in ourselves, for whoever experiences it will find that the whole physical part of our nature shares in this delight and sweetness. (IV, Chapter 2, 4, 5)

She then tells us what happens in the heart is what she calls the prayer of quiet, or divine consolations, and continues to use the metaphor of the fountains and water to describe this state of prayer:

In the prayer of quiet, when the water flows from the spring itself and not through the conduits, the mind ceases to act; it is forced to do so, although it does not understand what is happening, and so wanders hither and thither in bewilderment, finding no place for rest.

Meanwhile the will, entirely united to God, is much disturbed by the tumult of the thoughts: no notice should be taken of them, or they would cause the loss of a great part of the favour the soul is enjoying.

Let the spirit ignore these distractions and abandon itself in the arms of divine love: His Majesty will teach it how best to act, which chiefly consists in its recognising its unworthiness of so great a good and occupying itself in thanking Him for it. (IV, Chapter 3, 7)

So, for Teresa, these experiences come from the divine source, and can in no way be manufactured. Our part is to persevere in prayer and in willingness to surrender to God. Here, in the deepest interior we are letting go of the intellect and memories. We are learning, by experiencing a growing non-attachment to our thoughts, that God is so much more than we could imagine, and that we possess more human dignity than we could know.

A modern Orthodox monk talks of:

achieving the stillness of prayer in the heart, with the mind, free from reflections, keeping quiet watch like a sentry to make sure that nothing enters into the heart from without. Where this state of sacred silence exists, heart and mind feed on the Name of Christ and His commandments. They live as one, controlling all happenings within, not by logical investigation, but intuitively, by a specific spiritual sense… As soon as the mind unites with the heart it can see every movement in the sphere of the subconscious… it is the striving after a state of uninterrupted mental attention in the heart – a state in which prayer becomes constant, imbued with a clear, robust feeling of God present and active, and the mind from much weeping becomes strong enough to push back every attack by passionate intrusive thoughts.[4]

Our will is being united with God's will for our life. What does this really mean? Teresa explains that our human will and understanding relate to our material being, our 'life in the flesh' so to speak. What is happening in this mansion is the beginning of transcending this materiality, with its emphasis on life in the world and our fleshly existence.

A new dimension of being is evolving, where the primary emphasis is on spiritual things and our life in God. We are encountering the Grace of God in the depths of our being, in the growing point of the Spirit, and our ego-based human consciousness can know nothing of it directly.

Although Teresa speaks of progression within to what is already there, there is now a totally new state of being and life evolving, which is emphasising the things of the Spirit. This new life in God has its own needs, its own operations and laws, which are not circumscribed by material limitations. It isn't that we have a deeper will or a more searching understanding than we had before.

Rather, our more surrendered heart is being given a Divine knowledge of God, by His Grace, which we are inevitably leaping up to embrace. As this Divine contact is *utterly other* than our bodily existence, this part of us cannot know what is happening in the deeper recesses.

Our evolving spiritual self is occupied with Love. Our

mind and our ordinary thoughts, however, find themselves increasingly redundant, and can become indignant and rebellious, and make a lot of unnecessary fuss! We know that something is fundamentally transforming our heart in this fourth mansion, but we do not know *how we know, or what we know.*

We do not know what is happening at the time it is happening. Only in looking back, sometimes after many years, at the fruits that grow from the living tree do we 'understand', or 'see' in a very different way what has actually happened. Teresa is clear that she did not really understand what was happening to her at the time until she had reached the innermost mansion.

She recalls the scriptural verse 'Thou has dilated my heart' *('Dilatasti cor meum')* to explain the dilation of heart which is begun by the celestial waters of the Holy Spirit acting within:

> This joy does not appear to me to originate in the heart, but in some more interior part and, as it were, in the depths of our being. I think this must be the centre of the soul... I discover secrets within us which often fill me with astonishment: how many more must there be unknown to me!
>
> Oh my Lord and my God! How stupendous is Thy grandeur! We are like so many foolish peasant lads: we think we know something of Thee, yet it must be comparatively nothing, for there are profound secrets even in ourselves of which we know nothing... The dilation begun by the celestial waters in the depths of our being – they appear to dilate and enlarge us internally, and benefit us in an inexplicable manner, nor does even the soul itself understand what it receives. It is conscious of what may be described as a certain fragrance, as if within its inmost depths were a brazier sprinkled with sweet perfumes.
>
> Although the spirit neither sees the flame nor knows where it is, yet it is penetrated by the warmth, the scented fumes, which are even sometimes perceived by the body. Understand me, the soul does not feel any real heat or scent, but something far more subtle, which I use this metaphor to explain... clearly it does not arise from the base coin of human nature, but from the most pure gold of

Divine Wisdom. I believe that in this case the powers of the soul are not united to God, but are absorbed and astounded at the marvel before them. (IV, Chapter 2, 5, 6)

His Love is filling us to overflowing from the deepest regions within our heart. The mysterious paradox is that this only occurs in a deep state of inner surrender. At these early stages it is usually happening unconsciously and we are not aware of it until afterwards. It is nothing to do with our personality or our worldly existence. It is as if the deepest region of our being is beginning to dissolve, and be absorbed into a vast, limitless ocean of God's Presence and Being.

It is not of our body, of the ego, the mind or any faculties – it concerns the deepest part of our heart. All this is quite a mystery to ordinary human understanding and we can only lovingly accept what is happening to us. These expansions, or dilations, of the heart are something that cannot be imagined beforehand. Miraculously, through these experiences, God is drawing the soul closer to Himself in ways that are only known to Him.

Teresa details the different spiritual gifts that God gives to those in both active and passive prayer, and discusses the similarities and differences between them. The gifts associated with active prayer are called spiritual consolations, and those associated with passive prayer are spiritual delights. What is the difference?

The Spanish *contentos* is translated as 'consolations', which are experiences of joy, peace, satisfaction, happiness and other related pleasant sensations, similar to those experienced in ordinary everyday life. They are naturally acquired experiences and sensations that evolve from prayer, meditation, leading a God centred life, and doing good works for others.

Spiritual delights come from the Spanish *gustos*, and are 'infused mystical gifts' that come directly from God. Human nature or events cannot initiate them. Spiritual delights can only be present when God is acting on the individual in a special and blessed way – in infused, supernatural or mystical prayer.

She is emphatic in this dwelling place about the increasing role of deepening humility towards God and the transforming action of the Holy Spirit in the heart, which is becoming more and more essential. The degree of humility tests the purity and genuineness of the seeker's love for Him and Him Alone.

The essential accompaniment of the 'dilation of the heart' will be real humility:

> **humility, humility! For God lets Himself be vanquished by this and grants us all we ask. The first proof that you possess humility is that you neither think you now deserve these graces and consolations from God, nor that you ever will as long as you live. You ask me: 'How shall we receive them, if we do not try to gain them?'** (IV, Chapter 2, 8)

Another important manifestation that is developing is the growth in our generosity towards others and the world. In her own day and writings, 'penances' described corporal acts of mortification in the religious life which were much in vogue and were considered the hallmarks of generosity. For Teresa, generosity of spirit means going far beyond what is expected or usually obligatory. True mystical grace shows itself in increasing generosity, in a real giving of ourselves to others.

It also shows itself in the growing resolution and practical ability to put our own desires, wishes and hopes aside and devote ourselves, completely, to others. Most importantly, it manifests in the gift of ourselves that will persevere in prayer in spite of all the hindrances and difficulties. As Teresa stresses, profound faith, humility and generosity are not normally the fruit of a single mystical encounter – this 'dilation of the heart' is the result of our faithful response to many such encounters.

Teresa gives important spiritual guidance on the mysterious paradox of how to cultivate longing for God and the hope of obtaining His favours, while having no expectations or desires. She gives several reasons why such favours should not be striven after.

Firstly, the essential motivation of the soul needs to be our love of God without self-interest. This tests our purity of intent and surrender. The spiritual favours that Teresa herself experienced inspired her with greater courage and generosity and bred humility, and she is clear that she did not consciously look for these favours.

She is adamant that no matter what we do, we can never acquire infused contemplation, because this mystical grace is precisely the *opposite* of self-interest, and attention on ourselves. Infused contemplation means forgetfulness of self, not a watching of self in order to see how we are praying.

The second reason against striving after favours is that it can demonstrate a lack of humility towards God, in thinking that any importance or personal attributes of the little 'I' or ego cause automatic rights or obligations with respect to anything so great as spiritual blessings:

> **It is a slight lack of humility to think that our wretched services can win so great a reward.** (IV, Chapter 2, 8)

Thirdly, the true preparation for receiving such spiritual blessings is our conscious desire to surrender. We prepare by struggling and giving up the thousand attachments and identifications that keep us in bondage to our own limitations, expectations and egotism:

> **The real preparation for them is to desire to suffer and to imitate our Lord, rather than to receive consolations, for indeed we have all offended Him.** (IV, Chapter 2, 8)

Fourthly, and most importantly, God is not obliged to bestow Heavenly gifts or blessings, and in no way are we to expect them either:

> **His Majesty has not promised to give us these favours in the same way as He has bound Himself to bestow eternal glory on us, if we keep His commandments. We can be saved without these special graces: He sees better than we do what is best for us and which of us love Him sincerely.** (IV, Chapter 2, 8)

THRESHOLD

Teresa introduces the prayer of quiet here, which is the connecting bond between active and passive prayer, and refers to 'this kind of recollection being supernatural'. This deepening stillness and quiet allows us to listen more attentively, silently and obediently, and is based on the growing capacity to love and be loved and works best without effort, labels or expectations. We cannot understand passive prayer with our rational faculties, as it appears to be mysterious, paradoxical and unrelated to any effort on our own part.

Now the senses and passions are beginning to lose their hold on the soul as the spirit is becoming much stronger:

> There is no occasion to retire nor to shut the eyes, nor does it depend on anything exterior; involuntarily the eyes suddenly close and solitude is found. Without any labour of one's own, the temple of which I spoke is reared for the soul in which to pray; the senses and exterior surroundings appear to lose their hold, while the spirit gradually regains its lost sovereignty. Some say the soul enters into itself; others, that it rises above itself. (IV, Chapter 3, 1)

Teresa tells of her own experience at this stage and gives careful spiritual guidance, saying that the call comes from God when He hears our ardent longing and desire for Him. Realising how much has been lost, the soul wishes to re-enter the vicinity of the castle again:

> Let us imagine that the senses and the powers of the soul have fled and joined the enemy outside. After long days and years of absence, perceiving how great has been their loss, they return to the neighbourhood of the castle, but cannot manage to re-enter it, for their evil habits are hard to break off.
>
> The King, Who holds His Court within it, sees their good will and out of His great mercy desires them to return to Him. Like a good Shepherd, He plays so sweetly on His pipes, that although scarcely hearing it they recognise His Call and no longer wander, but return, like lost sheep, to the mansions. (IV, Chapter 3, 1, 2)

Teresa goes into some detail about how the prayer of quiet works, and about the particular threshold where reason and the mind operate, and will tend to dominate, until '**we are called to recollection by love**' (IV, Chapter 3, 5). She is fairly emphatic that it is not possible to enter into these states of spiritual recollection unless God gives the soul this particular grace. God only bestows such favours on those who have renounced worldly and earthly desire on an inner level, even if our station in life, or service to our community does not permit us to appear to be doing so in an obvious or open way.

Nowadays, as many people are called to live and work in large cities, it is perfectly possible, though difficult, to live in big metropolitan areas and maintain these interior states of stillness, prayer and inward silence. In one of the famous nineteenth-century Russian monasteries outside Moscow, it was noted that:

> Although the spiritual fathers of Optino [monastery]… were compelled by their vocation to receive an unending stream of visitors – dozens and even hundreds in a single day – they did not thereby forfeit their inner hesychia [the orthodox term for sacred silence, mental quiet and stillness]. Indeed it was precisely because of this inner hesychia that they were enabled to act as guides to others. The words that they spoke to each visitor were words of power because they were words that came out of silence.[5]

Few are called, or able, to be completely monastic or ascetic in our own age. Our journey to, and in, God occurs within our heart and soul whilst we are in the midst of work, relationships and the marketplace. The essential spiritual meaning here relates to what is happening in the depths of the heart wherever we are in life, as one Orthodox theologian notes: 'One person can appear to be keeping silent and yet condemns others in their heart; such a person is speaking all the time. Another person talks from morning till evening and yet keeps silent; that is, he says nothing except what is helpful to others.'[6]

At this stage, the action of God begins to suspend our rational faculties as we prepare to hear 'what our Lord may say to us' (IV, Chapter 3, 4). How can we be more responsive to this delicate interior calling of our Lord in the centre of our heart? Teresa describes several conditions to help us understand, mysteriously and paradoxically, what is happening in these states of prayer.

Those who progress the most in spiritual matters are those whose reason and efforts are increasingly quiescent:

> **When He secretly shows us He hears our prayers, it is well to be silent, as He has drawn us into His presence; there would then be no harm in trying to keep our minds at rest... I believe that human efforts avail nothing in these matters, which His Majesty appears to reserve to Himself, setting this limit to our powers.** (IV, Chapter 3, 5, 6)

Teresa emphasises the exquisitely gentle and peaceful nature of these deepening interior states of prayer. Doing anything at all is painful or destructive and can spiritually cause more harm than good. No interior development can be forced, and our transforming heart must be left entirely in the hands of God. It is even impossible to force the mind to stop, to 'not think' because this only encourages resistance, agitation and further over-stimulation.

She says that no effort should be made to suspend the intellect and imagination. This prayer will only occur effortlessly when the time is right and the soul begins to be transported out of herself into absorption in God. We can only become more abandoned, receptive, open, passive and surrendered to God – states of being which are very much beyond discursive reasoning and the faculties of the human mind. Nothing can be forced or willed at this stage.

Teresa is quite clear about what begins to happen at this very important spiritual threshold. While the faculties are becoming more passive and dead to the ordinary world of the senses, the soul, in a state of spiritual absorption, is beginning to be graced by a taste of His Divine Light, knowledge of Him and wisdom far above anything natural:

When His Majesty wishes the mind to rest from working He employs it in another manner, giving it a light and knowledge far above any obtainable by its own efforts and absorbing it entirely into Himself. Then, though it knows not how, it is filled with wisdom such as it could never gain for itself by striving to suspend the thoughts.

Let the spirit ignore these distractions and abandon itself in the arms of Divine Love: His Majesty will teach it how best to act, which chiefly consists in its recognising its unworthiness of so great a good and occupying itself in thanking Him for it. (IV, Chapter 3, 6, 7)

What is this state of being which is becoming more absorbed and intoxicated by the Holy Spirit? Purely at the will of God, and when He wishes human understanding to cease, He enters the soul and illuminates her with His Light and Wisdom, which are quite different to what can be attained in our ordinary state. We continue to remain intoxicated in His Love, and without knowing how, find ourselves in possession of a mysterious knowing far deeper than any the human faculties can give.

It is as if God's Love is beginning to be infused into the very core of the heart of the pilgrim, and where the differences and separations between 'I' and 'Thou', 'me' and 'Him' begin to dissolve, however imperceptibly. Barriers and veils on all sorts of levels, inner and outer, begin to melt away and become meaningless.

There is the unmistakable sense in prayer that the depths of our heart are becoming more and more absorbed into God:

If transported out of itself by its feelings, well and good; but let it not try to understand what is passing within it, for this favour is bestowed on the will which should be left to enjoy it in peace, only making loving aspirations occasionally.

Although in this kind of prayer, the soul makes no effort towards it, yet often, for a very short time, the mind ceases to think at all... They [God's favours] must be received continually, for it is on their frequent reception that the whole welfare of the soul depends. (IV, Chapter 3, 7, 9)

In these states of absorption, we may lose all awareness of our body and the material world around us. It is impossible to say how this occurs, but this is the spiritual threshold that Teresa is describing in this dwelling place. Whilst engrossed in prayer, we might not notice anything, but in some way that we may be ignorant of, we are caught up into another sphere of being and forget the earth.

The Divine Hand can perform this with such caution and discretion that the soul does not detect the moment itself; just as one does not catch the moment of falling in love, or falling asleep. It is only after returning to her normal awareness of the world that the soul realises that she had departed from her usual state, and has been united with God. After such an event, all the things of the earth are seen as transient and temporary. The soul recognises that the point of her existence is to be with God, in Him, in Eternity.

Teresa describes the effects and signs in the soul of these mystical states. A dilation or enlargement of the heart takes place, as if the waters proceeding from the spring had no means of running away. It is as if the fountain had a device ensuring that the more freely the water flows, the larger becomes the chalice within the heart for the Holy Spirit to pour into.

Sometimes, miraculous gifts are bestowed. The gentle movement and interior dilation allow the soul to be less constrained in thought, feelings, activities, and in communication and service pertaining to spiritual matters. It is as if there is now liberation – more of our fears, anxieties and concerns are dissolving.

Such inner expansion has lasting effects, and begins to totally transform our whole life. We are able to become spontaneously much more open, generous and giving in a sort of automatic and obvious way. The soul has now tasted the Presence of God, which is changing our entire perspective and quality of living, and giving us confidence and faith in our ability to enjoy His Presence more fully as we go deeper into the castle. Fear of trials and tribulations is greatly moderated, because our faith, through direct experience, is now unshakeable and unmoveable.

Teresa counsels us on the prayer experiences of this mansion, reminding us that this is only the early beginnings of true mystical experience. The sense of virtue, of thinking and acting righteously, even in our smallest deeds becomes more imperative. We must trust, discern and surrender on the increasingly subtle, invisible and imperceptible spiritual levels.

Father Sophrony, an Orthodox monk who was a disciple of St Silouan of Mount Athos, describes this particular spiritual threshold:

> I once read a newspaper account of an engineer testing the jet engine of a plane who had carelessly stepped into the air stream, which caught and lifted him high off the ground. Seeing what had happened, his assistant quickly switched off the engine. The mechanic fell to the ground, dead.
>
> Something similar happens to the man of prayer; after being caught up into another sphere he returns to earth 'dead' to fleshly interests and worldly gains. He will not seek any career. He will not be too upset if he is rejected, nor will he be elated by praise. He forgets the past, does not cling to the present or worry about his earthly future.
>
> A new life full of Light has opened before him and in him. The infantile distractions that occupy the vast majority of people cease to interest him. And if we judge the quality of life, not by the quantity of pleasurable, psychophysical sensations, but by the extent of our awareness of cosmic realities, and most important of all, of the First and Last Truth, we shall understand what is hidden behind the words of Christ, 'My peace I give unto you'.[7]

NOTES: FOURTH MANSION

1. Melloni, J. *op.cit*, p.21
2. Sophrony (Sakarov) Archimandrite, *The Monk of Mount Athos*, St Vladimir's Seminary Press, Crestwood, New York, 1973, pp.96-97
3. Ware, K. *op.cit*. p.107
4. Sophrony, *op.cit*. pp.76-77
5. Ware, K. *op.cit*. p.95
6. Ibid, p.95
7. Sophrony (Sakarov) Archimandrite, *We Shall See Him as He Is*, Stavropegic Monastery of St John the Baptist, Essex, 1988, p.68.

THE FIFTH MANSION

Betrothed to Christ

Oh, my sisters, how shall I describe the riches, treasures, and joys contained in the fifth mansions! Would it not be better to say nothing about them? They are impossible to depict, nor can the mind conceive, nor any comparisons portray them, all earthly things being too vile to serve the purpose. Send me, O my Lord, light from heaven that I may give some to these Thy Servants.

St Teresa, Fifth Mansion

FRAGMENTS OF HEAVEN

From this point in the text – from the fifth dwelling place to the end of the text – Teresa is concerned with describing the perils and delights of union of the soul with God. She does not attempt to explain the spiritual treasures in these dwelling places, as human reasoning or comprehension cannot understand what is now happening. The fifth mansion has many levels, which represent different degrees of the manifold supernatural gifts that God is giving to the soul.

She is clear that it is not necessary to experience every level within this dwelling place – for some, it will be enough to 'stand at the front door', so to speak, and others will be content to be aware of some of the spiritual delights of this mansion. God shows His Mercy and showers His Gifts to different pilgrims in different ways, according to how we are praying, loving and working to become more Christ-like in all we do, think and feel.

She notes that most of the religious people she had known during her lifetime had 'at least gained some admittance to these rooms', and reiterates the central calling and vocation of the Carmelites which is to prayer and contemplation. Of course, her reform of the Order was founded on a return to the basic spiritual principles and practice of the early days of the founding of the order in the Holy Land:

> **All who wear the holy habit of the Carmelites are called to prayer and contemplation. This was the object of our Order, to this lineage we belong. Our holy fathers of Mount Carmel sought in perfect solitude and utter contempt of the world this treasure, this precious pearl, of which we speak, and we are their descendants. How little do most of us care to prepare our souls, that our Lord may reveal this jewel to us!**
> (V, Chapter 1, 2)

It is interesting that she begins to describe this deeper

spiritual dwelling place by referring to the early foundations of her religious order, the Carmelites. Mount Carmel, near Haifa in Israel, has been a sacred mountain for thousands of years and is best known as the location of the acts of Elijah, who is regarded as the greatest and holiest of the prophets of the Old Testament.

The Order was founded in the twelfth century during the period of the crusades, when a group of Latin crusaders established themselves on Mount Carmel aiming to live the eremitical life as hermits and ascetics in the grottoes of the sacred mountain, following in the ancient Elijan tradition.

Carmel is also known as the mountain of Mary. The attributes of beauty and sanctity, typical of Carmel, converge, through the comments of the Fathers of the Church and ecclesiastical writers, in reverence for the Mother of God on the mountain. Even from earliest times, churches dedicated to the Virgin Mary existed on Carmel.

This has been a constant factor in the tradition and consciousness of the Carmelite Order – that from the time of Elijah there has existed an uninterrupted series of religious followers perpetuating the presence of the prophet on Mount Carmel, even up to present times.[1]

These early hermits left almost nothing in the way of written records, and when history first took notice of them in the early 1200s, they were already a functioning community. The earliest recorded communication from the Carmelites themselves is preserved in the opening lines of their constitutions of 1281, and possibly dates back as early as the 1230s.

This response was to be given by members of the order when questioned about their heritage, particularly on returning to Europe:

> We declare, bearing testimony to the truth, that from the time when the prophets Elijah and Elisha dwelt devoutly on Mount Carmel, holy Fathers both of the Old and the New Testament, whom the contemplation of heavenly things drew

to the solitude of the same mountain, have without doubt
led praiseworthy lives there by the fountain of Elijah in holy
penitence unceasingly and successfully maintained.[2]

This is the ancient religious Carmelite tradition which
Teresa felt called by God to reform – to return to its
essential spiritual roots of the centrality of prayer and
contemplation. What Teresa refers to as: **'this precious
pearl… some foretaste of heaven [which] may be had on
earth'** (V, Chapter 1, 2), is the spiritual treasure which has
been long revered and sought after by those who love God
and seek to be wedded to Him. Teresa definitely felt
herself to be the heir to a spiritual patrimony and responsible
for the transmission of its values.

The significance of this connection with Carmel is not
primarily geographical or historical. Carmel, for Teresa, is
a family. Above all it represents the people who lived on
the biblical mountain of Elijah and who now form the
choir of the saints of the Carmelite Order in glory. She
writes in the *Book of Foundations*: 'How many saints have
we in heaven that wore this habit?'[3]

The remembrance of the saints of Carmel is a motive of
pride and joy, and a definite stimulus towards the mystical
journey. Elsewhere in the *Book of Foundations* one of her
poems expresses the desire to journey together towards the
Mount of Glory as an image of the interior pilgrimage
towards the ascent of Mount Carmel – 'Let us journey on
to heaven, nuns of Carmel.'[3]

In this dwelling place, she describes the deepening prayer
of quiet which is becoming a prayer of union. She is
adamant that if we seek to purchase these spiritual treasures,
we cannot hold anything back from Him:

> **He will have it all; in proportion to what you know you have
> given will your reward be great or small.** (V, Chapter 1, 3)

This is a deeper and more difficult level of surrender and
abandonment to God's will and plan for our lives. The
pilgrim is now beginning to enjoy fragments of heaven

while living on earth. Here, the soul is beginning to undergo a deeper state of interior spiritual transformation, a time of betrothal of the soul to Christ. Teresa explains that in this increasing state of spiritual absorption is the beginning of the prayer of union, where the soul is becoming betrothed before marriage.

She describes the soul in the prayer of union as being:

> asleep, fast asleep, as regards the world and itself; in fact, during the short time this state lasts it is deprived of all feeling whatever, being unable to think on any subject, even if it wished. No effort is needed here to suspend the thoughts, if the soul can love – it knows not how, nor whom it loves, nor what it desires.
>
> In fact, it has died entirely to this world, to live more truly than ever in God. This is a delicious death, for the soul is deprived of the faculties it exercised while in the body; delicious because it seems to have left its mortal covering, to abide more entirely in God. (V, Chapter 1, 3)

The soul can be, more often than not, doubtful and even confused as to what is actually happening until we gain more experience, and develop more subtle spiritual discernment about these deeper mystical states of absorption and infusion by the Holy Spirit. Questions constantly assail the mind – is it only over-active imagination, is it the senses gone wild, is it only sleep, am I deceiving myself? The whole area of careful and experienced discernment is critical at these stages.

Teresa tells us that the prayer of union in the fifth mansion cannot be imagined, manipulated or manufactured:

> The mind feels a thousand misgivings, and well for it that it should, because, as I said, nature may sometimes deceive us in this case. Although there is little chance of the poisonous reptiles entering here, yet agile little lizards will try to slip in, though they can do no har... these are the trivial fancies of the imagination.
>
> However active these small lizards may be, they cannot enter the fifth mansion, for neither the imagination, the understanding, nor the memory has power to hinder the graces bestowed on it.

I dare venture to assert that, if this is genuine union with God, the devil cannot interfere nor do any harm, for His Majesty is so joined and united with the essence of the soul, that the evil one dare not approach, or nor can he even understand this mystery. (V, Chapter 1, 5, 6)

Our mental faculties are becoming passive and quiescent, as if corpse-like, in order to perceive and be infused by Divine Love and magnetised by the Holy Spirit. The depth of spiritual joy, of awe and bewilderment, of being absorbed in the truly numinous sense of God and creation, of the Holy Spirit of God incarnating into our heart, is difficult to communicate:

These heavenly consolations are above all earthly joys, pleasure, and satisfaction. As great a difference exists between their origin and that of worldly pleasures as between their opposite effects, as you know by experience… the one seems only to touch the surface of the body, while the other penetrates to the very marrow. (V, Chapter 1, 6, 7)

During this time of increasing absorption and union in prayer there can be such a sense of profound stillness that the body is scarcely moving. The distractions of ordinary consciousness – thoughts, memories and imagination – cannot disturb the profound inner silence.

The distinctive prayer of the fifth mansion is a brief spell of increasing absorption in God. An extraordinary experience of joy can be felt, combined with a desire for complete submission to His will for our life. We are slowly becoming softer, more malleable, more consenting, much more peaceful in the deepening rest of His Presence and Light.

How do we know if the prayer of union is genuine or not? How do we know we are not being deluded? In fact, we don't know at the time of the ecstasy or rapture, but we can see and feel it more and more afterwards when we return to our ordinary state:

God then deprives the soul of all its senses that He may the better imprint in it true wisdom; it neither sees, hears, or

understands anything while this state lasts, which is never more than a very brief time; it appears to the soul to be much shorter than it really is.

God visits the soul in a manner which prevents its doubting, on returning to itself, that it dwelt in Him, and that He was within it, and so firmly is it convinced of this truth, that although years may pass before this favour recurs, the soul can never forget it nor doubt the fact... the conviction felt by the soul is the main point. (V, Chapter 1, 8)

We know that the prayer of union is genuine, not because of the clarity of the spiritual vision or experience that the soul might have had, but because of the absolute certainty that remains afterwards. This can only be the case if there has been direct experience of, and absorption in, God. God is placing Himself in the innermost centre of our heart, and when we return to our normal state there is no way we can doubt that it was actually God acting within our soul.

Our faith is deepening and becoming ever more alive, as we know the certainty of God's infusion in our hearts. From a human perspective we can still be confused, disorientated, or overawed, as the deeper sense of the Holy allows us to be more wholly human. The power and presence of God's Love and Radiance are being so impressed on the interior of the soul, so implanted within, that it can never be erased or forgotten. This is the beginning of His Betrothal to the soul.

The memory and experience of the Taste, the Sight and the Sound of the Holy Spirit is unmistakable. Teresa is clear that, at this stage, the conviction of God's Presence, Love and Glory does not depend on anything that is corporeal or material.

She wonders how it is possible to have such a conviction of the indwelling of God in the depths of our soul, how can we see and know these things if we are incapable of sight and hearing? She says that she doesn't know how this is possible, but it is '**the certitude which remains in the heart, which God alone gives**' (V, Chapter 1, 9).

She is very clear that if there is not the certainty that 'the soul dwelt in Him, and that He was within it', if there is not that unshakeable knowledge that God is in all things by His Presence and Power, then she would query and test the validity of such spiritual experience.

Teresa believes that, in cases where this certainty is absent, what has been experienced is not a union of the soul with God, but only a union with one of the faculties of the soul. Either that or what has been received is one of the many other graces and favours which God can grant.

She is clear that in these deeper dwelling places, the soul is more and more asleep to things of the world and is abandoning itself more and more to God, Who, for the time being, is taking complete possession of it. We cannot enter these deeper realms of the heart and soul by any of our own efforts:

> In all such matters we must not seek to know how things happened; our understanding could not grasp them, therefore why trouble ourselves on the subject? It is enough to know that it is He, the all-powerful God, Who has performed the work. We can do nothing on our part to gain this favour; it comes from God alone; therefore let us not strive to understand it. (V, Chapter 1, 9)

In the Old Testament Song of Songs, one of the most powerful love poems ever written, Teresa finds two verses that refer to this dwelling place and the spiritual espousals which are preparing the soul for union: 'Draw me, we will run after thee: the king hath brought me into his chambers: we will be glad and rejoice in thee, we will remember thy love more than wine: the upright love thee' (Song 1:4 KJV) and 'He brought me to the banqueting house, and his banner over me was love' (Song 2:4 KJV).

John of the Cross also makes use of the metaphor of the wine cellar in his mystical poem *The Spiritual Canticle* written in the 1580s. It is probably one of the greatest contemplative love poems in Christian literature. In lyric verse, John tells of the loving exchange that takes place, in all its richness and diversity, between the soul and Christ, the Bridegroom.

In this section of the poem (Stanzas 26 and 27), John writes:

> In the inner wine cellar,
> I drank of my Beloved, and when I went abroad
> Through all this valley
> I no longer knew anything,
> And lost the herd which I was following.
>
> There He gave me His breast;
> There He taught me sweet and living knowledge;
> And I gave myself to Him,
> Keeping nothing back;
> There I promised to be His bride.
>
> *Spiritual Canticle*, 26-27[4]

It is the Holy Spirit who now pervades the soul with wisdom, penetrating to the innermost 'wine cellar' of her being. For John, the image of the wine cellar represents the last and most intimate degree of love in which the soul can be placed in this life. Here, John says that 'God is recollecting the soul in the intimacy of His Love' and that, accordingly, this degree of love, the inner wine cellar, is the most interior.[5]

He also points out that at this stage, even though 'the soul is always in this sublime state of spiritual marriage once God has placed her in it, the faculties are not always in actual union, although the substance is, where God is recollecting the soul in one of these actual unions in the intimacy of His love.'[6]

Here, John is emphasising another principle of spiritual growth – that the wisdom of God is not acquired through natural learning processes, but through infusion of His Love into our heart – 'Naturally, it is impossible to love without first understanding what is loved, but super-naturally, God can easily infuse and increase love without the infusion or increase of particular knowledge. By means of this faith, God infuses charity in them, and augments this charity and its act, which means greater love, although their knowledge is not increased. Thus the will can drink love without the intellect again drinking knowledge.'[7]

John further explains, in his commentary on Stanza 27, that the 'Bride is telling of the mutual surrender made in this spiritual espousal between the soul and God, saying that in that interior wine cellar of love, they are joined by the communication He has made of Himself to her, by freely offering the soul the breast of His love.' John tells us that that is where God is now 'teaching her wisdom and secrets, and by the complete surrender she has made of herself to Him, she is keeping nothing back for herself nor for any other, promising to be His forever.'[8]

Teresa equates the prayer of union with the metaphor of the wine cellar, based on the book of the Song of Songs. She says that it is the beginning of the betrothal of the soul to God, the beginning of the union of human and divine will. She emphasises that it is not possible to enter these more interior dwelling places by personal effort, but only by the grace of God, effortlessly:

> **I think the prayer of union is the 'cellar' in which our Lord places us, when and how he chooses, but we cannot enter it through any effort of our own. His Majesty alone can bring us there and come into the centre of our souls.**
>
> **In order to declare His wondrous works more clearly, He will leave us no share in them except complete conformity of our wills to His, and abandonment of all things; He does not require the faculties or senses to open the door to Him; they are all asleep.**
>
> **He enters the innermost depths of our souls without a door, as He entered the room where the disciples sat, saying '*Pax vobis*' and as he emerged from the sepulchre without removing the stone that closed the entrance.** (V, Chapter 1, 10)

Some of the Orthodox mystics and saints have described this stage as the true magnetisation or gravitation towards God, where we are becoming wholeheartedly turned towards Him. St Theophan the Recluse, in the nineteenth century, talked of spiritual betrothal in terms of magnetisation and gravitation to God:

> It is only clear that God is touching us when we experience this living aspiration; when our spirit turns its back on everything else and is fixed on Him and carried away. At first, this will not happen; the zealous person is still turned wholly to himself. Even though he has 'decided' for God, this is only in his mind.
>
> The Lord does not yet let Himself be tasted, nor is the man yet capable of it, being impure. All he can do is to serve God without tasting Him, so to speak. Then as his heart begins to be purified and set right, he begins to feel the sweetness of a life pleasing to God, so that he begins to walk in His ways gladly and with love. Then the soul starts to withdraw from everything else as from the cold, and to gravitate towards God, Who warms it.
>
> This principle of gravitation is implanted in the fervent soul by divine grace. By its inspiration and guidance the attraction grows in natural progression, inwardly nourished even without the knowledge of the person concerned. The sign of this birth is that where the spirit in someone previously acted compulsively, it now begins to abide in God's presence willingly and quietly without strain, with feelings of reverence, fear and joy.
>
> Once the spirit was cramped within him, but now it is settled and stays there permanently. Now it is bliss for him to be alone with God, away from others and oblivious of external things. He acquires the kingdom of God within himself, which is peace and joy in the Holy Spirit. This immersion in God is called 'silence of the mind' or 'rapture in God'. It may be very fleeting at first, but the ultimate aim is that in time it should become constant.[9]

THE SILKWORM AND THE BUTTERFLY

The fifth dwelling place is explicitly associated by Teresa with the New Testament text, Colossians 3:3 – 'You have died and your life is hid with Christ in God', hiddenness being the keynote. We have reached the stage where we have done everything we could on our own to grow spiritually and now find it impossible to make any more progress, having reached the limits of our own efforts.

Interior transformation, which has begun in the fourth mansion, continues in this dwelling place as we prepare ourselves for a deeper abandonment to God's mysterious action:

> **Although we can take no active part in this work of God within us, yet we may do much to prepare ourselves to receive this grace.** (V, Chapter 2, 1)

Teresa amplifies her understanding of the prayer of union by using the metaphor of the transformation of silkworms into butterflies to represent the interior change from a natural ordinary condition into something supernatural, extra-ordinary, by the action of the Holy Spirit. She is quite taken by this metaphor and goes to some length to make this analogy with the contemplative soul.

The silkworm feeds off the natural world of mulberry leaves (which is the general help given to us all by God), and when full grown it has the capacity to transform this very natural substance into silk. Enclosed within the darkness of a temporarily constructed cocoon it spins this rather extraordinary substance of silk out of sight of the world. The worm itself is released at the end of its work, no longer the same species, but miraculously transformed into another species entirely – the butterfly.

The analogy to the contemplative soul being transformed by the Love of God is clear. Our deepening relationship with God is the container, or cocoon, for transformation:

> **The silkworm symbolises the soul which begins to live when, kindled by the Holy Spirit, it commences using the ordinary aids given by God to all, and applies the remedies left by Him in His Church… then it comes to life and continues nourishing itself on this food and on devout meditation until it has attained full vigour… When the silkworm is full grown, it begins to spin silk and to build the house where it must die.**

> **By this house, when speaking of the soul, I mean Christ…
> our life is hid in Christ, or in God (which means the same
> thing), or that Christ is our life. He is in the prayer of
> union… He is our home.** (V, Chapter 2, 3, 4)

The silkworm represents our soul on her spiritual journey
in the first three mansions. There has been much growth
and development through all of our own efforts – our
prayer, longing, waiting and stillness have formed the dark
cocoon that has been spun around our own self. The
cocoon represents our life in Christ which has been slowly
building and in the fourth dwelling place our life has
become hidden with Christ in God.

By emptying ourselves and eliminating the parts of
ourselves that detract from becoming immersed in the
Love of God and adding all of that which enhances His
Love in our life, we are slowly building the presence of
God around us. Here, the soul is in the process of spiritual
metamorphosis, becoming so filled with Christ, that she
emerges like the butterfly, as the transformed soul, fragile
and restless, but beautiful as she was not before.

By using this profound metaphor, Teresa is also referring
to how open the soul is now becoming, filling with the
radiation of the Light and Presence of Christ. I came to
understand this much more deeply, when, at the end of a
recent pilgrimage to the important places in Spain related
to the lives of Teresa and John, I had a dream. During and
after the trip, I had the sense of His light, heat, love and
warmth much more strongly within my heart and being,
and was much more at rest, in solitude, in God.

In the dream I saw clearly the stained glass, in my
private home, of Christ enthroned in Glory. When I
began to focus on the figure of Christ, I became aware of
a bird, or large butterfly that was hovering in front of
the figure. What was so strange is that I could see the bird
very clearly, but it was completely transparent, and I could
see right through the bird to Christ in Glory shining
behind it.

Teresa was constantly impatient with her nuns about deepening their surrender and abandonment to God:

> **Hasten over your work and build this little cocoon. Let us renounce self-love and self-will, care for nothing earthly, do penance, pray, mortify ourselves, be obedient, and perform all the other good works of which you know.**
>
> **Act up to your light; you have been taught your duties. Die! Die! As the silkworm does when it has fulfilled the office of its creation, and you will see God and be immersed in His greatness, as the little silkworm is enveloped in its cocoon. Understand that when I say 'you will see God', I mean in the manner described in which He manifests Himself in this kind of union.** (V, Chapter 2, 5)

The butterfly feels more and more of a stranger to the things of the earth, and constantly seeks new resting places. She cannot regress or return to her former natural state. Internal attachments and identifications to family, society and material possessions are naturally falling away, without effort. The pilgrim surrenders to continual spiritual transformation:

> **All that it can do for God seems nothing to the soul compared with its desire. It no longer wonders at what the saints bore for Him, knowing by experience how our Lord aids and transforms the soul, until it no longer seems the same in character and appearance... no wonder this pretty butterfly, estranged from earthly things, seeks repose elsewhere. Where can the poor creature go? It cannot return to whence it came, for, as I told you, that is not in the soul's power, do what it will, but depends on God's pleasure.** (V, Chapter 2, 7, 8)

Once the sacred wine of intoxication with love and being loved has been tasted, the soul is dissatisfied with everything that is not of God. How can she be content any longer to crawl and be motionless in the dark cocoon now that His Light has started to irradiate her being and perception? She wants to use her newly developed wings and ascend to become His Betrothed, the new creation in Christ. She wants to leave the gravity of the earth and consummate her love for God.

Teresa writes that the purpose of the different trials and suffering, which can seem to increase and intensify in these more interior dwelling places, is to enable us to more deeply submit to His impression on the soul:

> Have you not heard how the Bride says that God 'brought her into the cellar of wine and set in order charity in her'? This is what happens here. The soul has so entirely yielded itself into His hands and is so subdued by love for Him, that it knows or cares for nothing but that God should dispose of it according to His will. I believe that He only bestows this grace on those He takes entirely for His own.
>
> He desires that without knowing how, the spirit should come forth stamped with His seal, for indeed it does no more than does the wax when impressed with the signet. It does not mould itself, but need only be in a fit condition – soft and pliable; even then it does not soften itself, but must merely remain still and submit to the impression.
>
> All is done for us by Thee, Who dost but ask us to give our wills to thee, that we may be plastic as wax in Thy hands. (V, Chapter 2, 11, 12)

The peace in the fifth mansion is very deep, but so are the trials, which may be suffered in abundance. A more intense level of pain and suffering can often occur as we are becoming much more sensitive to and aware of the effects on others of even our smallest thoughts, feelings and actions, and on how our innermost betrothed state of 'being in God' is affected by them.

Even the most insignificant action, thought or feeling which is negative, damaging, self-centred, critical or destructive can sabotage the action and work of the Holy Spirit. We are more aware of what has been unconscious, and of the effect of every thought, word, and deed on the mystical body of Christ. The pilgrim can only radiate the Love of God more and more, although we may feel even more abandoned and bereft.

LOVE UNITING TO LOVE

Teresa describes the great spiritual treasures to be found in this mansion. She is clear that such supernatural gifts are not granted to everyone, but neither are they particularly important because union with God can be achieved without experiencing them. In this mansion, the old personality is dying, in order to be reborn into a new resurrected and transfigured life and existence in Christ.

Teresa describes this process carefully:

> **Is it necessary, in order to attain to this kind of divine union, for the powers of the soul to be suspended? No; God has many ways of enriching the soul and bringing it to these mansions besides what might be called a 'short cut'.**
>
> **But, be sure of this, my daughters, in any case the silkworm must die, and it will cost you more in this way. In the former manner this death is facilitated by finding ourselves introduced into a new life; here, on the contrary, we must give ourselves the deathblow.**
>
> **I own that the work will be much harder, but then it will be of higher value, so that your reward will be greater if you come forth victorious… there is no doubt it is possible for you to attain this true union with the will of God. This is the union I have longed for all my life and that I beg our Lord to grant me; it is the most certain and the safest.**
> (V, Chapter 3, 5)

Some of the obvious effects of such transformation in the soul are her changing and developing relationships with, and deepening ability to love and be charitable towards, others. Her love and her desire to give to others in increasing capacity are some of the signs of this state. We may not be sure that we love God as fully as we can, but we certainly can be sure whether or not we love others.

We begin to desire, and feel empowered to share and express more intensively a love of truth, mercy and justice, as if Christ were standing in front of us. We increasingly want to know and reflect what is true and highest in others. Teresa is clear about the effect on our lives:

> **I think the most certain sign that we keep these two commandments is that we have a genuine love for others. We cannot know whether we love God, although there may be strong reasons for thinking so, but there can be no doubt about whether we love our neighbour or not. Be sure that**

in proportion as you advance in fraternal charity, you are increasing in your love of God. (V, Chapter 3, 8)

In these chambers of the heart, the transforming butterfly soars and spreads her wings, **'taking a higher flight'** (V, Chapter 4, 1), moving ever deeper within the heart and higher to His Light. From the outside, others can observe a greater radiance of being. The soul is finally being prepared to be united in spiritual marriage in the depths of her heart with her Beloved.

Teresa found that the closest metaphor to describe spiritual betrothal of the soul to Christ was to compare it to the preliminaries before human marriage, although she is very clear to say that the two are very different and quite unlike each other:

> **In divine union, everything is spiritual and far removed from anything corporal, all the joys our Lord gives and the mutual delight felt in it being celestial and very unlike human marriage, which it excels a thousand times. Here, all is love united to love; its operations are more pure, refined and sweet than can be described, though our Lord knows how to make the soul sensible of them.**
>
> **It resembles the preliminaries that take place when two people are contemplating a betrothal. Their suitability and willingness for the alliance are first discussed; then they may be allowed to see one another sometimes, so as to come to a decision.**
>
> **Thus it is in the spiritual espousals: when the preliminary agreement has been made, and the soul thoroughly understands what great advantages she will gain, having resolved to fulfil the will of her Spouse in all things and to do all she can to please Him, His Majesty Who knows well whether this is so in reality, wishes in return to gratify His bride. He therefore bestows this favour upon her, visits her, and draws her into His presence, as He wishes her to know Him better.** (V, Chapter 4, 2)

There are long and intimate discussions concerning what suits both partners who are deeply in love. They meet many times to learn to appreciate and more intimately know each other. It is exactly the same with the Divine

Betrothal. The marriage contract has been drawn up, and the soul is given to understand the happiness of her situation.

She is determined to do the will of her Spouse in every way. His Majesty is becoming pleased with the soul, and granting her His Mercy, desires that she should get to know Him more and more intimately. It is not possible to understand the mystery of spiritual union from any rational or human perspective – it is quite inexplicable and paradoxical to mind or the faculties.

In essence, the grace of the Holy Spirit is being given as a token of her impending betrothal, in preparation to becoming His Bride. The soul is now becoming much more intimately acquainted during the spiritual betrothal, and is so fired by the momentary intoxication of His Presence, by His Touch, that all she wants is to do anything and everything not to hinder the betrothal.

Having once been filled by His Ecstatic Touch, all else seems secondary and unimportant. Teresa goes on to say:

> There is no longer any question of deliberation, but the soul in a secret manner sees to what a Bridegroom it is betrothed; the senses and faculties could not, in a thousand years, gain the knowledge thus imparted in a very short time.
>
> The Spouse, being Who He is, leaves the soul far more deserving of completing the espousals, as we may call them; the enamoured soul in its love for Him makes every effort to prevent their being frustrated. (V, Chapter 4, 2)

The soul can be in spiritual or ethical danger at this stage because of the deeper level of temptation and purification that is occurring. In this dwelling place, the soul has set her eyes on becoming a Bride of Christ, and is beginning to have intimate spiritual relations with His Majesty, and she must remain watchful and wakeful. Spiritual testing becomes increasingly subtle and invisible. Usually no one else would be aware of it, as it occurs deep in the heart and is known only to God.

There are manifold dangers and trials that present

themselves at every stage, and there are particular temptations and difficulties in this fifth mansion. It is important to grow in caution, wakefulness and alertness, and to be under the very careful eye of a spiritual director. Teresa strongly advises us to:

> **beg God constantly in our prayers to uphold us by His hand; we should keep ever in our minds the truth that if He leaves us, most certainly we shall fall at once into the abyss, for we must never be so foolish as to trust in ourselves.**
>
> **After this, I think the greatest safeguard is to be very careful and to watch how we advance in virtue; we must notice whether we are making progress or falling back in it, especially as regards the love of our neighbour, the desire to be thought the least of all, and how we perform our ordinary, everyday duties. If we attend to this, and beg our Lord to enlighten us, we shall at once perceive our gain and loss.**
> (V, Chapter 4, 8)

God calls the heart and makes it exult; then He disappears; and then He reveals Himself again. By the test of renunciation and a more lively 'feeling' of God, a person escapes gradually from the attacks of evil: light penetrates and protects his or her nature more and more. But God refuses to provide an overwhelming proof of His Presence – if He did He would actually be destroying the very possibility of a meeting and the free offer of His love.

The more the Inaccessible shares with us, the more inaccessible He shows Himself to be. By reminding us of the distance between Him and us He keeps us from idolising the mystical state. It is spirituality not of fusion or commixture but of communion, in which the Other remains the more unknown the more He makes Himself known. This is the way into a living eternity where progress in love never comes to an end.[10]

NOTES: FIFTH MANSION

1. Giordano, Silvano, (ed). *Carmel in the Holy Land – From its beginnings to the Present Day*, Il Messaggero di Gesu Bambino, Arenzano, 1995 p.34
2. Welch, J. *The Carmelite Way*, Gracewing, UK, p.8
3. Giordano, S. *op. cit.* p.49
4. Kavanaugh, K. and Rodriguez, O. (trans), *op. cit.* p.413
5. Ibid, p.511
6. Ibid, p.407
7. Ibid, p.513
8. Ibid, p.518
9. Amis, R. *op. cit.* p.293
10. Clement, O. *op.cit.* p.191.

THE SIXTH MANSION

Becoming His Bride

The Uncreated Light is Divine Energy. Contemplation of this Light begets, first and foremost, an all absorbing feeling of the living God – an immaterial feeling of the Immaterial, an intuitive not rational perception – which transports man with irresistible force into another world, but so warily that he neither realises when it happens nor knows whether he is in or out of the body.

This supramental sensation of the living God is accompanied by a vision of light, of light essentially different from physical light. Man himself then abides in light, becomes assimilated with the light, which he contemplates, and is spiritualised by it. He then neither sees nor feels his own materiality, or the materiality of the world.

Archimandrite Sophrony, *The Monk of Mount Athos*[1]

TESTS AND TRIALS

The sixth dwelling place occupies nearly a third of *The Interior Castle* text, where Teresa continues to discuss interior states of prayer and the intensification of the spiritual life. She covers the nature of the suffering and the various visions, locutions and ecstasies that can occur. The sixth mansion is a time of great trials and tests, possibly worse than anything we have experienced so far.

The most important amongst the trials that can develop in response to our deepening prayer life is what has been called the dark night of the soul. Teresa takes the dangers very seriously, hence the length of this part of the text. She methodically goes through many of the new spiritual experiences the soul can receive and gives guidelines on how to deal with them, in order to discern if we are on the right path or not.

Since entering the previous mansion and experiencing the prayer of union, a sense of a renewed spiritual life is emerging as God is slowly beginning to take over. Teresa symbolises this as the emergence of the 'little butterfly'. Our old self is breaking down and falling away, together with many of our old identifications, attachments, ways of thinking, living and relating, but the new mode of existence isn't in place yet.

The soul is still in a place of spiritual transition:

> **Formerly it feared penance, now it is strong: it wanted courage to forsake relations, friends or possessions: neither its actions, its resolutions, nor separation from those it loved, could detach the soul, but rather seemed to increase its fondness. Now it finds even their rightful claims a burden, fearing contact with them, lest it should offend God. It wearies of everything, realising that no true rest can be found in creatures.** (V, Chapter 2, 7)

There is now an increasing hunger for solitude, to be alone in prayer as much as possible. The graces, the taste and vision of God, which are being given to the soul, are by now:

so deeply imprinted on the spirit that its only desire is to behold Him again... The soul is now determined to take no other Bridegroom than our Lord, but He disregards its desires for its speedy espousals, wishing that these longings should become still more vehement and that this good, which far excels all other benefits, should be purchased at some cost to itself. (VI, Chapter 1, 1, 2)

The soul is becoming betrothed to her Bridegroom in this dwelling place, and the deeper tests and trials of our love for God, and God alone, can begin with a vengeance.

Interior trials multiply and increase as the soul journeys closer to His Divine Love and Power. Teresa is explicit about her own experience of such acute sufferings, which can only be borne from the long preparation gone through already, and from being so much closer to His Knowledge and Presence, which is protecting and sustaining the soul.

One of the most painful trials is the experience of being rejected or betrayed by others – even, sometimes, by close friends or family. When it comes to the more crucial tests of real and lasting spiritual companionship, few remain steadfastly alongside.

A critical separation must be developed between true and false companions, irrespective of status, rank or external appearances. Even professed religious persons can initiate persecution and rejection, as Teresa found.

It is a painful, heart-rending experience to be personally betrayed by those who have been closest and dearest. The journey towards the heart of our Beloved can often feel very lonely and perilous. Teresa became the subject of increasing attacks and gossip as it grew clear that she was being called to reform the Carmelite Order.

There can also be general ridicule and anything from minor sabotage to out-and-out persecution. In Teresa's experience:

Persons she thought were her friends desert her, making the most bitter remarks of all. They take it much to heart that her soul is ruined, that she is manifestly deluded, that it is all the devil's work, that she will share the fate of

so-and-so, who was lost through him, and she is leading virtue astray. (VI, Chapter 1, 5)

The worst fears of others can be aroused, as the collective shadow and resistance to the things of God and the deeper spiritual life can be activated. The experiences of the mystic can stir the strongest irrational anxiety and panic in many. The saints and those who love Him must endure these things, both inwardly and outwardly, as mirror reflections of the soul's resistance to surrendering to Him.

Teresa is frank about her own experience:

The worst of it is, these troubles do not blow over, but last all her life, for one person warns the other to have nothing to do with people of her kind! You will say that, on the other hand, some speak in her favour. Oh, my daughters, how few think well of her in comparison with the many who hate her! (VI, Chapter 1, 6)

However, such experiences, shocking and painful though they are at first, can be opportunities to learn greater spiritual discrimination, in order to become indifferent to suffering or praise.

Teresa explains that it is precisely the rejection, envy and antipathy which, when aroused so strongly in others, can serve to demonstrate how people can be quite unconscious of what they are saying, speaking of good and evil in the same breath. So the pilgrim is able to develop more subtle spiritual discernment as to the intent and motivation behind such attacks and to learn to attach no more importance to one reaction than to another.

Also, whatever is happening in the kernel of the heart belongs to God and is being returned to Him. The Holy Spirit is giving the soul greater illumination: '**causing her to take a far higher flight**' (VI Chapter 2, 1). These are His free gifts which He is giving the soul, to enable her to become more oblivious to her personal self, in order to be able to praise God for His graces.

Teresa warns that it is the same, if not worse, if the soul is showered with adulation, praise or personal worship.

This can cause even more havoc if it is actually believed to be true, or if there is any personal identification with such praise or worship. It can be a dangerous temptation, as inflation, fanaticism and power seeking can be fuelled.

The pilgrim at this stage needs to become totally objective and disidentified, praise and contempt commanding an equally detached response. Tests and temptations can always be turned around and used as opportunities for spiritual growth.

Greater trials of a more personal and physical kind can be experienced, in the form of serious illness and disease. No one knew this better than Teresa. For most of her life, she experienced great physical pain after the paralysis resulting from her attack of catalepsy in her twenties.

Although her health improved to some degree in later life, she remained weak:

> **Our Lord now usually sends severe bodily infirmity. This is a far heavier cross, especially if acute pain is felt; if this be violent, I think it is the hardest of earthly trials. I speak of exterior trials, but corporal pains, if of the worst kind, enter the interior of our being also, affecting both spirit and body, so that the soul, in its anguish, knows not what to do with itself, and would far rather meet death at once by some quick martyrdom than suffer thus.**
>
> **However, these paroxysms do not last long, for God never sends us more than we can bear, and always gives us patience first.** (VI, Chapter 1, 13)

Other trials include the agonising experience of the dark night of the soul, of being in an arid lonely wilderness, feeling completely cut off from everyone and everything, where all is blackened and any inner illumination gone. The soul can feel even more lost and confused than ever, completely unable to understand or comprehend how this can be after all that has gone before.

It is as if, for all the Touch of His Presence that we have been blessed with, the anguish of His Absence becomes ever more acute. Teresa describes her own suffering:

> What can the poor soul do if such trial lasts for many days? Prayer makes no difference as far as comforting the heart, which no consolation can enter, nor can the mind even grasp the meaning of the words of vocal prayer; mental prayer is out of the question at such a time, since the faculties are unequal to it.
>
> Solitude harms the soul, yet society or conversation is a fresh torment. Strive as the sufferer may to hide it, she is so wearied and out of sorts with all around that she cannot but manifest her condition. How can the soul possibly tell what ails it? Its pains are indescribable; it is wrought with nameless anguish and spiritual suffering.
>
> The best remedy for these crosses – I do not mean for gaining deliverance from them, for I know of nothing that will do that, but for enabling one to bear them – is to perform external works of charity and to trust in the mercy of God, which never fails those who hope in Him. (VI, Chapter I, 23, 24)

On the journey, these dark nights are not merely loss of contact with the visible and intelligible but can be extreme trials of anguish and despair. We identify ourselves with the passion and journey of Christ in his agony, when He not only cried, with a loud voice *'E'lo-i, E'lo-i, lama sabachtha'ni?* which means, 'My God, my God, why hast thou forsaken me?' (Mk 15; 34 RSV), but also 'Father, into thy hands I commit my spirit!' (Lk 23; 46 RSV).

Trials such as these are the crucible of humility, the exodus into the desert that is *faith alone*. Each of them is the introduction to a consolation – that is, to a perceptible presence of the Consoler, of the Holy Spirit – and the greater the nakedness in which one welcomes Him, the greater the consolation received.

The practical aspect of the life in Christ conceals the most complex mystery in human life. Two titanic forces, linked together in man, create an immense and unbreakable tug-of-war with the essence of our heart and being in the middle. Two loves, standing in opposition and turned towards opposite poles, form the motive power of these two forces; love towards God and love of this world.

In this uninterrupted tug-of-war, trials and temptations are constantly present, and none of us remain untouched by the struggle with them. They serve to habituate us to the correct stance in relationship to God, which is the dependence of all things upon the watchful eye of the Divine wisdom and justice.

DARK NIGHT OF THE SPIRIT

The first purgation or night is bitter and terrible to the senses. But nothing can be compared to the second, for it is horrible and frightful to the spirit.

If God intends to lead the soul on, He does not put it in this dark night of spirit immediately after its going out from the aridities and trials of the first purgation and night of the sense... In this new state, as one liberated from a cramped prison cell, the soul goes about the things of God with much more freedom and satisfaction of spirit and with more abundant interior delight than it did in the beginning before entering the night of the sense... Nonetheless, since the purgation of the soul is not complete, certain needs, aridities, darkness's and conflicts are felt. These are sometimes far more intense than those of the past and are like omens or messengers of the coming night of the spirit. These morsels of dark contemlation though, are never as intense as is that frightful night of contemplation, in which God places the soul purposely in order to bring it to divine union.

Thus, to reach union, the soul must enter the second night of the spirit. In this night, both the sensory and spiritual parts are despoiled of all these apprehensions and delights, and the soul is made to walk in dark and pure faith, which is the proper and adequate means to divine union.

(John of the Cross, *Dark Night*, II, Chapter 1, 2)

In John's imagery, the night of the spirit – midnight in the journey of faith – is the most intense phase of darkness. All our support systems are totally inadequate, and only our naked faith can sustain us during this time, where our trust in God, and God alone, is tested and tried to its utmost limits. This midwinter, or midnight, of the soul is a period of utter emptiness and aridity, which can be experienced as a complete disinterest in all things spiritual, without having any of the usual pleasures of ordinary life.

This phase or state can be drastic and devastating. The very ground of our being is being purified. Of those who have come through it John writes, without exaggeration, 'These are the ones who go down into hell alive.' In this 'purgatory' the soul is becoming detached from all its last attachments and identifications, which is the perceptible and spiritual 'experience' of the Presence of God. It is now forced to abandon the one support that sustained it through all the hardships and purgation of the ascent of Carmel. The *experience* of God's love must make room for God alone.

For that experience is not God and erects a screen between the soul and God's *naked* Presence. The last traces of the 'witness', the 'spectator', the self-referential human 'I' are now dying, being annihilated and utterly transformed, in order for the splendour of the resurrected and transfigured Christ and the glory of His Light and Divine Love to be revealed.

In illumination, the soul begins to 'know', become 'conscious of' and 'merge with' the mysteries of His Kingdom. Now, through traversing the dark night, the soul is being prepared to *become one* with the Love and Light of God, through our love and devotion to Christ, our Bridegroom. This is a vast, vast step, and a step that the soul, on its own, is totally unable to take. After knowing and merging with God in the earlier mansions, this dark abyss is traversed in order to wholly *become one with Him* in divine union.

It is a crucifixion of the self – a willing dying 'on the cross', an experiencing of all the torments of Gethsemane and Calvary, all the feelings of persecution, utter illusionless isolation and sense of abandonment by God as the necessary preparation for the revelation of the Resurrection. The self that comes forth from the night is no longer a 'separated' self, but a 'new person in Christ', transfigured and transmuted in intimate union with the source of Love.

The dark night can be a truly terrifying experience, and when it is the real thing it will stretch the pilgrim to the very limits of human comprehension. The experience usually brings a sense of ultimate crisis – of collapse of all hope, of all meaning in life. It is accompanied by a sense of dryness in all things religious and an inability to find delight in prayer and contemplation.

Only supreme love and faith can take the soul through this horrifying experience. The starved and tortured self has to learn to accept lovelessness for the sake of love, nothingness for the sake of the fullness in which all things ultimately come to rest, and has to profoundly accept annihilation without the security of any sure promise of life.

As Evelyn Underhill explains:

> So long as the subject still feels himself to be 'somewhat', he has not yet annihilated selfhood and come to that ground where his being can be united with the being of God... only when he learns to cease thinking of himself at all, in however deprecatory a sense, when he abolishes even such selfhood as lies in a desire for the sensible presence of God, will harmony be attained.
>
> This is the 'naughting of the soul'... Here, as in purgation, the condition of access to higher levels of vitality is a death; a deprivation, a detachment, a clearing of the ground. Poverty leaps to the Cross; and finds there an utter desolation without promise of spiritual reward. The satisfactions of the spirit must now go the same way as the satisfactions of the senses. Even the power of voluntary sacrifice and self-discipline is taken away. A dreadful ennui, a dull helplessness, takes its place.[2]

This condition of godlessness is essentially distinct from atheism only by it's feeling of utter bereavement and lasting faith, which may persist for years. It may be accompanied by obsessions of profanity, temptations to despair, feelings of total rejection. The pilgrim finds himself or herself suspended between heaven and earth without gaining access to either one.

The worldly life holds no more attraction, nor can even a minimum of past spiritual fervour be recovered. All that once filled the soul with happiness has lost its meaning and taste; God as well as the world. Nor has anything replaced it. Yet deep down we are able to retain the conviction that God is still there, through pure faith.[3]

John tells us what happens in this destruction of the self:

> Wishing to strip them in fact of this old man and clothe them with the new which is created according to God in the newness of sense… God divests the faculties, affections, and senses, both spiritual and sensory, interior and exterior. He leaves the intellect in darkness, the will in aridity, the memory in emptiness and the affections in supreme affliction, bitterness and anguish, by depriving the soul of the feeling and satisfaction it previously obtained from spiritual blessings.
>
> For this privation is one of the conditions required that the spiritual form, which is the union of love, may be introduced in the spirit and united with it. The Lord works all of this in the soul by means of a pure and dark contemplation. (*Dark Night*, II, 3:3)

John goes on to detail the different kinds of afflictions, and the depth of absorption that occurs in the dark night:

> Since the divine extreme strikes in order to renew the soul and divinise it by stripping it of the habitual affections and properties of the old man to which it is strongly united, attached and conformed, it so disentangles and dissolves the spiritual substance – absorbing it in a profound darkness – that the soul at the sight of its miseries feels that it is melting away and being undone by a cruel spiritual death; it feels as if it were swallowed by a beast and being digested in the dark belly, and it suffers an anguish comparable to Jonah's when in the belly of the whale.
>
> It is fitting that the soul be in this sepulchre of dark death in order that it attain this spiritual resurrection for which it hopes.' (*Dark Night*, II, 6:1)

The dark night is the experience that will finally open us to eternal life. Our extreme suffering is able to be profoundly valued as central and essential to our relationship with God. This act of complete surrender gives the soul a footing in Eternity.

It is the most dramatic and devastating of the spiritual manifestations of the sixth mansion – yet if the mystics are to be believed, it is the greatest gift that God can bestow on us, although it won't seem like a gift at the time. It is His special way of preparing us for eternal life with Him alone.

Why does God allow the dark night to happen? Iain Matthew, in his book *The Impact of God* says:

> If night first tells us that there is somewhere to go, it also announces that we cannot get there on our own. 'Night' presents suffering, not as the only place, but as a privileged place of God's inflow. In it, love not only comes; love also opens a space for its coming. That is the God-content of pain – it has power to unlock us at the point we cannot unlock ourselves... Healing comes particularly in situations that take us out of our own control, in the kind of pain that is bewildering.

Teresa writes of the bewildering pain of the sixth dwelling place:

> **Her understanding being too obscured to discern the truth, she believes all that the imagination, which has now the upper hand, puts before her mind, besides crediting the falsehoods suggested to her by the devil, whom doubtless our Lord gives leave to tempt her.**
>
> **The evil spirit even tries to make her think God has rejected her. Many are the trials which assault this soul, causing an internal anguish so painful and so intolerable that I can compare it to nothing save that suffered by the lost in hell, for no comfort can be found in this tempest of trouble.** (VI, Chapter 1, 18)

LOCUTIONS, ECSTASY AND RAPTURE

Teresa is known for her extreme and unusual spiritual experiences that she records in these chapters in the sixth dwelling place. She writes about the various ways by which God is arousing, or waking the soul, through different types of visions, locutions, wordless prayer, 'flight of the spirit' and levitations. It is difficult for those with no experience of such mystical states to make sense of them.

When God is arousing the soul through *locutions,* He is doing this:

> **by means of words addressed to the soul in many different ways; sometimes they appear to come from without, at other times from the inner depths of the soul, or again, from its superior part, while other speeches are so exterior as to be heard by the ears like a real voice.** (VI, Chapter 3, 1)

Locutions represent a voice from the deepest part of our heart, rising and emerging to give us advice, or to keep us on the spiritual track, which our conscious mind has either forgotten, repressed, mislaid or otherwise pushed away. The tests to the soul of discriminating between what is true and real, and what is false, are now becoming ever more critical, interior and knife-edged on this narrow road.

Here, we have to have a spiritual guide or teacher to help us with spiritual discernment. Teresa gives good, solid advice and guidance by which to distinguish and discriminate in such subtle spiritual matters. She knows that such words addressed to the soul may come either from God, the devil or the imagination.

How can we discern the difference? As with all supernatural phenomena, she suggests that at the beginning it is better to '**resist these communications**', for '**if they come from God this is the best way of obtaining more, for when they are discouraged, they increase**' (VI, Chapter 3, 3).

If they continue, she suggests some guidelines by which we can distinguish genuine locutions from false ones. She says it is irrelevant whether we perceive them as coming from inside, outside or elsewhere. What matters is the effect they are having on our lives and how we are dealing with them.

The main characteristics of true locutions are their strength, their sincerity, and the ability of the message to bring a sense of relief, peace and comfort:

> **The first and the truest is the power and the authority they carry with them... for example, a soul is suffering all the sorry and disquiet I have described, the mind is darkened and dry; but it is set at peace, freed from all trouble and filled with light, merely by hearing the words 'Be not troubled'... or she hears a single sentence which says 'It is I, be not afraid' and is at once freed from all fears and filled with consolation.** (VI, Chapter 3, 7, 8)

If the experience is truly from God, it carries a weight of power and authority in both word and action which is unmistakable. The direct power granted by the Holy Spirit changes and lifts our state of being spontaneously and unforgettably, like a bolt of light that penetrates anxiety, fear, or confusion.

If the words and spiritual contact truly come from God, then their effects are unmistakable. A great calm begins to flood the soul and we have the sense of being carried over an abyss.

The power and authority of the Spirit has such force and conviction that no human faculty can create it. It is outside, and above, and deep within the soul. It interpenetrates all parts, but its source is not from her. The Holy Spirit is working upon her.

These spiritual states have a particular effect on memory. The force, intensity and meaning of what is experienced in the depths of our being ensure that they are never forgotten. In essence, they are our remembrance of Him. They are imprinted, almost burnt on the soul permanently, and seem to be accessible very quickly if we turn our attention to His unforgettable imprint on our soul.

Teresa describes her increasing confidence that the source of her own experiences was God:

> These divine locutions leave us so convinced of their truth that, although their fulfilment sometimes seems utterly impossible, and we vacillate and doubt about them, there still remains in the soul a certainty of their verity which cannot be destroyed.
>
> Perhaps everything may seem to mitigate against what was heard, and years pass by, yet the spirit never loses its belief that God will make use of means unknown to men for the purpose, and that, finally, what was foretold must surely happen; as indeed it does. (VI, Chapter 3, 11)

To the human mind, the things of God seem miraculous and incredible. All the soul can do is try to remain attentive and objectively observe. Interior visions and experiences can seem terrifying, mysterious and overwhelming.

Yet we cannot forget what has been revealed. If they truly come from the Spirit of God, it is only a matter of time before they are realised. It is best to talk about such interior states only to those with whom we share intimate spiritual companionship.

If these experiences, words, visions and locutions are, in fact, products of the imagination, then what has been described is not present. If they are not truly from the Holy Spirit, they bring no lasting conviction that stands the test of authority, of time, or of what others might say about such things. More importantly, we have very little peace, comfort or interior joy as a result.

The Holy Spirit has other methods of speaking to the soul that can point to whether the words originate from God. Teresa tells us that such words can be accompanied by intellectual visions:

> God speaks to the soul in another way, by a certain intellectual vision... it takes place far within the innermost depths of the soul, which appears to hear distinctly, in a most mysterious manner, with its spiritual hearing, the words spoken to it by our Lord Himself.
>
> The way in which the spirit perceives these words, and

> **the results produced by them, convince us that they cannot
> in any way come from the devil. Their powerful after effects
> force us to admit this, and also clearly show they do not
> spring from the imagination.** (VI, Chapter 3, 19)

She expands her spiritual guidance here. Firstly, because of
the clarity of the words and spiritual vision, they are
remembered exactly, as if burnt or imprinted within. Words
from the imagination, reason or the mind are not so clear
or distinct:

> **those locutions that are divine are so distinct that the hearer
> remembers if there were a syllable missing, and also what
> special words were made use of, although a whole sentence
> may have been spoken.** (VI, Chapter 3, 20)

Secondly, such experiences and words from the Holy Spirit
occur spontaneously in His time, not in ordinary time. He
can come at any moment, often when the soul is least
prepared or expectant. It can often seem miraculous. The
soul cannot be deceived about such things, nor could the
imagination fabricate them.

Knowledge cannot be created – it can only be heard,
received, infused into the soul, and corroborated from
Christian tradition and from those who have walked the
path towards union with our Lord:

> **it is impossible for the imagination to have framed such
> speeches and deceived the mind by the fancies about what it
> had never wished, nor sought for, nor even thought about.**
> (VI, Chapter 3, 21)

Thirdly, when the words come from Him, the soul can
only receive and listen, because their quality, their touch
and taste are quite different. If they come from the
imagination, they are of a much inferior quality, as it
originates from the will of the hearer.

Fourthly, and most importantly, the words are accompanied by a comprehension of more than they actually
mean. The words are only gateways, directives and signs to
something greater than themselves. If such words come

from a deceiver, or an imitation of the Holy Spirit, they may be pronounced clearly but they create doubt about whether they proceed from the Spirit of Truth or not.

False locutions cannot duplicate these effects, nor can they produce in the soul the same peace or light. Indeed, on the contrary, we are left with discomfort, disquiet, confusion and conflict, feeling as if something is not right, or is deeply wrong. If the soul learns to actively and accurately discern and discriminate, alongside remaining humble and surrendered, waiting to see the effects of such experiences, no lasting harm accrues.

The soul is becoming blessed by the grace of God and is increasingly less concerned for her personal life. The more she wants to honour and fulfil the will of God alone, the less she cares for her personal self:

> **Unless self-abasement increases with God's expression of love, they [the locutions] do not come from the Holy Spirit. Inevitably, when they are divine, the greater the favours, the less the soul esteems itself, and the more keenly it remembers its sins. It becomes more oblivious of self-interest; the will and memory grow more fervent in seeking solely God's honour with no thought of self.** (VI, Chapter 3, 25)

Thus, in summary, any locution, series of words or advice received in prayer should be treated with the utmost caution, and perhaps with a degree of disregard. If the advice is authentic, it will be repeated. If it is of such a power and quality as to convince us of its true spiritual origins, we should look at it from many angles for qualities of strength, wholesomeness and spontaneity. If it satisfies these conditions, Teresa then suggests talking it over with a trusted advisor to get a second opinion.[4]

ECSTASY AND RAPTURE

Teresa often goes beyond images and words into a region where wordless prayer alone is sufficient. At different times she calls these moments ecstasies, raptures and transports, and they can occur in this mansion. She is clear that we need more courage than we can imagine in our journey to these innermost regions, needing to dig deeper for greater spiritual strength than ever before.

The tiny mortal soul feels so undeserving of the blessings of such rapturous states of God. We feel complete awe. Gifts from an earthly king would be difficult enough to handle, but when it concerns the Divine King we usually feel faint-hearted.

Teresa knows our anxiety at approaching the Divine King:

> **Our nature appears too timid and base for anything so high; without doubt, unless God gave us the grace, it would be impossible for us, however much we might appreciate its benefits.** (VI, Chapter 4, 1)

Ecstatic and rapturous states can continue more deeply in this mansion. Teresa tells of how His Light and Power can so overwhelm the soul that for moments we can lose consciousness of, and orientation in, ordinary time and space, although we have not entirely lost the use of our faculties.

It is like beginning to touch and be filled with a blinding Light, or the soul being set wholly on Fire. The interior Life, like the phoenix, is set ablaze, His Love consuming her like a great fire:

> **In one sort of rapture, the soul, although perhaps not engaged in prayer at the time, is struck by some word of God which it either remembers or hears. His Majesty, touched with pity by what He has seen it suffer for so long past in its longing for Him, appears to increase the spark I described in the interior of the spirit until it entirely enflames the soul, which rises with new life like a phoenix from the flames.**
>
> **The soul being thus purified, God unites it to Himself in a way known only to Him and the spirit, nor does even the latter so understand what happens as to be able to explain it to others afterwards. The mind, however, had not lost the use of its faculties, for this ecstasy does not resemble a swoon**

> **or a fit, in which nothing either interior or exterior is felt.**
> **What I do understand is that the soul has never been so**
> **alive to spiritual things, nor so full of light and of knowledge**
> **of His Majesty as it is now.** (VI, Chapter 4, 3, 4)

These are Divine Mysteries, having nothing to do with ordinary modes of perception or normal faculties. This is entirely supersensible. In her own rapturous states, Teresa writes of her immersion in God, where she became faint breathed, was unable to speak, and experienced almost complete sensory deprivation and suspension of her faculties.

The Divine Knowledge being imparted to the soul in these last two mansions belongs to the Creator and to Him Alone. How are we able to experience the Presence of the Divine, whilst all the senses and faculties of the outer mansions are quiescent?

Teresa guides us:

> **While the soul is in this suspension, our Lord favours it by**
> **discovering to it secrets, such as heavenly mysteries and**
> **imaginary visions, which admit of description afterwards,**
> **because they remain so imprinted on the memory that it**
> **never forgets them.**
>
> **'But,' you ask me, 'if the very sublime favours our Lord**
> **bestows in this mansion cannot afterwards be remembered,**
> **what profit do they bring?' Oh, daughters! Their value**
> **cannot be overrated; for though the recipient is incapable**
> **of describing them, they are deeply imprinted in the centre**
> **of the soul and are never forgotten.**
>
> **'How can they be remembered if no image is seen and**
> **the powers of the soul do not comprehend them?' I, too, do**
> **not understand this, but I know that certain truths of the**
> **greatness of God remain so impressed on the spirit by this**
> **favour, that, did not faith teach Who He is and that it is**
> **bound to believe He is God, it would henceforth worship**
> **Him as such, as did Jacob, when he saw the ladder.** (VI, Chapter 4, 5, 6)

It is a total mystery. All the soul can really know and be sure of is the burning of His Light and Glory in our heart. Nothing much more can be said. The Radiance and Light that begins to shine just is what is. That is why Teresa warns us not to try to understand these mysterious workings of His Love in our heart.

She insists that these states of rapture and ecstasy cannot be feigned, willed, created by themselves or imitated. If this has happened, then their signs and effects will not correspond to what she has carefully described.

The rapture is allowing the radiance, the ecstatic joy and the intoxication of His Love to penetrate ever deeper within our soul, His Bride:

> When the spirit is very closely united to God, it is introduced into this mansion of the empyrean heaven, which must be in the centre of our souls – for since God resides in them; He must own one of the mansions.
>
> While the soul is in ecstasy, our Lord does not appear to wish it to apprehend these mysteries, and its inebriation of joy in Him suffices it. Sometimes, however, He is pleased to withdraw it from this rapture, and it at once perceives what the mansion contains.
>
> On returning to itself, the mind can recall what has been seen, but is unable to describe it, nor can it, by its natural abilities, attain to see more of the supernatural than God has chosen to show it. (VI, Chapter 4, 10)

FLIGHT OF THE SPIRIT

The most mystifying spiritual phenomenon Teresa describes in the sixth mansion is *flight of the spirit*, where she tells of a deeper surrender of the soul into the hands of God:

> There is another form of rapture, which, though essentially the same as the last, yet produces very different feelings in the soul. I call it 'flight of the spirit' for the soul suddenly feels so rapid a sense of motion that the spirit appears to hurry it away with a speed which is very alarming, especially at first.
>
> She does not know where the spirit is going, who is raising her, nor how it happens; for at the first instant of this sudden movement one does not feel sure that it is caused by God.

> **Resistance only accelerates the motion – God now appears to be teaching the soul, which has so often placed itself absolutely in His hands and offered itself entirely to Him, that it no longer belongs to itself.**
>
> **This person, therefore, resolved to resist no more than does a straw when attracted by amber; she therefore yielded herself into the hands of Him who is Almighty, seeing it is best to make a virtue of necessity.** (VI, Chapter 5, 1-2)

How much closer is the soul to His Radiant Divine Being, as we are merging into His great Ocean of Living Waters. This is not like the fourth mansion, where the waters were more distant and silently controlled. Here, the Living Waters are let loose, and can be dangerous and overwhelming to the unprepared. The little vessel of the soul must know how to ride the spiritual waves of our Bridegroom, Christ the King.

From Teresa's description, we have the sense of a great spiritual power operating and of being swept up by a force of Love much greater than ourselves. To illustrate her point, she returns to the analogy of water to explain further what happens in this mystical state:

> **It seems that the cistern of water of which I spoke in the fourth mansion, was formerly filled gently and quietly, without any movement. Now, however, this great God, who restrains the springs and the waters, and will not permit the ocean to transgress its bounds, lets loose the streams, which with a powerful rush flow into the cistern and a mighty wave rises, strong enough to raise on high the little vessel of our soul.**
>
> **Neither the ship herself, nor the pilot and sailors, can at their choice control the fury of the sea and stop it from carrying the boat where it will; far less can the interior of the soul now stay where it chooses, or force its senses or faculties to act more than He Who holds them in His dominion decrees; as for the exterior powers, they are here quite useless.** (VI, Chapter 5, 3)

Other kinds of 'flight of the spirit' can be different. Here, she describes her experience of the Divine world of Light and Being, and her partaking of the communion of saints:

> The soul really appears to have quitted the body, which, however, is not lifeless, and though, on the other hand, the person is certainly not dead, yet she herself cannot, for a few seconds, tell whether her spirit remains within her body or not.
>
> She feels that she has been wholly transported into another and a very different region from that in which we live, where a Light so unearthly is shown that, if during her whole lifetime she had been trying to picture it, and the wonders seen, she could not possibly have succeeded.
>
> In an instant, her mind learns so many things at once that if the imagination and intellect spent years in striving to enumerate them, it could not recall a thousandth part of them.
>
> This vision is not intellectual but imaginary and is seen by the eye of the soul more clearly than earthly things are seen by our bodily eyes. Although no words are pronounced, the spirit is taught many truths; if for instance, it beholds any of the saints, it knows them at once as well as if intimately acquainted with them for years. (VI, Chapter 5, 8, 9)

However, there are constant reminders of the great dangers and pitfalls to those who are unprepared for such awesome spiritual perceptions and experiences. The psychological foundation in the earlier mansions must be firmly developed, rooted in perseverance, humility and self-knowledge, in order to be safely applied in the journey to these regions of God.

Preliminary levels of experience and understanding must have been adequately tested and lived out in the crucible of everyday life. No level, stage, or mansion can be missed or avoided, without causing serious imbalance and incurring consequences. Essential aspects of experience for the soul must be gone through, struggled for, tested and built on solid foundations, so that the latter stages of the ascent can be traversed.

There is no substitute for the long, long years of conscious effort and psychological preparation to become living, reliable Brides of Christ, enabling the Holy Spirit to act and intervene at the right time, in His Time, at the right place in the right conditions. Vast efforts, tremendous labours, about which Teresa guides the soul, are needed to come into possession of those spiritual wings on which it is possible to ascend Mount Carmel.

In these tumultuous waters of the Spirit great courage, faith, confidence, alongside humble and conscious resignation and surrender, are required so that God may do with the soul what He wills. And if she is graced by such visions of the Living Waters of the Spirit, it is not for her alone. Each soul is called, drawn to give, to serve God even more selflessly and compassionately.

What is the purpose of such ecstatic visions and raptures? Teresa says that there are three main ones. Firstly, to give direct experience and knowledge of the Greatness of God, for the more the soul sees, the more she knows is in store, and the more deeply conscious she is becoming of those realms.

Secondly, greater self-knowledge is attained and more and more humility is developing from seeing and knowing how tiny and insignificant is the soul, in comparison to such Divine Grandeur.

Thirdly, to encourage a greater detachment from earthly, physical things, except for those that can be turned to the service of God. Teresa describes these mystical gifts as jewels with which:

> **the Bridegroom begins to deck His Bride; they are too valuable for her to keep them carelessly. These visions are so deeply engraved in her memory that I believe she can never forget them until she enjoys them for evermore… the Spouse Who gave her these gifts has power to give her grace not to lose them.** (VI, Chapter 5, 13)

The various supernatural phenomena already discussed by no means exhausts the range and type of occurrences that she suggests could be experienced at this stage. We can receive experiences in any sense or dimension, as there appears to be no arena in which God cannot act.

Thus, we can have a peculiar sensation of a delicious smell filling the air:

> **Our Lord also uses other means of rousing the soul; for instance when reciting vocal prayer, without seeking to penetrate the sense, a person may be seized with a delightful fervour, as if suddenly encompassed with a fragrance powerful enough to diffuse itself through all the senses.**
> (VI, Chapter 2, 14)

Teresa obviously had a keenly developed sense of smell and she often uses descriptions of perfumes when trying to express some of the more subtle mystical states. It is interesting that when she lay on her deathbed, the other nuns noted a beautiful smell of fresh roses filling the house.[5]

As well as sensations of smell, we may have bodily sensations of warmth, cold, comfort and discomfort. We may cry a great deal – Teresa gives a whole section to a discussion of this. It is often referred to as 'the gift of tears' and is considered a sign of great blessing in many traditions. It is common amongst many of the Orthodox monks and saints from Mount Athos.

It seems that the 'little butterfly' of the fifth dwelling place, which is our renewed and transformed soul, can become very restless and disturbed on account of all the different and unusual experiences that can occur now.

Teresa goes to some length to give good and wise advice concerning supernatural occurrences. In general, she advises that we remain vigilant and clear, staying close at all times to the guidelines that she lays out for assessing the authenticity of all supernatural occurrences.

Visions, locutions, and tears are actually superfluous in themselves. It is the effects they produce on our lives which are far more important. Do they allow a greater peace and openness to grow and develop, or are we becoming more disturbed, anxious and closed-minded? If the latter is the case over the long term, although they may not necessarily be destructive, caution and discretion should be exercised and our spiritual director consulted.

All true spiritual phenomena lead to a greater sense of humility in the person who receives them. Any visions or locutions that tend towards a greater sense of pride or inflation are very suspect. Supernatural phenomena will become very destructive if they are used, in any way, to serve the ego – for our own self-aggrandisement or if there is any identification whatsoever with such experiences. We can never ask for or expect these experiences – we should accept them as part of God's gifts, and certainly not as something to be taken for granted.

All authentic spiritual experiences lead towards a greater awareness of others and their difficulties and to a greater concentration on and awareness of God. We have much to learn from the witness of God in the experiences of all Christian denominations and other faiths. We should question spiritualities and approaches that close us to the experience of God in other people's lives, whether they are Christian or not: fundamentalism has no place in authentic spirituality.[6]

As we approach these deeper spiritual levels, Teresa constantly exhorts us to find a sound and wise guide. Time and again she urges:

> **Be perfectly candid and straightforward with your confessor…**
> **in giving him an account of your prayer. Unless you do this**
> **I cannot assure you of your safety, nor that you are led by**
> **God.** (VI, Chapter 9, 10)

The spiritual director has a specific task, which is to help clarify the action of God in the life of those seeking guidance. To this end, the only spiritual director is the Holy Spirit, and the two people in the guidance session are listening to what the Holy Spirit has to say.

VISIONS OF GOD

The Holy Mother tells us of her own mystical visions of the Presence of Christ:

> **A person who is in no way expecting such a favour, nor has**
> **ever imagined herself worthy of receiving it, is conscious**
> **that Jesus Christ stands by her side, although she sees Him**

neither with the eyes of the body nor of the soul. This is called an intellectual vision, I cannot tell why.

At first it distressed her, for she could not understand it; she could see nothing, yet so convinced did she feel that Jesus Christ was thus in some way manifesting Himself, that she could not doubt that it was some kind of vision, whether it came from God or not. Its powerful effects were a strong argument that it was from Him; still she was alarmed, never having heard of an intellectual vision, nor was she aware that such a thing could be. She, however, felt certain of our Lord's presence, and He spoke to her several times in the way that I have described.

She was frightened by this vision, which, unlike an imaginary one, does not pass away quickly, but lasts for several days and even sometimes for more than a year. She went, in a state of great anxiety to her confessor, who asked her how, if she saw nothing, did she know that our Lord was near her, and bade her describe His appearance.

She said that she was unable to do so, nor could she see His face, nor tell more than she had already done, but that she was sure it was the fact, that it was He Who spoke to her, and it was no trick of her imagination. Although people constantly cautioned her against this vision, she, as a rule, found it impossible to disbelieve in it, especially when she heard the words: 'It is I, be not afraid.'

Whenever she desired to speak to His Majesty in prayer, or even at other times, He seemed so close that He could not fail to hear her. He did not, however, speak to her whenever she wished, but unexpectedly, when necessity arose. She was conscious of His being at her right hand, although not in the way we know an ordinary person to be beside us, but in a more subtle manner, which cannot be described. This Presence is, however, quite as evident and certain, and indeed far more so, than the ordinary presence of other people about which we may be deceived; not so in this, for it brings with it graces and spiritual effects which could not come from melancholia.

This brings with it a special knowledge of God; a most tender love for Him results from being constantly in His company, while the desires of devoting one's whole being to His service are more fervent than any hitherto described. The conscience is greatly purified by the knowledge of His perpetual and near presence for, although we know that God sees all we do, yet nature inclines us to grow careless and forgetful of it. (VI, Chapter 8, 2, 3, 4, 6)

He is just as close, tender and intimate in our own time as He has ever been and ever will be. This divine secret, of His Presence and intimate Betrothal to the soul, is a most precious jewel in the cave of our heart. These treasures of heaven are becoming available to more and more individuals, but who will receive them and allow them to penetrate deeply within? It is as if a great invisible treasure chest is being opened in these deeper chambers, for those Brides who are preparing and making themselves ready to receive His gifts.

He is ever nearer, but can the heart receive Him? Our fear, trembling and anticipation grows. What the soul has been longing for is now so near, so intimate, so terrifyingly close. The intensity of love, the longing to merge, the desire of the soul to fuse with His Radiance is becoming so strong.

The Holy Mother describes this directly:

> **The presence of our Lord... may thus be symbolised – let us suppose that we have in our possession a gold locket, containing a precious stone of the highest value and powers, which, although we have not seen it, we are certain is in the case, and its virtues benefit us when we wear the pendant. Although we have never gazed on it, we value it highly, knowing by experience that it has cured us of maladies for which it is remedial.**
>
> **However, we dare not look at it, nor open the locket, nor could we do so even if we wished, for the owner of the jewel alone knows the secret of unfastening its casket. Although he lent it us for our use, yet he kept the key for himself; he will open the trinket when he chooses to show us its contents, and close it again when He sees fit to do so.**
> (VI, Chapter 9, 1)

These are brief moments of intimacy with our Beloved, to aid our journey onwards, to awaken further our memory of the jewels of Paradise.

Teresa writes of her awesome vision:

> **Suppose the owner of this locket suddenly opened it at times for the benefit of the person to whom he has entrusted it... This may be compared to what happens when our Lord is pleased to caress the soul. He shows it in vision His**

most sacred Humanity, under whatever form He chooses; either as He was during His Life on earth, or after His Resurrection.

The vision passes as quickly as a flash of lightning, yet this most glorious picture makes an impression on the imagination that I believe can never be effaced until the soul at last sees Christ to enjoy him for ever. Although I call it a 'picture', you must not imagine that it looks like a painting; Christ appears as a living Person, Who sometimes speaks and reveals deep mysteries.

The image is seen by the interior sight alone; but of bodily apparitions I can say nothing, for the person I know so intimately never experienced anything of the kind herself, and therefore could not speak about them with certainty. The splendour of Him Who is revealed in the vision resembles an infused light, as of the sun, covered with a veil as transparent as a diamond, if such a texture could be woven, while His raiment looks like fine linen.

The soul to whom God grants this vision almost always falls into an ecstasy, nature being too weak to bear so dread a sight. I say 'dread', though this apparition is more lovely and delightful than anything that could be imagined, even though anyone should live a thousand years, and spend all that time in trying to picture it, for it far surpasses our limited imagination and understanding; yet the presence of such surpassing majesty inspires the soul with great fear. (VI, Chapter 9, 2, 3)

Teresa continues her instructions on the differences between true and false raptures and visions. The capacity to be deceived is ever present, and must be guarded against constantly by ever increasing humility. There are certain characteristics of such visions of His most sacred Humanity, and His Resurrection Body, which help to discriminate between what is true and false.

She describes how it is not possible to gaze on the Lord's Radiance for very long. It is too awe-inspiring, terrifying and all encompassing. In true mystical states, this radiance is totally alive, like the burning, fiery radiance of the Sun. The physical exterior Sun is difficult for our natural eyes to gaze on. How much more so is the Emanation and Glory of Jesus Christ our Lord.

If, however, the gaze is continuous, then it is the result of psychological experience, with none of the power, or blinding, awe-inspiring radiance. Teresa says that such visions are probably caused by ardent meditation, which can evoke such inner images. Weak overactive imagination or gullible personalities can become absorbed with the contents of their own subconscious mind.

Such experiences, though, are like dead, repetitive things in comparison to the Real. When something of the Holy Spirit is truly granted, it is not difficult to see the difference. Deception, both within ourselves and in others, becomes increasingly obvious with greater spiritual discernment. The false has a personal, empty ring to it, even if we ardently believe, aor are absorbed in, such raptures and visions.

Teresa says there is a great difference:

> **A large number of people have spoken to me on the subject, therefore I know by experience that there are souls which, either because they possess vivid imaginations or active minds, or for some other reason of which I am ignorant, are so absorbed in their own ideas as to feel certain they see whatever their fancy imagines. If they had ever beheld a genuine vision, they would recognise the deception unmistakably.**
>
> **They themselves fabricate, piece by piece, what they fancy they see; no after effects are produced on the mind, which is less moved to devotion than by a sight of a sacred picture. It is clear that no attention should be paid to such fancies, which pass more quickly than dreams from the memory.** (VI, Chapter 9, 6)

If it is true and real, physical descriptions are inadequate. It is deeply grafted in the cave of our heart, and it is obvious that the soul has been abiding in the Presence of God. The peace and radiance of the Holy Spirit, which is infusing the core of our being, is evident. It is not a factor of our willing it, or of anything being manufactured by the ego, the mind or the psyche. It is a gift, depending on the quality of our receptivity to Him, as an unexpected favour of His Love.

Teresa makes a scriptural analogy:

> In the favour I am speaking about, the case is very different.
> A person is far from thinking of seeing anything, no idea of
> which has crossed the mind, when suddenly the vision is
> revealed in its entirety, causing within the powers and senses
> of the soul a fright and confusion soon changed into a
> blissful peace.
>
> Thus, after St Paul was thrown prostrate on the ground,
> a great tempest and noise followed from heaven; so, in the
> interior world of the soul, there is a violent tumult, followed
> instantly, as I said by a perfect calm. Meanwhile, certain
> sublime truths have been so impressed on the mind that it
> needs no other master, for, with no effort of its own, Wisdom
> Himself has enlightened its former ignorance.
>
> The soul for some time afterwards possesses such
> certainty that this grace comes from God, that whatever
> people may say to the contrary it cannot fear delusion. (VI,
> Chapter 9, 7, 8)

And how should the soul behave and react to such visions:

> Caution is necessary, and time should be allowed to see
> what effects follow. Day by day, the progress of the soul in
> humility and in the virtues should be watched: if the devil
> is concerned in the matter, he will soon show signs of himself
> and will be detected in a thousand lies.
>
> If the confessor is experienced and has received such
> favours himself, he will not take long in discovering the
> truth. In fact, he will know immediately, on being told of
> the vision, whether it is divine or comes from the imagination
> or the demon: more especially if he has received the gift of
> discerning spirits. (VI, Chapter 9, 9)

How do we begin to integrate and adjust to such indwelling
Radiance? If it truly is the gift of God, then the Light from
the innermost mansions to the outer mansions will reveal
the fruits of His gifts in time. Are we becoming less ego-
centred and more immersed in our common humanity
and service? Do we seek ever more righteousness in our
thoughts, speech and action as the spontaneous, natural
outflowing of our being?

There is really no mistaking if it truly is the Holy Spirit
of God indwelling in the innermost chamber of our soul.

Real interior transformation is unmistakable. The Light of God has the capacity to transform and transmute, in the depths of the soul, fear, hatred, envy, possessiveness, jealousy, compulsions and obsessions.

Teresa stresses that there are many individuals of a deep and abiding spirituality and love of God who have never known what it is to receive even one of these visions or raptures, or to have had any of these types of experiences. Conversely, others do have these favours and do not benefit as such, as they are not of a profoundly spiritual disposition.

Such mystical visions and states of being, by themselves, do not signify glory or advantage to the soul. It is actually to the contrary – such souls are even more obliged to surrender to, and serve, Him. Much more is incumbent on those who have been given such blessings. For any who might feel envious and yearn for such spiritual favours, Teresa's advice is never to encourage such desires, attitudes and wishes.

Firstly, she says it shows want of humility to wish to be given what may not have been deserved. It can never be known why one person has such favours bestowed on them, and the next has none. God has His Purposes and Intent for all things that occur, and His Will cannot be questioned or quizzed.

Secondly, if there is not the great longing in the soul for God, there is certain to be deception, delusion and dangerous pitfalls in these mystical states. Thirdly, if there is great personal desire, human imagination becomes very suggestible and:

> **makes them fancy they see or hear it, just as when a man's mind is set upon a thing all day, he dreams of it at night.**
> (VI, Chapter 9, 15)

Fourthly, the right way of spiritual development for each of us can never be known purely from our own desires and yearnings. This must be left to the wisdom of God, in our further surrendering to His greater Knowledge and

Understanding for each of us. He knows our soul more intimately than we know ourselves, and He creates the most appropriate experiences, situations and conditions specifically for each of us.

Fifthly, jealousy of such favours and blessings is both futile and dangerous. The interior trials which go hand in hand with them can be severe and numerous. How can we know if such trials and difficulties could be borne? It would be like asking to enter an atomic reactor! Much preparation, conscious suffering, detachment and preliminary testing are required to survive such direct power and exposure to His Divine Glory and Presence.

Humility, detachment, surrender and the ever-burning love in her heart for God are the constant keys of the soul to unlock the doorway to Paradise:

> **I believe that these desires are supernatural, and proper to very fervent souls who wish to prove to God that they do not serve him for pay; so, as I said, such people do not urge themselves to work harder for Him by the thought of the glory they will gain, but rather labour to satisfy their love, of which the nature is to toil for the Beloved in a thousand ways.**
>
> **Such souls would fain find a way to consume themselves in Him, and were there need that, for the sake of God's greater glory, they should be annihilated forever, they would count it great gain.** (VI, Chapter 9, 21)

The Holy Mother goes on to describe many of the other kinds of visions that are likely to occur, their consequences, how they take place and what effects they leave behind. This is to help us discriminate more acutely, to know that not all mystical states derive from heavenly spheres.

However, there are other hidden ways that God communicates with the soul which are more refined and subtle. Among other favours that are bestowed is deepening understanding of the profound differences between the supreme truth of His Divine Mysteries and our own mortality and ignorance:

I desire that, as far as possible, we should act with perfect truth before God and man, and above all that we should not wish to be thought better than we are; that in all our deeds we should ascribe to God what is His, and attribute what is ours to ourselves, and that we should seek for verity in all things. (VI, Chapter 10, 6)

The soul is even more shocked and repelled by mortal ignorance and egotism, which stands so resistant to seeing Divine Beauty and Grandeur mirrored in all of Creation. How shocking it is for the soul to become increasingly conscious of, and sensitive to, the travesty of false pride.

These are supernal mysteries about which the human personality is totally ignorant. It is like the worm, the little 'I', committing abominations, insults and lies in the majestic palace of a great King. The worm doesn't know where it is, being caught up in fantasies, ideas, and blind assumptions. It is unable to stop, listen and take an objective look at where it *really is*. The worm can only prepare the cocoon for the soul to gestate, to become re-woven and re-born into real existence in the Presence of the Heavenly King.

When the soul begins to wake up, she realises in shock and horror, that all that is left for her to do is to die herself, in that form, state and level of being; to die in order to be transformed, from her very core, into His Image and Likeness; to prepare herself to be impregnated by His Light, the Light of Christ, so as to reflect, like a translucent mirror, the beauty and majesty of these innermost mansions.

Teresa is clear – how could a worm ever think it could appropriate or reflect Divine Grandeur from the standpoint and 'beingness' of a worm? So she continues to emphasise the necessity of humility even more strongly:

Short as the time lasts, yet, in a manner impossible to describe, God also manifests that in Him there is a verity which makes all in creatures seem obscure. He convinces the soul that He alone is that Truth which cannot lie, thus demonstrating the meaning of David's words in the psalm: 'Every man is a liar', which could never be thus realised by any other means, however often we might hear that God is

> **truth infallible... Once, while I was wondering why our Lord so dearly loves the virtue of humility, the thought suddenly struck me, without previous reflection, that it is because God is the supreme Truth, and humility is the truth, for it is most true that we have nothing good of ourselves, but only misery and nothingness: whoever ignores this lives a life of falsehood.** (VI, Chapter 10, 5, 6)

The soul is not bestowed with gifts or favours for the sake of curiosity or enthusiasm. Those heavenly things that have been hidden from the soul before are now becoming perceptible by the *interior* spiritual senses, as we begin to consciously live and flow within the great river of His Living Waters.

Teresa is, as before, strict in her criteria for accepting the veracity of visions and has strong guidance for those whose claims are not authentic. As with locutions, ecstasies, raptures and flight of the spirit, she counsels us to examine the after-effects of visions and ask ourselves whether they leave us in a state of peace and joy, or whether they depress and disturb us.

We should not ask for them or court them, but should let them come of their own accord and simply accept them. Most importantly, we should have a trusted spiritual director or friend with whom we can discuss our experiences and who can give an objective perspective.

THE WOUND OF LOVE

> **For these past trials cause her to take a far higher flight. I will now describe the way in which the Spouse treats her before uniting her entirely to Himself. He increases her longing for Him by devices so delicate that the soul itself cannot discern them; nor do I think I could explain them, except to those who have personal experience. These desires are delicate and subtle impulses, springing from the inmost depths of the soul.** (VI, Chapter 2, 1)

What is this Divine Love that all mystics speak of? Teresa exclaims:

I am at my wits' end, sisters, as to how to make you understand this operation of love; I know not how to do so. It seems contradictory to say that the Beloved clearly shows He dwells in the soul and calls by so unmistakable a sign, and a summons so penetrating, that the spirit cannot choose but hear it, while yet He appears to reside in the seventh mansion. He speaks in this manner, which is not a set form of speech, and the inhabitants of the other mansions, the senses, the imagination and the faculties dare not stir.

O Almighty God! How profound are Thy secrets, and how different are spiritual matters from anything that can be seen or heard in this world! I can find nothing to which to liken these graces, insignificant as they are compared with many others Thou dost bestow on souls. (VI, Chapter 2, 4, 5)

From my own diary:

I begin to feel very uncomfortable, in pain and distress, as I surrender to His Love. I feel something pulling me into a powerful all-encompassing Presence. It starts to feel more difficult and agonising, as I let go more and more. I tremble with something and I don't know what it is and why it has come. I am shaking. My heart is beating faster. I feel on the threshold of something momentous.

Teresa says that these spiritual states take the soul unawares, when we least expect or want them. The whole body can quiver in anticipation or fear. We feel so powerless, broken, out of control, so weak. It's where we feel the most vulnerable and in pain. Our resistance is broken to nothing. He must have everything of us.

From my own diary:

Nothing left. Only His Sound that penetrates everything. I hear the Sound. He is calling. I am reduced to nothing. I don't know the source of this pain in my heart. It's just that my heart is more and more broken. Something is penetrating to the core of my heart. Something is piercing my essence. His Shaft of Light is penetrating into my heart.

The Bridegroom enters into my intimate chamber. As He starts to penetrate, the heavens begin to open above. Vast shafts of Light bursting from above, down through an exquisitely tiled ceiling of a religious building into my innermost core. His Light is exploding above as the Bridegroom is piercing me.

It is like a Fire that burns through everything. His Fire is ignited in our heart. It starts to burn like a coal being set alight. It comes and goes as He wills, occurring deep within our being. From her own experience of these mystical states, Teresa says that:

> **There is no suspension here of the senses or other faculties: they wonder at what is happening, without impeding it. Nor do I think that they can either increase or dispel this delightful pain. Anyone who has received this favour from our Lord will understand my meaning on reading this; let her thank Him fervently: there is no need to fear deception, but far more fear of not being sufficiently grateful for so signal a grace being able in any way, it seems to me, either to increase or to deprive the soul of that delicious pain.** (VI, Chapter 2, 8)

Can the source of such Divine Effect be other than of God? The Holy Mother talks of the decreasing likelihood of deception at this stage. Firstly, the powers that obstruct such unifying states of being do not grant these types of experiences:

> **The devil cannot give such delicious pain: he may cause pleasure or delight, which appears spiritual, but is unable to add suffering…his power is limited to what is external; suffering produced by him is never accompanied with peace, but with anxieties and struggles.** (VI, Chapter 2, 10)

The mark of authenticity that the grace comes from God is '**especially the suffering of so keen a sort, [which] is so united to peace and joy of soul**' (VI, Chapter 2,10). If it is imaginary or delusional, there won't be the unique conjoining of suffering and joy together. It does not produce conflict, worry, anxiety or disturbance. It is of a totally different quality and order.

Secondly, the soul experiences such peace and ineffable blessings that can only come from regions and principalities over which obstructing powers do not rule. Teresa is clear that '**this welcome storm comes from no region over which Satan has control**' (VI, Chapter 2, 11). It comes from a purely spiritual source, over which destructive powers no longer have influence or dominion.

Thirdly, she is even more resolved to journey on to the innermost mansion. This experience is so real and unforgettable that only those who know it can have any sense of what is being communicated. Everything is coming together in one unified body. It is the joining together of all that has been disparate into one.

This type of pain and suffering encourages and motivates us to develop even greater spiritual courage and resolve to journey further into our interior castle. The spiritual pain suffered is so conjoined to ineffable tranquillity, joy and peace that it is unmistakable.

If this is not the case, Teresa says that the source of the suffering is not from God:

> **It is very clear that this is no fiction; the imagination may counterfeit some favours, but not this, which is too manifest to leave room for doubt. Should anyone still remain uncertain, let her know that hers were not genuine impulses, that is, if she is dubious as to whether or not she experienced them, for they are as certainly perceived by the soul as is a loud voice by the ears.**
>
> **It is impossible for these experiences to proceed from melancholy, whose whims arise and exist only in the imagination, whereas this emotion comes from the interior of the soul.** (VI, Chapter 2, 12)

The soul may experience different types of visionary, ecstatic or rapturous states, being awakened by God in many ways. There are other supernatural gifts that can be bestowed. Echoing the five physical senses, our interior spiritual senses are now awakened by the Holy Spirit, whether interior sight, interior taste, smell, touch or hearing of His Sound.

The Holy Mother gives another example of the Spirit awakening the soul:

> When reciting vocal prayer, without seeking to penetrate the sense, a person may be seized with a delightful fervour, as if suddenly encompassed with a fragrance powerful enough to diffuse itself through all the senses.
>
> I do not assert that there really is any perfume, but use this comparison because it somewhat resembles the manner by which the Spouse makes His presence understood, moving the soul to a delicious desire of enjoying Him, and thus disposing it to heroic acts, and causing it to render Him fervent praise.
>
> This favour springs from the same source as the former, but causes no suffering here, nor are the soul's longings to enjoy God painful: this is what is more usually experienced by the soul. (VI, Chapter 2, 14,15)

Teresa elucidates on the Divine Fire that is ignited in the heart as the soul begins to be more consumed by His Love:

> I have been thinking that God might be likened to a burning furnace, from which a small spark flies into the soul, which feels the heat of this great fire, which, however, is insufficient to consume it.
>
> The sensation is so delightful that the spirit lingers in the pain produced by its contact. This seems to me the best comparison I could find, for the pain is delicious and is not really pain at all, nor does it always continue in the same degree; sometimes it lasts a long time, and on other occasions passes quickly.
>
> In fact, it is never permanent and therefore does not wholly inflame the spirit; but when the soul is ready to take fire, the little spark suddenly dies out, leaving the heart longing to suffer anew its loving pangs.
>
> Undoubtedly, this movement of the heart comes from God, Who is unchangeable; nor do its effects resemble those of other devotions, in which the strong absorption of delight makes us doubt their reality. (VI, Chapter 2, 6, 7)

The agony and ecstasy of the kindling of Divine Fire in the smouldering coal of our heart! The total aloneness of the soul in this state of being, naked and vulnerable in her surrender to union with God:

> She feels a strange loneliness, finding no companionship in any earthly creature; nor could she, I think, among those

> who dwell in heaven, since they are not her Beloved;
> meanwhile, all society is a torture to her.
>
> She is like one suspended in mid-air, who cannot touch
> the earth or mount to heaven; she is unable to reach the
> water while parched with thirst, and this is not a thirst that
> can be borne, but one which nothing will quench-nor would
> she have it quenched, save with that water of which our
> Lord spoke to the Samaritan woman, but this is not given
> her. Alas, O Lord, to what a state dost Thou bring those
> who love Thee! (VI, Chapter 11, 5)

She is torn asunder. The soul cannot go back to her former
state, which is even more repellent and distant to her than
before. She can only live in the middle of the paradox of
death and union:

> Seeing what she has gained, the sufferer would gladly endure
> frequently the same pains, but can do nothing to help herself
> in this matter. There are no means of reaching that state
> again until God chooses to decree it, when neither resistance
> nor escape is possible.
>
> The mind feels far deeper contempt for the world than
> before, having learnt that nothing earthy can succour it in
> its torture; it is also much more detached from creatures,
> having learnt that no one but its Creator can bring it
> consolation and strength. (VI, Chapter 11, 10)

She knows now that she is destined for Divine Union and
His Blessings:

> At last, ah, at last! before they die, He repays them for
> all they have suffered, as you shall now learn. May He be
> forever blessed, and may all creatures praise Him! (VI, Chapter
> 11, 12)

NOTES: SIXTH MANSION

1. Sophrony *op.cit.* p.108
2. Harvey, A. *The Son of Man – the Mystical Path to Christ*, Jeremy Tarcher/Putnam, NY, 1999, p.114
3. Dupre, L. *op. cit.* p.72
4. Tyler, P. *The Way of Ecstasy*, Canterbury Press, Norwich, 1997, p.95
5. Ibid, p.100
6. Ibid, p 102.

THE SEVENTH MANSION

The Mystery of Union

What we do know is this; when he is revealed, we will be like him, for we will see him as he is.

1 John 3:2

When our Lord is pleased to take pity on the sufferings, both past and present, endured through her longing for Him by this soul which He has spiritually taken for His bride, He, before consummating the celestial marriage, brings her into this His mansion or presence chamber. This is the seventh mansion, for as He has a dwelling place in heaven, so has He in the soul, where none but He may abide, and which may be termed a second heaven.

St Teresa, Seventh Mansion

THE WEDDING

From my own diary:

> I have entered a deep state of prayer, asking to be shown His deepest secrets of Love. He begins to reveal Himself in the innermost chamber of my heart. Time and space begin to change. In my depths, I begin to crouch down smaller and smaller, my essence seeming to be beckoned, to be drawn, into a type of childlike position like a foetus ready to be born anew.
>
> 'I' am becoming more transparent, as nothing, as somehow my essence is becoming more absorbed into another dimension of Being. I am becoming more and more contained and absorbed within a huge, throbbing Heart, which grows bigger and bigger, pulsating all around me. I become totally enveloped within an enormous, throbbing heart of Love. This overwhelming force, this Love, penetrates from all directions, as vast shafts of Light open up from above.

Teresa expresses acute anxiety on speaking about this innermost mansion:

> **Oh, great God! Surely such a miserable creature as myself should tremble at the thought of speaking on a subject so far beyond anything I deserve to understand. Indeed I felt abashed, and doubted whether it would not be better to finish writing about this mansion in a few words, lest people might imagine that I recounted my personal experience. I was overwhelmed with shame, for, knowing what I am, it is a terrible undertaking.** (VII, Chapter 1, 2)

Teresa is very clear how difficult it is to describe what is happening, human language being limited and fairly meaningless here. Any description can only serve as a pointer, a tiny glimpse into the heart of these profound spiritual mysteries:

> **Who can recount His mercies and His greatness? It is impossible, so do not be amazed at what I write about them, which is but a cipher of what remains untold concerning God... May His Majesty be pleased to guide my pen, and to teach me to say somewhat of the much there is to tell of His revelations to the souls he leads into this mansion.** (VII, Chapter 1, 1)

From the place of the soul, our personal will, wishes and desires are now entirely quiescent. Our spiritual journey towards the gradual abandonment to the will of the Lord has taken us out of the sphere of egocentricity to awakening to the existence, and living reality, of the different dwelling places of our interior castle. It has taken us towards this final dwelling place, unification with Him in the Heavenly Realms.

The previous mansions are different to this innermost mansion. Teresa writes that:

> **The little butterfly, then, has died with the greatest joy at having found rest at last, and now Christ lives in her.**
> (VII, Chapter 3, 1)

After the transformation of the middle mansions and the turbulence, agony and ecstasies of the fifth and sixth mansions, all comes to an end now. There is a sense of completion, peace and rest. The soul is entering the bridal chamber of our Lord.

The mystical marriage of Christ to the soul is being consummated:

> **You must not think of the soul as insignificant and petty, but as an interior world, containing the number of beautiful mansions you have seen; as indeed it should, since in the centre of the soul there is a mansion reserved for God Himself.**
>
> **When His Majesty deigns to bestow on the soul the grace of these divine nuptials, He brings it into His Presence chamber, and does not treat it as before, when He put it into a trance. I believe He then unites her to Himself, as also during the prayer of union; but then only the superior part was affected, and the soul did not feel called to enter its own centre as it does in this mansion. Here it matters little whether it be in the one way or the other.** (VII, Chapter 1, 6, 7)

Teresa expresses her deepening mystical relationship with Christ in terms of visions, where she now has the certainty that she is 'endowed with life by God'. Everything within her soul is now taking place in the deepest interior place, which is inaccessible to all but God.

The soul's intimacy with Him is now completely independent of human faculties:

> In the former favours our Lord unites the spirit to Himself and makes it both blind and dumb, like St Paul after his conversion, thus preventing it from knowing whence or how it enjoys this grace, for the supreme delight of the spirit is to realise its nearness to God. During the actual moment of divine union the soul feels nothing, all its powers being entirely lost. (VII, Chapter 1, 8)

In this seventh mansion, there is now the direct spiritual perception of the knowledge, love and wisdom of God. It is as if the soul is able to directly hear, perceive and become infused by the innermost recesses of His Mysteries. Now she is knowing, and becoming united to, the essence of His Love with all the threads of her existence.

It is as if she is now able to flow totally with, and be in, the reality of all His creation, which continually pulsates with His Knowledge, Love and Light. Veils and separation from His Divine Being are being lifted, as all levels of His creation are becoming unified through His Endless Tapestry of Light.

The Holy Mother is clear that in this mansion everything is different. The spiritual truth of the doctrine of faith is being revealed to the soul in a direct, immediate, personal encounter with the Living God:

> Now, however, He acts differently; our pitiful God removes the scales from its eyes, that it may see and understand somewhat of the grace received, in a strange and wonderful manner in this mansion, by means of an intellectual vision.
>
> By some mysterious manifestation of the truth, the three persons of the most Blessed Trinity reveal themselves, preceded by an illumination, which shines on the spirit like a most dazzling cloud of light. The three Persons are distinct from one another; a sublime knowledge is infused into the soul, imbuing it with a certainty of the truth that the Three are of one substance, power, and knowledge, are one God.
>
> Thus that which we hold, as a doctrine of faith, the soul now, so to speak, understands by sight, although it beholds the Blessed Trinity neither by the eyes of the body nor of the soul, for this is no imaginary vision.

> **All the three Persons here communicate Themselves to the soul, speak to it, and make it understand the words of our Lord in the Gospel, that He and the Father and the Holy Ghost will come and make their abode with the soul which loves Him, and which keeps His commandments.**
> (VII, Chapter 1, 8, 9)

Teresa is now speaking about that interior place where both our spirit and our body are able to be penetrated through and through by the Holy Spirit and the Love of God, bonding them together as one, united to Christ – spirit to spirit, body to body, flesh to flesh.

Her amazement at the difference between just hearing and believing the tenets of faith in God, and being led to realise their living spiritual truth, is clear:

> **Oh, my God, how different from merely hearing and believing these words is it to realise their truth in this way! Day by day a growing astonishment takes possession of this soul, for the three Persons of the Blessed Trinity seem never to depart; it sees with certainty, in the way I have described, that They dwell far within its own centre and depth; though unable to describe how, for want of learning, it is conscious of the indwelling of these divine Companions.**
> (VII, Chapter 1, 10)

It is the knowledge of the three Persons of the Blessed Trinity dwelling in the centre of our being. When His Light enters and unites with the soul, however, it is not permanent nor forever, and when it departs we do not know when He will return.

But the understanding, knowledge and love for God remains so carved in our essence that it is truly unforgettable and transforms everything for us. How much of the brilliance of His Divine Light can a soul bear?

In this first flowering of interior union it is important to remember that this is the *beginning* of a marriage relationship. This sacred marriage is not the end of love but the new beginning of a Love relationship that continually deepens into eternity.

There is no end to His Love for us. It is without measure and limit:

> This presence is not always so entirely realised, that is, so distinctly manifest, as at first, or as it is at times when God renews this favour, otherwise the recipient could not possibly attend to anything else, nor live in society. Although not always seen by so clear a light, yet whenever she reflects on it she feels the companionship of the Blessed Trinity. This is as if, when we were with other people in a very well lighted room, someone were to darken it by closing the shutters; we should feel certain that the others were still there, although unable to see them. (VII, Chapter 1, 12)

> You may ask: 'Could she not bring back the light and see them again?' This is not in her power; when our Lord chooses, He will open the shutters of the understanding: He shows her great mercy in never quitting her and in making her realise it so clearly. His divine Majesty seems to be preparing His bride for greater things by this divine companionship: which clearly helps perfection in every way, and makes her lose the fear she sometimes felt when other graces were granted her. (VII, Chapter 1, 13)

> It also appears to me that the soul and its faculties are not identical. There are so many and such transcendental mysteries within us, that it would be a presumption for me to attempt to explain them. If by God's mercy we enter heaven we shall understand these secrets. (VII, Chapter 1, 16)

UNION

> We now come to speak of divine and spiritual nuptials, although this sublime favour cannot be received in all its perfection during our present life, for by forsaking God this great good would be lost. The first time God bestows this grace, He, by an imaginary vision of His most Sacred Humanity, reveals Himself to the soul, that it may understand and realise the sovereign gift it is receiving. (VII, Chapter 2, 1)

In this dwelling place, Teresa has a vision of the Sacred Humanity of Jesus, and knows, with all certainty and assurance, that the mystical marriage now being consummated is with Him, and it is through Him, in the Holy Spirit, that she has fellowship with the Father.

She is offering the vision, the possibility and the essential spiritual guidance for those who are surrendering to His Will and Intent in their lives to become saints of our Lord, the Brides of Christ.

In guiding the soul in these matters, Teresa describes the intricacies of the divine marriage. She writes of her own transformation:

> He may manifest Himself in a different way to other people; the person I mentioned, after she had been to Holy communion, beheld our Lord, full of splendour, beauty and majesty, as He was after His Resurrection. He told her that henceforth she was to care for His affairs as though they were her own, and He would care for hers: He spoke other words, which she could understand better than repeat. (VII, Chapter 2, 1)

She is clear that these visions are very different to anything that has gone before, as mystical union with Christ belongs to the non-corporeal world. She tells us how and why things are now so different:

> Our Lord had thus revealed Himself to her at other times; yet this was so different that it left her bewildered and amazed, both on account of the vividness of what she saw and of the words heard at the time, and also because it took place in the interior of the soul, where, with the exception of the one last mentioned, no other vision had been seen.
>
> You must understand that between the visions seen in this and in the former mansions there is a vast difference; there is the same distinction between spiritual espousals and spiritual marriage as between people who are only betrothed and others who are united forever in holy matrimony. (VII, Chapter 2, 1, 2)

In approaching the very centre of the castle, there is now a mysterious sense of inner peace arising from our sacred union that exists, side by side, with the turmoil of the outer mansions. As we reach, and rest in, this final place of union, we realise that everything on our journey through the mansions to our resting place in God has contributed to the fullness and completion of becoming truly human.

By choosing to open ourselves totally to God, and surrender to life in the Holy Spirit, we become what we truly are, what we are meant to be – made in the image and the likeness of God. It is only when we are able to be totally open and transparent to God, and only when He has been able to love us, totally, intimately, as a friend, as a lover, that we are able to be wholly present, real and alive in Him. It is only when we are able to become God-filled that we are able to become fully and truly human.

In spiritual betrothal, the soul can still repudiate His Love and the impending union:

> **Spiritual espousals are different, and like the grace of union are often dissolved; for though two things are made one by union, separation is still possible, and each part then remains a thing by itself. This favour generally passes quickly, and afterwards the soul, as far as it is aware, remains without His company.** (VII, Chapter 2, 4)

In mystical union, what happens in betrothal is now impossible. Christ, His Divine Majesty, appears to the soul in a totally interior way, His Essence fusing with our essence, as one Burning Light. Teresa is adamant that this sacred marriage is independent of human faculties, reason or physical sensations:

> **This is even more true of the spiritual marriage, for this secret union takes place in the innermost centre of the soul, where God Himself must dwell: I believe that no door is required to enter it. I say, 'no door is required', for all I have hitherto described seems to come through the senses and faculties, as must the representation of our Lord's Humanity, but what passes in the union of the spiritual nuptials is very different.**
>
> **Here God appears in the soul's centre, not by an imaginary but by an intellectual vision, far more mystic than those seen before, just as He appeared to the Apostles without having entered through the door when He said: *Pax vobis.* [Peace be with you]** (VII, Chapter 2, 2)

So mysterious is the secret and so sublime the favour that God thus bestows instantaneously on the soul, that it feels a supreme delight, only to be described by saying that our Lord vouchsafes for the moment to reveal to it His own heavenly glory, in a far more subtle way than by any vision or spiritual delight.

As far as can be understood, the soul, I mean the spirit of this soul, is made one with God, Who is Himself a spirit, and Who has been pleased to show certain persons how far His Love for us extends, that we may praise His greatness. He has thus deigned to unite Himself to His creature; He has bound Himself to her as firmly as two human beings are joined in wedlock, and will never separate Himself from her. (VII, Chapter 2, 3)

The soul is totally surrendering to His Divine Current of Life, knowing that His Ocean with no horizon is constantly transforming her into a spiritual being. We have thrown ourselves into the Ocean of God's Existence. In this state, we are in direct contact with Him, as His spiritual waters flow through her.

Teresa uses symbols of candles, water and light to try to express, however inadequately, these mysteries of spiritual union. She uses the metaphor of two candle flames that momentarily become one, *one Flame, one Light*, but can be separated.

She also describes union as raindrops falling into a river, or as a stream flowing into the ocean – the two separate flows of water become *one indissoluble Living Water:*

In the spiritual marriage with our Lord, the soul always remains in its centre with its God. Union may be symbolised by two wax candles, the tips of which touch each other so closely that there is but one light; or again, the wick, the wax and the light become one, but the one candle can again be separated from the other, and the two candles remain distinct; or the wick may be withdrawn from the wax.

Spiritual marriage is like rain falling from heaven into a river or stream, becoming one and the same liquid, so that the river and the rainwater cannot be divided; or it resembles a streamlet flowing into the ocean, which cannot afterwards be disunited from it.

This marriage may also be likened to a room into which

a bright light enters through two windows – though divided when it enters, the light becomes one and the same. (VII, Chapter 2, 4, 5)

The Fire and Love of Christ is burned into the soul, which is now united to the Sacred Heart of Jesus, whose Love fills our whole being to overflowing. Teresa speaks now, in this seventh mansion, about her realisation that, through Christ, she has been totally and effortlessly absorbed into that still, silent, rapturous vortex of Life that endlessly revolves between the Father and the Son:

> The same Apostle says: 'To me, to live is Christ and to die is gain.' This, I think, might here be uttered by the soul, for now the little butterfly of which I spoke dies with supreme joy, for Christ is her life. This becomes more manifest by its effects as time goes on, for the soul learns that it is God Who gives it 'life', by certain secret intuitions too strong to be misunderstood, and keenly felt, although impossible to describe.
>
> These produce such overmastering feelings that the person experiencing them cannot refrain from amorous exclamations, such as 'O Life of my life, and Power which doth uphold me!' with other aspirations of the same kind. For from the bosom of the Divinity, where God seems ever to hold this soul fast clasped, issue streams of milk, which solace the servants of the castle. I think He wishes them to share, in some ways, the riches the soul enjoys; therefore from the flowing river in which the little streamlet is swallowed up, some drops of water flow every now and then to sustain the bodily powers, the servants of the bride and Bridegroom. (VII, Chapter 2, 6, 7)

She talks of the unmoving centre of the soul, which has united with Christ, allowing Him to direct our heart, mind and action, as if there were *one body, one mind, one spirit in Him:*

> The soul itself, as I said, never moves from this centre, nor loses the peace he can give Who gave it to the Apostles when they were assembled together. I think this salutation of our Lord contains far deeper meaning than the words convey, as also His bidding the glorious Magdalene to 'go in peace'.

> **Our Lord's words** *act* **within us, and in these cases they must have wrought their effect in the souls already disposed to banish from within themselves all that is corporal and to retain only what is spiritual, in order to be joined in this celestial union with the uncreated spirit. Without doubt, if we empty ourselves of all that belongs to the creature, depriving ourselves of it for the love of God, that same Lord will fill us with Himself.** (VII, Chapter 2, 9)

She describes how the innermost mansion of the castle of the soul has now been reached, where the Heavenly King makes his permanent abode in the depths of our pilgrim's heart. It is no longer a passing, fleeting visit, as in the spiritual espousals.

It is now the mutual and permanent abiding of The Lover in His beloved in the throne room of the King:

> **God places the soul in His own mansion, which is in the very centre of the soul itself. They say the empyrean heavens, wherein our Lord dwells, do not revolve with the rest; so the accustomed movements of the faculties and the imagination do not appear to take place in any way that can injure the soul or disturb its peace.**
>
> **The Lord introduces the soul into His own mansion, which is the centre of the soul herself. The empyrean heaven where Our Lord dwells is said not to move like the rest. Thus, once she has entered this heaven, there seems to be no movement in this soul, such as there is in the faculties and imagination, which can prejudice or take away her peace.** (VII, Chapter 2, 12)

She emphasises that the royal union in the seventh mansion is nothing to do with the sensory world. The body may still experience many difficulties, crises and imbalances through such a process of profound internal spiritual transformation. However, these do not affect the consummation of His Light in the centre of our soul as they occur in the outermost mansions:

> **It is not intended that the powers, senses and passions should continually enjoy this peace. The soul does, indeed, but in the other mansions there are still times of struggle, suffering and fatigue, though as a general rule, peace is not lost by**

them. This 'centre of the soul' or 'spirit' is so hard to describe or even to believe in, that I think, sisters, my inability to explain my meaning saves you from being tempted to disbelieve me; it is difficult to understand how there can be crosses and sufferings, and yet peace in the soul.

Let me give you one or two comparisons. A king resides in his palace; many wars and disasters take place in his kingdom, but he remains on his throne. In the same way, although tumults and wild beasts rage with great uproar in the other mansions, yet nothing of this enters the seventh mansions, nor drives the soul from it. Although the mind regrets these troubles, they do not disturb it nor rob it of its peace, for the passions are too subdued to dare to enter here, where they would only suffer still further defeat. Though the whole body is in pain, yet the head, if it be sound, does not suffer with it. (VII, Chapter 2, 14, 15)

MYSTERY OF THE KISS

Teresa emphasises the nature of the profound spiritual certainty and security that the soul now rests in – we have truly come home. Our choice has been irrevocably made – we have become one with Him and He is united in the depths of our heart. There is now a very particular type of interior security, a security in God that has no need of deep suffering and yearning anymore, no need for visions, raptures, ecstasies and the like.

The spiritual reassurance that we received previously has been the product of our needing constant reminders of the eternal Presence and Love of God. We have now arrived home, and can rest, and *be* in the centre of our castle, where His Presence and Love is now a permanent, indissoluble, fused, part of our being. She writes elsewhere of this innermost mansion: 'I firmly believe that no strong attachment to any creature or to all the glory of Heaven has any dominion over me. My one attachment is to the love of God…' (*Spiritual Relations* VI).

What is this new spiritual life? What does it consist of? How does it differ from our former life? The Holy Mother is explicit in answering these questions. First and foremost, she says that forgetfulness of self is so entire that personal ambitions, desires and aspirations seem no longer to exist. This self-forgetfulness that is now occurring is, at times, so complete that it seems as though we no longer exist, as if there has been a loss of soul. We are changing and transforming, no longer identified with, or attached to, a 'personal identity'.

Our desire is to be fully employed in procuring the glories of the spiritual realms whilst on earth. We know now the truth of His Words – that if we cared for His interests He would take care of ours. Constant divine companionship is now assured, and the silence, peace, rest and 'being in God' is everything.

We have been transformed, and our attachments to, and identification with, worldly ambitions or aspirations have been dissolved:

> **For such a transformation has been worked in her that she no longer recognises herself, nor does she remember that heaven, or life, or glory are to be hers, but seems entirely occupied in seeking God's interests... Thus she recks nothing, whatever may happen, but lives in such strange oblivion that, as I said, she seems no longer to exist, nor does she wish to be of any account in anything –** *anything!* **unless she sees that she can advance, however little, the honour and glory of God: for which she would most willingly die.**
>
> **Do not fancy I mean, daughters, that she neglects to eat and drink, though it brings no small torment to her, nor to perform the duties of her state. I am speaking of her interior; as regards her exterior actions, there is little to say, for her chief suffering is to see that she has hardly strength to do anything.** (VII, Chapter 3, 1, 2, 3)

Secondly, there is the yearning to further sacrifice and surrender what is left of our personal self. This can include further trials, persecutions and suffering, but we now experience a greater detachment from such situations. In fact, there can be interior joy in the face of persecution.

Teresa describes her own transformed attitude:

> She feels a great interior joy when persecuted, and is far
> more peaceful than in the former state under such
> circumstances: she bears no grudge against her enemies,
> nor wishes them any ill. Indeed she has a special love for
> them, is deeply grieved at seeing them in trouble, and does
> all she can to relieve them, earnestly interceding with God
> on their behalf. (VII, Chapter 3, 4)

There develops a strange otherworldly objectivity, where
no one or nothing can deeply affect or disturb our inner
life. We are more objective towards the outer world and
what goes on outside the castle. They don't affect the
innermost mansions.

Teresa describes this state of being, in all its subtlety,
peace and tenderness:

> Such a soul, thoroughly detached from all things, wishes to
> be either always alone, or else occupied on what benefits
> the souls of others: she feels neither aridity nor any interior
> troubles, but a constant tender recollection of our Lord,
> Whom she wishes to praise unceasingly. When she grows
> negligent, the same Lord arouses her in the way that I told
> you, and it is easy to see that this impulse comes from the
> interior of the soul, like the former impetuous desires.
>
> It is now felt very sweetly, but is neither produced by
> the intellect nor the memory, nor is there any reason to
> believe the soul itself has any share in it. This is so usual
> and so frequent that any one who has been in this state
> must have noticed it. However large a fire may be, the flame
> never burns downwards, but upwards, and so this movement
> is seen to come from the centre of the soul whose powers it
> excites. (VII, Chapter 3, 7)

Teresa is describing the final transformation into the *new
man/woman*, the moment when our sacrifice, the sacrifice
of ourselves and our ego-bound life, is brought to its
completion in this mansion. This is the state of complete
acceptance and surrender into the hands of God.

The soul is now totally open to the fullness of the
Father's life, through the Son and His final and complete
gift of the Holy Spirit. It is this gift, which brings about the
theosis, the divinisation, of the old man/woman as we are

transformed into the *new man/woman* in the mystical marriage. This is a great mystery – that we only truly become human, become ourselves, when we have fully surrendered to God.

Teresa goes on to explain how it is possible to be totally attentive to the strength and power of His Love in this unitive state, as well as being occupied with external matters. The union of her love with the Great Love is unabated:

> I think that for the sake of these sweet and penetrating touches of His love all our past pains were well spent... When these impulses are given you, remember that they come from the innermost mansion, where God dwells in our souls. Praise Him fervently, for it is He Who sends you this message, or love letter, so tenderly written, and in a cipher that only you can understand and know what He asks. (VII, Chapter 3, 8)

What is the difference between this mansion and all other mansions? Teresa explains:

> This mansion differs from the rest in that, as I said, the dryness and disturbance felt in all the rest at times hardly ever enters here, where the soul is nearly always calm.
>
> It does not fear that this sublime favour can be counterfeited by the devil, but feels a settled conviction that it is of divine origin, because, as above stated, nothing is here perceived by the senses or faculties, but His Majesty reveals Himself to the spirit, which He takes to be with Himself in a place where I doubt not the devil dare not enter, nor would our Lord ever permit him.
>
> All the graces here divinely bestowed on the soul come, as I said, through no action of its own, save its total abandonment of itself to God. (VII, Chapter 3, 8, 9)

In this state, the peace of union and total abandonment to His Love is effortless and occurs in silence:

> They are given in peace and silence, like the building of Solomon's Temple, where no sound was heard. It is thus with this temple of God, this mansion of His where He and the soul rejoice in each other alone in profound silence.
>
> The mind need not act nor search for anything, as the Lord Who created it wishes it to be at rest, and only to

> watch, through a little chink, what passes within. Though
> at times it cannot see this, yet such intervals are very short,
> because, I believe, the powers are not here lost, but only
> cease to work, being, as it were, dazed with astonishment.
>
> I, too, am astonished at seeing that when the soul arrives
> at this state it does not go into ecstasies, except perhaps on
> rare occasions – even then they are not like the former
> trances and the flight of the spirit, and seldom take place in
> public as they did before…this may be either because the
> spirit has at last found repose, or that it has seen such
> wonders in this mansion that nothing can frighten it, or
> perhaps because it no longer feels solitary, since it rejoices
> in such Company. (VII, Chapter 3, 9, 10)

This divine marriage is consummated with His Kiss that
unites the soul to God:

> These effects, with all the other good fruits I have mentioned
> of the different degrees of prayer, are given by God to the
> soul when it draws near Him to receive that 'kiss of His
> mouth' which the bride asked for, and I believe her petition
> is now granted. (VII, Chapter 3, 12)

The peace and profound contentment given to the soul are
quite beyond human understanding or reasoning:

> Here, the overflowing waters are given to the wounded
> hart: here she delights in the tabernacles of God: here the
> dove sent out by Noah, to see whether the flood had
> subsided, has plucked the olive branch, showing that she
> has found firm land amongst the floods and tempests of
> this world. O Jesus! Who knows how much in Holy Scripture
> refers to this peace of soul! (VII, Chapter 3, 12)

Teresa attempts the impossible in describing the land of
transforming union. When the summit of the mountain
has been reached, what more is there to describe? What can
be seen and talked about are the pathways up the mountain.
When the top has been reached we can say nothing more
about it – there is no 'further on' from where we may look
back and see what it was like. The mountain tip, the
seventh mansion can be seen only from heaven, for it
belongs there.

Resting in Eternity, Living in the World

And the effect of righteousness will be peace, and the result of righteousness, quietness and trust forever. My people will abide in a peaceful habitation in secure dwellings, and in quiet resting places. (Isaiah 32:17-18)

Then I saw a new heaven and a new earth; for the first heaven and the first earth had passed away, and the sea was no more. And I saw the holy city, new Jerusalem, coming down out of heaven from God, prepared as a bride adorned for her husband; and I heard a loud voice from the throne saying, 'Behold the dwelling of God is with men. He will dwell with them, and they shall be his people, and God himself will be with them; he will wipe away every tear from their eyes, and death shall be no more, neither shall there be mourning, nor crying nor pain anymore, for the former things have passed away. And he who sat upon the throne said, 'Behold, I make all things new.' (Rev 21:1-5)

We have come to the final resting place of our contemplative journey. In the outermost mansions of our soul we remain rooted in the everyday world of practicalities, pressure, service, charity and challenges, whilst in the innermost mansion we are 'being, and resting', in eternity, in union with God. Teresa makes sure we know that, as the journey comes to rest in the peace, love and fullness of Christ, we have not received these spiritual gifts and blessings for our own personal use.

The contemplative life is certainly not an end in itself. We can only truly rest in God's Presence and abundance when we are also impelled and empowered to selfless action, charity and service. The double movement of Transcendent Love constantly draws us inwards to unity and fruition, and simultaneously flows out again, urging us to become humble, selfless, supple servants of His Divine Love in the world.

The *living waters are for the flowers*, and the purpose of the contemplative journey is to be even more engaged in the world around us in activities and works of service, charity and loving action, whilst simultaneously united with the Lord in the innermost dwelling places.

The soul is united with God in order to imitate, and live, the life of Christ in the world. Teresa is emphatic about this:

> **This is the aim and end of prayer, my daughters; this is the reason for the spiritual marriage, whose children are always good works. Works are the unmistakable sign that shows these favours come from God, as I told you.**
>
> **It will do me little good to be deeply recollected when alone, making acts of the virtues, planning and promising to do wonders in God's service, if afterwards, when occasion offers, I do just the opposite.** (VII, Chapter 4, 10)

We are now able to be in peace, and radiate love in the midst of coping with all the demands and expectations that the world makes on us. We always have the indwelling presence and love of God to guide us. We are able to find rest in that peace, silence, stillness and tranquillity that 'passes human understanding' and dwell in His Eternal Presence.

The desire and urge to communicate, to give to and serve others from the abundance of Divine Love and Life that has been bestowed is even stronger and more compelling, more urgent than ever before. If we love God and have given ourselves to Him, we are able to love and give ourselves to others and the whole world entirely naturally, effortlessly, willingly, humbly and unself-consciously.

In ordinary life, we are able to live in an extraordinary way, in the fullness of the peace and love of God. Our defences and resistances have fallen away and we can rest in peace, deep within ourselves, without effort. We now have very little interior identification with the world, and its constant demands, pressures and expectations. Worldly influences, fears, anxieties and concerns have lost their seductive and manipulative power over our heart and soul.

The centre of our soul has become subservient, in full consciousness and humility, to the power and energy of His Love. This state of consciousness, of peace and repose, does not necessarily manifest itself in outward states of ecstasy or visions, although sometimes it may. The extraordinary events that Teresa writes about tend to be the exception rather than the rule.

On the contrary, our mystical experiences of intimacy and love become more and more introverted, more and more contained and interior. At this stage of inner peace and surrender, we live in a state of receptivity, fluidity, suppleness, transparency, humility and constant attentiveness to His Divine Providence. We have a particular stillness, a constant sense of meaningfulness, a final resting in eternity.

This is certainly the emphasis that Teresa conveys in the final section:

> I think it may console you to enjoy yourselves in this interior castle, where you can enter, and walk about at will, at any hour you please… It is true you cannot enter all the mansions by your own power, however great it may appear to you, unless the Lord of the Castle Himself admit you… He dearly loves humility; if you think yourselves unworthy to enter the third mansion, He will grant you all the sooner the favour of entering the fifth.
>
> Then if you serve Him well there, and often repair to it, He will draw you into the mansion where He dwells Himself, whence you need never depart. When once you have learnt how to enjoy this castle, you will always find rest, however painful your trials may be, in the hope of returning to your Lord, which no one can prevent.
>
> Although I have only mentioned seven mansions, yet each one contains many more rooms, above, below and around it, with fair gardens, fountains and labyrinths, besides other things so delightful that you will wish to consume yourself in praising the great God for them, Who has created the soul in His own image and likeness. (Epilogue)

Any activity can deepen our contemplative experience as long as it is done with a contemplative attitude. Joseph Chu

Cong, a Trappist monk and Prior of St Joseph's Abbey in
Spencer, Massachusetts, writes of his conversation with
Mother Teresa of Calcutta which demonstrates this perfectly:

> Some years ago I had the joy of welcoming Mother Teresa
> of Calcutta into our monastery at Spencer. During my lovely
> exchange with Mother, I asked her a naïve question: 'Mother,
> being so busy working all day and travelling all over the
> world non stop, where in the world do you find time to pray
> and to contemplate?'
>
> With her loving eyes, she looked at me and said 'Father,
> my contemplation is when I touch the sick, when I embrace
> the dying child, when I wash the wounds of a leper. Jesus
> told us that whenever you do these things to the least of my
> brothers and sisters, you do it to me; and I know Jesus
> always tells the truth. To me the dying child or the lepers are
> only Jesus in disguise.'[1]

We are able to love others and the world for the sake of
Love, and Love, alone. We can bear the weakness,
disappointment, fears, terrors, hatred, difficulties, and pain
of others and the world patiently, quietly, uncritically,
generously and unconditionally in faith, hope and love.

This is a depth of love that will face all obstacles, endure
all pain and purifications, hope for all things. We express
the constant deepening of our love and charity to others
and the world. The virtues are now no longer actively
sought and practised. Our true love given and expressed
always enriches others, brings them happiness, and gets
reborn again and again in life.

There is a growing depth of compassion, goodness,
limitless faith in God, prayer and the helping of others.
Real kindness and generosity freely given to others is a
reflection of the Love we have received that immeasurably
exceeds and precedes our own personal love.

Love in individual hearts always lights the fire of charity,
simplicity, kindness, compassion, justice and self-sacrifice.
Through prayer and constant longing, this growing capacity
for charity and service deepens that spiritual maturity that
unites both action and contemplation in our souls. The

transforming and utterly radical power of Love from the innermost mansions is especially directed as forgiveness, towards those we find most difficult to love.

One of the most important themes that Teresa emphasises at the end of her mystical text is the importance of balancing being active in the world with resting in contemplation. She, of course, was constantly aware of the need for contemplation, yet at no stage, especially in these final chapters of *The Interior Castle*, does she forget the crucial importance of the need to nourish our active, practical side.

She is clear about this:

> **Therefore, sisters, take care to lay a firm foundation, by seeking to be the least of all and the slave of others, watching how you can please and help them, for it will benefit you more than them. Built on such strong rocks, your castle can never go to ruin.**
>
> **I insist again: your foundation must not consist of prayer and contemplation alone: unless you acquire the virtues and practise them, you will always be dwarfs; and please God no worse may befall you than making no progress, for you know that to *stop* is to go *back* – if you love, you will never be content to come to a standstill.** (VII, Chapter 4, 13)

Teresa uses the story of Martha and Mary from St Luke's Gospel, which has been traditionally used to illustrate the difference between the contemplative and active callings. The Gospel passage reads:

> 'Now as they went on their way, he entered a certain village, where a woman named Martha welcomed him into her home. She had a sister named Mary, who sat at the Lord's feet and listened to what he was saying. But Martha was distracted by her many tasks; so she came to him and asked, 'Lord, do you not care that my sister has left me to do all the work by myself? Tell her then to help me.' But the Lord answered her, 'Martha, Martha, you are worried and distracted by many things; there is a need of only one thing. Mary has chosen the better part, which will not be taken away from her.' (Luke 10:38-43)

In the centre, between the two women, who seem so unlike each other, sits Christ. He is obviously aware of the situation and when Martha finally explodes, He is ready with His answer 'Martha, Martha, you are worried and distracted by many things; there is a need of only one thing.'

The story deals with the nature of the relationship of contemplation to action and the tensions that are often involved between them. In the balanced life of faith and works, the interior and ever deepening communion with God results in ever widening, outgoing action towards the world. We are tools and channels of God.

Teresa uses the story to help explain how being 'united with God' and also active in the world can create apparent divisions or tensions, and how the degree of integration between action and contemplation, between the moral and the mystical in our lives, is the crux. In the centre of contemplation is action, and in the midst of action is a deeply contemplative core.

If we want to derive a rhythm of life based upon Teresa's life and writings, then this integration and incorporation of the practical and the spiritual in our lives will be foremost:

> **Both Martha and Mary must entertain our Lord and keep Him as their Guest, nor must they be so inhospitable as to offer Him no food. How can Mary do this while she sits at His feet, if her sister does not help her?** (VII, Chapter 4, 17)

Commenting on the relationship between the active and contemplative callings using the Mary and Martha story, Rowan Williams notes that Mary *alone* cannot be a complete or perfect soul because we never free ourselves from temporal human responsibility while we live in time. Mary presupposes Martha, meaning that the mature contemplative is someone who has learned Martha's way, and the attempt to be Mary without this learning process is a mark of immaturity.[2]

If we are able to live creatively within the tension between action and contemplation, we are able to become fully human, fully alive. This tension can always be used to highlight the need for those constant hints and reminders in times in our lives when being and resting in God in the centre of our interior castle is being obscured by overactivity, identification, stress, anxiety or worry.

Fullness of the life in the Spirit means a constant observance and delicate holding of a balance between action and contemplation, between receiving and giving, between apprehending and expressing, between action and fruition. The perfect achievement of this twofold ideal is Christ – His deeds of power and mercy, His richly various responses to every level of human existence, His gift to others of new faith and life were directly dependent on the nights spent on the mountain in prayer.[3]

Others have closely mirrored Teresa's observations and spiritual wisdom. For the Flemish mystic, the Blessed Jan van Ruysbroec, union means a full, conscious participation in the entire life of God that is at once utterly peaceful and completely dynamic, at once at rest and in perpetual action. He tells us in his *Spiritual Espousals*:

> The divine persons who form one sole God are in the fecundity of their nature ever active; and in the simplicity of their essence they form the Godhead and eternal blessedness. Thus God according to the Persons is Eternal Work; but according to essence and its Perpetual stillness, he is Eternal rest. Now love and fruition live between this activity and this rest...the spirit of God himself breathes us out from himself that we may love, and may do good works, and again he draws us into himself that we may rest in fruition. And this is Eternal Life; even as our mortal life subsists in the indrawing and outgoing of our breath... Understand, God... demands of us both action and fruition, in such a way that the action never hinders the fruition, nor the fruition the action, but they strengthen one another. And this is why the interior man lives his life according to these two ways: that is to say, in rest and in work. And in each of them he is wholly and undividedly: for he dwells wholly in God in the virtue of his restful fruition and wholly in himself in virtue of his active love. And God, in his communications,

perpetually calls and urges him to renew both this rest and work.'[4]

For Teresa, the mystical union that matters is union with the Divine Will and going out from Him into the world, not primarily an experience of absorption in God. The paradox of Christian mysticism, which she emphasises throughout her writings, is that we cannot take refuge in a God that is detached from life and creation. The God with whom we are finally united is the God whose being is directed in Love towards the world.[5]

We need to be ready to continually surrender and give up our own solitude our 'being, resting in God's Presence' alone, in order to carry His Love into everyday life. As Teresa shows by her life and experience, hidden behind the activity and practicality of the person 'living in union with God' is the continual interior intimacy with Christ, the Bridegroom, who 'makes all things new'.

It *is* possible to live in the living waters and the burning fires of Divine Love, and rest in the continual and persistent awareness of God's Presence at all times, in all places, uninterrupted by life and activity. Most of us have the idea that to be actively in the world and at the same time wholly exposed to the Reality and Presence of God is something we can only yearn for, hope for, pray for and wait patiently and expectantly for.

However, the life, writings and experience of St Teresa of Avila show that it is possible, and indeed, is every person's spiritual birthright to be called into the deeper contemplative life, into unceasing prayer, into union with God, as the life of Jesus Christ and all of His saints throughout the centuries have shown and testified.

> And for their sake I consecrate myself, that they also may be consecrated in truth. I do not pray for these only, but also for those who believe in me through their word, that they may all be one; even as thou, Father, art in me, and I in thee, that they also may be in us, so that the world may believe that thou hast sent me.

The glory which thou has given me I have given to them, that they may be one even as we are one, I in them and thou in me, that they may become perfectly one, so that the world may know that thou has sent me and has loved them even as thou has loved me.

Gospel of John 17:19-23 (RSV)

NOTES
RESTING IN ETERNITY, LIVING IN THE WORLD

1. Chu-Cong, J. *The Contemplative Experience,* Crossroad, NY. 1999, p.103
2. Williams, R. *op. cit.* p.160
3. Underhill, E. *An Anthology of the Love of God,* Mowbray & Co, London, 1953, p.214
4. Harvey, A. *op. cit.* p.127
5. Williams, R. *op. cit.* p.160.

BIBLIOGRAPHY

Allison Peers, E. *Mother of Carmel – A Portrait of St Teresa of Jesus*, SCM Press, London, 1948.

Allison Peers, E. (trans). *The Complete Works of Saint Teresa of Jesus*, Vol 1-3, Sheed and Ward, London, 1946.

Amis, Robin. *A Different Christianity*, State University New York Press, NY, 1995.

Barry, William and Connolly, William. *The Practice of Spiritual Direction*, HarperCollins, San Franscisco, 1991.

Bishop of Nafpaktos Hierotheos. *A Night in the desert of the Holy Mountain*, Birth of the Theotokos Monastery, Greece, 1995.

Boosalis, Henry. *Orthodox Spiritual Life*, St Tikhon's Seminary Press, Pennsylvania, 2000.

Bryant, Christopher. *Jung and the Christian Way*, DLT, London, 1983.

Chu-Cong, Joseph. *The Contemplative Experience*, Crossroad Publishing, NY, 1999.

Clement, Oliver. *The Roots of the Christian Mysticism*, New City, London, 1993.

Coelho, Mary. *St Teresa of Avila's Transformation of the Symbol of the Interior Castle*, Teresianum Ephemeredes Carmeliticae, 1987, I.

Conn, Joann Wolski (ed). *Women's Spirituality*, Paulist Press, New Jersey, 1996.

Conroy, Maureen. *The Discerning Heart, Discovering a Personal God*, Loyola University Press, 1993.

Dupre, Louis. *The Deeper Life – An Introduction to Christian Mysticism*, Crossroad Publishing, NY, 1981.

Giordano, Silvano (ed). Beattie, Mark; Connolly, Stephan; Tulloch, Andrew (trans). *Carmel in the Holy Land – From its beginnings to the Present Day*, II Messaggero di Gesu Bambino, Arenzano, 1995.

Green, Thomas. *When the Well Runs Dry – Prayer beyond the Beginnings*, Ave Maria Press, Notre Dame, Indiana, 1998.

Gregory of Nyssa. *From Glory to Glory*, SVS Press, Crestwood, NY, 1979.

Griffiths, Bede. *The Golden String*, Templegate, Illinois, 1954.

Guenther, Margaret. *Holy Listening: the Art of Spiritual Direction*, DLT, London, 1993.

Harton, Frank. P. *The Elements of the Spiritual Life – A Study in Ascetical Theology*, SPCK, London, 1957.

Harvey, Andrew. *Son of Man – the Mystical Path to Christ*, Jeremy Tarcher/Putnam, NY, 1998.

Houdek, Frank. *Guided by the Spirit – a Jesuit Perspective on Spiritual Direction*, Loyola Press, Chicago, 1996.

Humphreys, Carolyn. *From Ash to Fire*, New City Press, NY, 1992.

Jacobi, Mario. *Individuation and Narcissism*, Routledge Kegan Paul, London, 1990.

James, William. *Varieties of Religious Experience*, Penguin, NY, 1985.

Judy, Dwight. *Embracing God*, Abingdon Press, Nashville, 1996.

Jung, Carl G. *Two Essays on Analytical Psychology*, Collected Works 7, trans R.F.C. Hull, Routledge Kegan Paul, London, 1953/1966.

Jung, Carl G. *Aion*, Collected Works 9ii, trans R.F.C. Hull, Routledge Kegan Paul, London, 1959.

Kavanaugh, Kieran and Rodriguez, Otilio (trans). *The Collected Works of St John of the Cross*, ICS Publications, Washington, DC, 1979.

Leech, Kenneth. *Soul Friend: Spiritual direction in the modern world*, DLT, London, 1994.

Lonsdale, David. *What is Spiritual Direction – A Discussion Paper*, Dec 1998.

Lonsdale, David. *Listening to the Music of the Spirit*, Ave Maria Press, Indiana, 1993.

Lopez Baralt, E. *Islam in Spanish Literature: From the Middle Ages to the Present*, E.J. Brill, Leiden, 1992.

Louf, André. *Tuning in to Grace – the Quest for God*, DLT, London.

Louth, Andrew. *The Origins of the Christian Mystical Tradition*, Clarendon Press, Oxford, 1981.

Matthew, Iain. *The Impact of God*, Hodder and Stoughton, London, 1995.

May, Gerald. *Care of Mind, Care of Spirit*, HarperCollins, San Francisco, 1992.

McGinn, Bernard. *Foundations of Mysticism*, Vol 1, SCM Press, London, 1990.

Melloni, Javier. *The Exercises of St Ignatius Loyola in the Western Tradition*, Gracewing, UK, 2000.

Monbourquette, John. *How to Befriend your Shadow*, Novalis, Ottowa, 2001.

Nicoll, Maurice. *The New Man*, Watkins, London, 1981.

Obbard, Elizabeth Ruth. *La Madre, the Life and Spirituality of Teresa of Avila*, St Pauls, 1994.

Orrel, Linda Henry. *Teresa's Jewish Mysticism, in Spiritual Life – A Quarterly of Contemporary Spirituality*, Vol 36, No. 2, Summer 1990.

Ruffing, Janet. *Spiritual Direction Beyond the Beginnings*, St Paul's, London, 2000.

Sherrard, Phillip. *The Sacred in Life and Art*, Golgonooza Press, 1990.

Sophrony (Sakarov) (Archimandrite). *The Monk of Mount Athos*, St Vladimir's Seminary Press, Crestwood, NY, 1973.

Sophrony (Sakarov) (Archimandrite). *We Shall See Him As He Is*, Starropegic Monastery of St John, Essex, 1988.

Teresa of Avila, *The Life of Saint Teresa of Avila by Herself*, trans J.M. Cohen, Penguin Classics, 1957.

Teresa of Avila, *The Interior Castle*, Fount/HarperCollins Religious, London, 1995.

Teresa of Avila, *The Interior Castle*, trans Discalced Carmelite, Sands and Co, London, 1945.

Tyler, Peter. *The Way of Ecstasy*, Canterbury Press, Norwich, 1997.

Ulanov, Ann. *Religion and the Spiritual in Carl Jung*, Paulist Press, New York/Mahwah, 1999.

Ulanov, Ann. *Picturing God*, Cowley Press, Cambridge, Mass, 1986.

Underhill, Evelyn. *An Anthology of the Love of God*, Mowbray & Co, London, 1953.

Underhill, Evelyn. *Mysticism – the Nature and Development of Spiritual consciousness*, Oneworld, Oxford, 1996.

Underhill, Evelyn. *An Anthology of the Love of God*. Mowbray & Co, London, 1953.

Wakefield, Gordon (ed). *Dictionary of Christian Spirituality*, SCM Press, 1983.

Ware, Kallistos (Bishop). *The Inner Kingdom*, St Vladimir's Seminary Press, NY, 2000.

Ware, Kallistos (Bishop) (ed). et al. *The Philokalia*, Vol 3, Faber and Faber, London, 1984.

Welch, John. *Spiritual Pilgrims: Carl Jung and Teresa of Avila*, Paulist Press, New York/Mahwah, 1982.

Welch, John. *The Carmelite Way*, Gracewing, UK, 1996.

Williams, Rowan. *Teresa of Avila*, Geoffrey Chapman, London, 1991.

Waaijman, Kees. *The Mystical Space of Carmel – A Commentary on the Carmelite Rule*, Peeters, Louvain, 1999.

Woods, Richard (ed). *Understanding Mysticism*, Athlone Press, London, 1981.

Yeats, W.B. *Collected Poems*, Picador, London, 1990.